INTRODUCING
SYMBOLIC LOGIC

INTRODUCING SYMBOLIC LOGIC

Robert M. Martin

broadview press

National Library of Canada Cataloguing in Publication

Martin, Robert M.
    Introducing symbolic logic / Robert M. Martin.

ISBN 1-55111-635-9

1. Logic, Symbolic and mathematical. I. Title.

BC135.M37 2004   160   C2004-902105-2

Broadview Press Ltd. is an independent, international publishing house, incorporated in 1985.

North America:

PO Box 1243, Peterborough, Ontario, Canada K9J 7H5
Tel: (705) 743-8990
Fax: (705) 743-8353
customerservice@broadviewpress.com
3576 California Road, Orchard Park, NY, USA 14127

UK, Ireland, and Continental Europe:

NBN Plymbridge
Estover Road, Plymouth PL6 7PY UK
Tel: 44 (0) 1752 202301
Fax: 44 (0) 1752 202331
Fax Order Line: 44 (0) 1752 202333
Customer Service: cservs@nbnplymbridge.com
Orders: orders@nbnplymbridge.com

Australia and New Zealand:

UNIREPS, University of New South Wales
Sydney, NSW, 2052
Tel: 61 2 9664 0999
Fax: 61 2 9664 5420
email: info.press@unsw.edu.au

Broadview believes in shared ownership, both with its employees and with the general public; since the year 2000 Broadview shares have traded publicly on the Toronto Venture Exchange under the symbol BDP.

www.broadviewpress.com

Broadview Press ltd. gratefully acknowledges the financial support of the Government of Canada through the Book Publishing Industry Development Program for our publishing activities.

PRINTED IN CANADA

ACKNOWLEDGEMENTS

The idea behind writing this was to produce a student-friendly logic text. Many students in the author's logic classes liked this idea enough to collaborate in the project by providing a long list of typos, unclarities, and flat-out mistakes in photocopied earlier versions of this book. The author apologizes to them for the earlier mess, and thanks them for providing so much help in cleaning it up. Special thanks in this regard are due to two A+ logic students, Dave Trennum and Sarah Brodbar-Nemzer. The collaboration with Broadview Press on this book began with a discussion between the author and Broadview's President, Don LePan, over (and abetted by) several glasses of Granite Brewery Peculiar Ale. Don's continuing sympathy with the author's unusual approach, and the helpfulness of the other nice folks at Broadview, are deeply appreciated.

CONTENTS

INTRODUCTION

CHAPTER ONE: SENTENCE LOGIC

CHAPTER TWO: SENTENCE DERIVATIONS

CHAPTER THREE: QUANTIFIER LOGIC

CHAPTER FOUR: QUANTIFIER DERIVATIONS

INTRODUCTION

You're about to enter the wacky and wonderful, thrilling world of Symbolic Logic!! It will change your life!!! It...

No, no, no, stoppit! That's easily recognizable stupid hype.

The truth is you can live without Symbolic Logic; but it can be interesting, fun, and somewhat useful. At least many students find that it is. Hope you do too.

Before we get down to business in Chapter One, a few words about what Symbolic Logic is, what it's good for, and what you should do when you read this book.

What Symbolic Logic Is

Very roughly speaking, Logic is the theory of good and bad reasoning. This book deals with Deductive Logic, which is one sort of reasoning. (In Chapter One, there's some talk about what deductive and non-deductive reasoning is.) Symbolic Logic gives a theory of reasoning by providing general forms of good and bad reasoning using symbols. It looks a bit like algebra, or other kinds of symbol-using mathematics, as you can see if you take a quick glance at the rest of this book. But don't worry if you have math-phobia. You don't need to know any mathematics, or to have any skill at doing it, to learn Symbolic Logic.

What It's Good For

Logic textbooks sometimes claim that working your way through their book is a very good way to learn how to reason better. That's probably a bit of an exaggeration. Finding out something about the theory of good and bad reasoning is not necessarily an effective way to improve your reasoning, any more than finding out about the physics of motion is a good way to improve your ability to catch a baseball. But there are, perhaps, some more modest practical payoffs to studying logic. It may make you a bit more sensitive to the logical ambiguities and mistakes involved in ordinary talk and reasoning. Or maybe not. Anyway, the real reasons for studying logic are the same as the real reasons for studying any sort of theory: it can be fascinating and fun. A lot of people just enjoy finding out how things work.

What You Should Do

Compared to most other textbooks, this one is not very long. Your reading assignments will be shorter than those in almost any other humanities class. But don't be misled by this into thinking that you can spend a lot less time on this. You can't just zip through it, the way you might rush through a novel. You'll have to read what's in here very slowly, and several times.

Do not plan to work on logic for long periods of time. After an hour or so your brain will simply refuse to do any more. You'll learn *far* more by doing six half-hour sessions than by attempting one three-hour session.

Always have pencil and paper handy when you read. Write down key concepts, in your own words. When samples of logical procedures are provided in the readings, try reproducing them yourself without looking at the text. Writing while reading is a far superior way to learn than just reading.

You'll find exercises scattered generously throughout this book. It's very important that you don't ignore these. You may sometimes feel that you've completely understood a section you've just read, so it would be a waste of time to do the exercises; but students have often found that this feeling is a mistake. Even though you seem to have understood the readings, you may still be unable to do the exercises. Being able to do the exercises is the true test of your grasp of the subject matter, so it's an excellent way to find out how you're doing. If you have trouble with an exercise, you should go back and read the preceding section again, and maybe ask about the exercise in class. Even if the first exercises in a group seem easy, finish doing that group. Sometimes they get harder.

A second reason why the exercises are important is that doing them is essential for learning the material. An important part of learning Symbolic Logic is learning *skills*, not facts. It's more like learning how to ride a bicycle than like learning the capitals of the European countries.

It's something you learn by trying to do it, by working your way from easier to harder tasks. That's why the exercises are so important.

Answers are provided to all the exercises, but it's extremely important that you consult them only after you've done your best to answer the questions on your own. That's why the answer sections are a bit hard to find, separated from the questions, at the end of each chapter—to discourage you from glancing at them when you try to do the exercises.

If you have trouble with some exercises, don't look up the answers right away. Go back and re-read the section preceding those exercises, and then try them again. Look at the answers only after you've tried hard to answer the questions, re-read the material, and tried again. This is the way to learn the subject matter. The way *not* to learn the subject matter is to look up the answers to the questions right away, after having given them no thought, or just a little.

If exercises seem easy to you, do them anyway, then look at the answer section. Sometimes you'll find that you've made mistakes. Sometimes your answers will be correct, but the answer section will suggest other ways of dealing with the questions, and you'll benefit from finding this out. Sometimes the answer section will add important notes about dealing with the exercise questions.

In a book with so much detailed stuff, it's inevitable that some mistakes and typos have slipped through. If something seems wrong to you, the author of this book would be extremely grateful if you tell him about this. He'd also very much like to hear your reactions: criticisms and questions. You can reach him by email: martin@dal.ca.

CHAPTER ONE

SENTENCE LOGIC

Sentences

A **sentence** is what is either true or false. Every sentence is either true or false, never neither, never both. This is a different notion of *sentence* from the one ordinarily used. These:

Please pass the salt.
Is it raining?
Awesome!

would ordinarily be called sentences, but since none of these is either true or false, they are not sentences in the sense that we will use that word.

> *Exercise 1.1* Which of the following are sentences?
>
> 1.1.1. Pierre Trudeau was the first Prime Minister of Canada.
>
> 1.1.2 Never let a dog sense that you are afraid.
>
> 1.1.3. Would you like coffee or tea?
>
> 1.1.4. Hooray for the Mooseheads!

It's easy to distinguish sentences from non-sentences, and you hardly need exercises to practice on for this. There are, however, some cases in which the answer is not quite so clear; consideration of these cases leads to interesting questions. We won't be talking about any of these questions in this book, but just in case you'd like to begin thinking about them, take a look at the answers to the following exercises for a very brief discussion of the problems raised in each case.

Exercise 1.2 *Which of the following are sentences?*

1.2.1.   You live in Halifax, don't you?

1.2.2.   My cousin lives in Moncton.

1.2.3.   The first human will land on Mars in the year 2049.

1.2.4.   I name this ship the *Joseph Stalin*.

1.2.5.   I would like some tea.

1.2.6.   This sentence is false.

1.2.7.   (Said while eating chocolate ice cream): "Delicious!"

1.2.8.   This chocolate ice-cream is delicious!

Every sentence thus has one of the two **truth values**. The two truth values are TRUE and FALSE.

A **set** of sentences is a collection of (one or more) of them.

Arguments

An *argument* is a set of statements one of which (the **conclusion**) is taken to be supported by the remaining sentences (the **premises**). This passage:

> *Fred must have been here; because the lights are on, and he is the only guy who leaves the lights on.*

Is an argument. The conclusion is

> *Fred must have been here.*

There are two premises:

> *The lights are on.*
> *He (Fred) is the only guy who leaves the lights on.*

We could just as well understand this as an argument with the same conclusion but only one premise:

> *The lights are on, and he (Fred) is the only guy who leaves the lights on.*

It doesn't make any difference, as far as we're concerned: we can treat this as an argument with two premises, or with one more complex premise. And sometimes (as in this example) premises and conclusion are joined together in one English sentence. In the following argument, however, the conclusion is given by a separate English sentence:

> *Robin's eggs are blue. That bird's nest has white eggs in it. So that can't be a robin's nest.*

Note that in the example concluding that Fred was here, the conclusion happens to comes first; but it can come anywhere. The word *because* here is a clue that the premises follow. You can sometimes tell when a passage contains an argument, and which are the premises and which is the conclusion, by such tip-off words. Premise-indicating words include

> *since*
> *for*
> *because*
> *on account of*
> *inasmuch as*
> *for the reason that*

Conclusion-indicating words include

> *therefore*
> *thus*
> *it follows that*
> *so*
> *hence*
> *consequently*
> *as a result*

But sometimes what looks like an argument isn't. For example,

> *The grass is brown because it hasn't rained.*

probably isn't an argument, because, it's reasonable to suppose, that sort of thing wouldn't be said in an attempt to convince the hearer that the grass is brown. The hearer, we'd guess, already knows that. What's said gives an explanation of the fact. But you can think of a situation in which this might be an argument: suppose that somebody knows that it hasn't rained, but doesn't know the current colour of the grass, and you want to convince that person that it's brown. This is an odd situation: why would an argument be necessary, when presumably one could just look at the grass?

In order to distinguish arguments from non-arguments, you can't rely on the presence or absence of conclusion- or premise-indicating words. You have to try to figure out what the speaker's intentions in producing that passage would be, in the most likely circumstances.

Exercise 1.3 *Determine which of the following are arguments; in each argument, underline the conclusion.*

1.3.1.   I'm not going to be at the party tonight because I have logic homework to do.

1.3.2.   It's likely to be sunny tomorrow, because the weather forecast said so, and they're usually right.

1.3.3.   That's not my car. My car's green.

1.3.4.   All Canadians know that Saskatchewan is flat. You won't find any Canadians going to Saskatchewan to ski, because nobody goes to ski to a place they know is flat.

1.3.5.   Fred had seventeen beers and consequently passed out.

1.3.6.   I'm really smart. So I'll surely get an A in logic.

1.3.7.   Since I already had lunch, I'm not going to the café with you.

1.3.8.   People raised in Mexico usually enjoy spicy hot food. I think José will like your cooking.

1.3.9.   Fred is home tonight, because every night he's always either at the pub or at home, and he's not at the pub.

1.3.10. Fred is home tonight, because the hockey playoffs are on TV.

To write an argument down in standard form, we arrange it like an addition, with the premises lined up, then a horizontal line, then the conclusion:

Fred is the only guy who leaves the lights on.
The lights are on.
Fred must have been here.

Validity and Invalidity

An argument is **deductively valid** (we'll just say **valid**, for short) if and only if it is not possible for the premises to be true and the conclusion false. An argument is **deductively invalid** (**invalid**, for short) if it is not deductively valid, that is, if it is possible for the premises to be true and the conclusion false.

Here are some valid arguments:

> *All dogs are mammals.*
> *Fido is a dog.*
> *Fido is a mammal.*

> *If it's raining, the picnic is off.*
> *It's raining.*
> *The picnic is off.*

> *Fred, Sally, and Seymour are the only people in the room.*
> *At least one person in the room is eating pizza.*
> *Neither Fred nor Sally is eating pizza.*
> *Seymour is eating pizza.*

> *Every pig can fly.*
> *Everything that can fly has propellers.*
> *All pigs have propellers.*

Note that some of these premises and conclusions are actually false, but that doesn't show that the arguments they're in are invalid. All that's relevant is whether it's possible that the conclusion be false if the premises were true. Can you imagine a world in which the premises are true but the conclusion is false? If you can't coherently imagine this, if it's impossible in this sense, then the argument is valid. Assure yourself that all the arguments above are valid. Stretch your imagination, for example, on the last of these examples, and imagine that every pig can fly and that every flying thing has propellers. In that imaginary world, it would have to be the case that pigs had propellers. It would be impossible that the premises be true, but the conclusion false.

What we're doing here can be thought of as investigating **possible worlds**. These are not other planets; they're ways things might have been. The actual world is a possible world, but there are many other possible worlds: ways things might have been but aren't, actually. So, for example, there are possible worlds in which pigs fly. In one possible world, pigs fly and all weigh over 1,000 kg. In another possible world, pigs fly, but some weigh under 1,000 kg. But there is no possible world in which pigs fly, all weigh over 1,000 kg., and some weigh under 1,000 kg.

This is an invalid argument:

> *Seymour has failed every test in all his classes so far this year.*
> *Seymour hasn't read any assigned readings in any of his classes.*
> *Seymour hasn't attended most of his class meetings.*
> *Seymour won't pass the logic test tomorrow.*

If those premises were true, it would be very likely that the conclusion was true. The premises would be very good evidence for the conclusion. So this argument is a good one—it would convince people. But it isn't valid: if those premises were true, it would be possible (though unlikely) that the conclusion be false. Because the truth of these premises would provide good evidence for the conclusion, it's said to be a *strong inductive* argument.

That argument about Fred and the lights being on (page 2) is also invalid, because it's remotely possible that the lights were on for some other reason, like a bizarre flaw in the electrical wiring that turned them on without human intervention. So it's possible that the conclusion could be false when the premises were true. But it's highly unlikely that the conclusion be false when the premises are true, so it's a strong inductive argument. But it's deductively invalid.

Here's another invalid argument:

> *New York is in the USA.*
> *Berlin is in Germany.*
> *Paris is in France.*

Here all the premises are true, and so is the conclusion. But that doesn't matter. It could be possible that the conclusion were false while the premises were true. Imagine, for example, that they re-drew the boundaries of France to exclude Paris (putting it in Spain), while the geography of the US and Germany remained as they actually are.

Soundness

You've noticed some valid arguments have one or more false premises, and some have false conclusions. The only thing that one can't have in a valid argument is premises that are all true and a false conclusion. This is a consequence of the definition of validity: a valid argument is one in which, if the premises were true, the conclusion couldn't be false.

The basic function of an argument is to establish the truth of its conclusion. A valid argument guarantees the truth of its conclusion when all the premises are true. But when one or more of the premises are false in a valid argument, the conclusion might be true or false. So valid arguments are useful only when they have true premises: in that case, we can be assured of the truth of the conclusion. The kind of argument we really value, then, is not just valid: it also has true premises. This sort of argument is called a **deductively sound** argument (we'll just simply call it **sound**, for short). An argument is **deductively unsound** (**unsound**, for short) if and only if it is not deductively sound—that is, if it has one or more false premises, or it's invalid, or both.

Exercise 1.4 *True or false?*

1.4.1. If an argument is valid, all its premises are true.

1.4.2. If an argument has a false conclusion, the argument is invalid.

1.4.3. If a valid argument has true premises, its conclusion must be true.

1.4.4. If a valid argument has a true conclusion, all its premises must be true.

1.4.5. If a valid argument has a false conclusion, all its premises must be false.

1.4.6. If a valid argument has a false conclusion, its premises can't all be true.

1.4.7. An invalid argument might have premises that are all true and a true conclusion.

1.4.8. An invalid argument might have premises that are all true and a false conclusion.

1.4.9. An invalid argument might have a true conclusion and at least one false premise.

1.4.10. A sound argument might have a false conclusion.

One of the main aims of deductive logic is to provide rigorous techniques for sorting out arguments into those that are valid and those that are invalid. We'll get to these. But, even before we get there, you should have some feeling for validity and invalidity in arguments. To tell whether an argument is valid or not, try to imagine a possible world (maybe quite different from the real world)—a coherent way things might have been—in which the premises are true but the conclusion is false. If you can imagine such a world, then the argument is invalid. If such a world is impossible, then the argument is valid.

Exercise 1.5 *Are these arguments valid or invalid?*

1.5.1.   If it's raining then the picnic is off.
         The picnic is off.
         It's raining.

1.5.2.   If it's raining then the picnic is off.
         The picnic is not off.
         It's not raining.

1.5.3.   No reptiles can fly.
         Pigs are reptiles.
         No pigs can fly.

1.5.4.   Every reptile can fly.
         Pigs are reptiles.
         Every pig can fly.

1.5.5.   Sally is extremely thirsty.
         Sally is offered a cold drink of water.
         Sally will drink the water.

1.5.6.   Fred buys Moosehead or Alpine at the liquor store.
         Fred bought Moosehead today.
         Fred didn't buy Alpine today.

1.5.7.   All Canadians are happy or handsome.
         No Canadian is silly.
         All happy people are silly or hardworking.
         All hardworking people are silly or handsome.
         All Canadians are handsome.

Consistency and Inconsistency

Validity and invalidity are not the only things logic deals with. Another topic is consistency and inconsistency. A set of sentences is **logically consistent** (we'll simply say **consistent**, for short) if and only if it is possible for all the members of that set to be true. It's **logically**

inconsistent (**inconsistent**, for short) if and only if it's not consistent—that is, if it's impossible that all the members of the set be true at once.

We'll indicate a set of sentences by putting them inside wiggly brackets { } and separating them by commas.

This set is consistent:

> { *Pigs can fly. , Cows are reptiles. , Paris is in Spain.* }

Each sentence is false, of course. But this doesn't matter. You can imagine a world—a very bizarre world, of course—in which each of these sentences is true at once. That makes them consistent.

This set is inconsistent:

> { *Fred is here or in the pub. , Fred isn't here. , Fred isn't in the pub.* }.

A world in which one of these sentences is true is possible, but there is no possible world in which all three of them are true at once.

Exercise 1.6 *Consider every set of two of those sentences about Fred. How many different sets of two are there? Write them down, and say whether each of these is consistent or inconsistent.*

Exercise 1.7 *Say whether each of the following sets is consistent or inconsistent:*

1.7.1. { Today is Monday. , It rains here every Monday. , It's raining today. }

1.7.2. { Today is Monday. , It never rains here on Monday. , It's raining today. }

1.7.3. { Today isn't Monday. , It always rains here on Monday. , It isn't raining today. }

1.7.4. { If it rains tomorrow, we'll go to the movies. , If we go to the movies, we'll eat popcorn. , It will rain tomorrow. , We won't eat popcorn tomorrow. }

Necessary Truth and Falsity

The next logical matter we look at is **necessary truth** and **necessary falsity**. A sentence is **necessarily true** if and only if it is not possible for the sentence to be false—if it's true in every possible world; that is, there is no possible world in which it is false.

Examples of necessarily true sentences are:

George Bush loves bologna sandwiches, or he doesn't.
Either no pig can fly, or else at least some of them can.
If every dog has its day, and Pluto is a dog, then Pluto has his day.
If Fred is a bachelor, then he's unmarried.

There aren't any possible worlds in which any of these sentences are false. You can't imagine a state of affairs—a possible world—in which any of these is false, and that's not a consequence of a limit on the powers of your imagination. These sentences are not just merely true: they *have to* be true: it's impossible that they be false.

A sentence is **necessarily false** if and only if it is not possible for the sentence to be true—if it's false in every possible world; that is, there is no possible world in which it is true. Here are some necessarily false sentences:

It's raining and it's not.
Every pig can fly, and Porky is a pig, but Porky can't fly.
Fred's in the pub or at home, but he's not in the pub, and he's not at home.
Fred has a sister who is male.

Most sentences you run into are neither necessarily true nor necessarily false. They're just plain true, or just plain false. Sentences that are just plain true are

Pigs can't fly.
It sometimes snows in Toronto.
Bananas grow in Costa Rica.

All of these sentences are true—that is, just plain true, true in the actual world. But for each of them, you can imagine a possible world in which it's false. Imagine, for example, a world in which pigs can fly. It's a weird world—one in which pigs are very different from what they're actually like, or in which the laws of aerodynamics are quite different.

Note that every necessarily true sentence is also (just plain) true. It's true in every possible world, including the actual world. (The actual world, remember, is counted as one of the possible worlds. And why not? It's clearly not impossible!)

These sentences are (just plain) false:

> *The main language spoken in Peru is Italian.*
> *An earthworm can beat an ostrich in a race.*
> *The moon is farther from the earth than the sun is.*

Logical Truth, Falsity, Indeterminacy

Most of the examples of necessary truths and falsehoods we have looked at so far all owe their necessity to the "logic" of the sentence. (Exactly what this means is hard to explain, but as we go on you'll understand it better.)

But it seems that there are necessarily true (and necessarily false) sentences where this is not a consequence of the logic of the sentence. Definitional truths (for example, *Every square has equal sides*) are usually taken to be necessarily true. Corresponding to these are definitional falsehoods (for example, *Somebody has a trombone which is not a musical instrument*). The necessary truth among the examples above, *If Fred is a bachelor, then he's unmarried,* is a definitional truth. It's necessarily true "by definition," in this case, because of the definition of the word *bachelor*. No man could correctly be called a bachelor, given the meaning of *bachelor* in English, unless he were unmarried. Likewise, *Fred has a sister who is male* is false, of course, but it's more than that: it's necessarily false, by definition of the word *sister*.

Some philosophers think that there are necessary truths that are neither a matter of logic nor of definition. A proposed example of this is the (supposed) fact that every event has a cause. The existence of this sort of necessary truth is controversial, and we can't go into the debate here.

In any case, it's only the **logical truths and falsehoods** we're going to be concerned with. *Fred's in the pub or at home, but he's not in the pub, and he's not at home* is a logically false statement. It's false, but more than that: it couldn't be true—it's necessarily false—because of the logic of the words *or* and *not*.

Any statement which says in effect,

> A *or* B, *but neither* A *nor* B

is logically false—false because of its logic. Similarly, *Either every pig can fly, or else at least some of them can't* is a logical truth: necessarily true because of the logic of the words *every* and *some*.

At this point, you're not expected to be able to do a very good job of distinguishing logical truths from ordinary ones (or logical from ordinary falsehoods). This is what the logic we're about to learn is for. Nevertheless, at this point you should have at least a rough idea of what the difference is.

Every sentence is true or false, of course. But those which are neither logically true nor logically false are called **logically indeterminate**. You should understand, however, that calling a sentence logically indeterminate does not mean that it's indeterminate whether it's true or false. Logically indeterminate sentences are perfectly true (like *No pigs can fly*) or perfectly false (like *Brazil is north of Canada*).

Here is a summary of what we have been saying:

- A sentence is **logically true** if and only if it is necessarily true because of its logic.

- A sentence is **logically false** if and only if it is necessarily false because of its logic.

- A sentence is **logically indeterminate** if and only if it is neither logically true nor logically false. Logically indeterminate sentences are either (just plain) true, or (just plain) false.

Here's a logical truth:

> *It's Tuesday or it's not.*

It's necessarily true, because of its logic. So it's also (just plain) true. Every logical truth is (just plain) true. A logical truth is true in every possible world, including the actual world.

This:

> *It's Tuesday and it's not.*

is a logical falsehood—it's necessarily false, because of its logic. So it's also (just plain) false. Every logical falsehood is (just plain) false. A logical falsehood is false in every possible world, including the actual world.

This sentence:

> *Pigs can't fly.*

is (just plain) true, but it's not logically true. It's true in the actual world, but its logic doesn't make it true in every possible world. There are some possible worlds in which it's false. You might want to say that it's impossible that a pig could fly: it's contrary to the laws of aerodynamics. Okay: it is impossible in that sense, but it's still logically possible. It's not contrary to the laws of logic. It's logically indeterminate.

This sentence:

> *There are people living on Mars.*

is (just plain) false, but it's not logically false. It's false in the actual world, but its logic doesn't make it false in every possible world. There are some possible worlds in which it's true. It's logically indeterminate.

It's getting tiresome to say "(just plain)" so often. From now on, when I say *true* I mean *(just plain) true*—that is, true in the actual world. Saying that a sentence is true, then, means that it's true in the actual world, but nothing is implied about the other possible worlds. Maybe it's also true in all the other possible worlds, in which case it's also necessarily true. And when I say *false* I mean *(just plain) false*—that is, false in the actual world; nothing is implied about its status in other possible worlds

Exercise 1.8   *State whether each sentence is logically true or logically false or logically indeterminate.*

1.8.1. Turtles can fly.

1.8.2. There are more than five coffee trees in Brazil.

1.8.3. Fred loves Zelda.

1.8.4. There is a pig which is not a mammal.

1.8.5. All pigs are mammals, and there is a pig which is not a mammal.

1.8.6. All unsupported heavier-than-air things fall toward the ground.

1.8.7. Either something is green or it isn't.

1.8.8. No pig can do algebra, but Porky is a pig and he can do algebra.

1.8.9.   There exists a machine that runs forever without using any power.

1.8.10.   If today is Tuesday, then today is not Tuesday.

1.8.11.   7 + 5 = 12

Logical Equivalency

Two sentences are **logically equivalent** if and only if it is not possible for them to have different truth values from one-another; that is, if it's not possible for one to be true while the other is false. To determine whether two sentences are logically equivalent, try to imagine a possible world in which one is true and the other is false. If there is such a logically coherent world, then they are not equivalent. If there is no logically coherent world in which they have different truth values, they're equivalent. So, for example,

> *It's Tuesday and it's raining.*
> *It's raining and it's Tuesday.*

Are logically equivalent, because if one of them were true, the other one would be also; and if one of them were false, the other one would be also. But

> *It's Tuesday and it's raining.*
> *It's Tuesday.*

is not a logically equivalent pair, because we can imagine a possible state of affairs in which one is true, but the other is false. Imagine, for example, that it's a sunny Tuesday. Then the first sentence would be false, and the second one true.

Here are some pairs of logically equivalent sentences:

> *It's Tuesday or it's raining.*
> *It's raining or it's Tuesday.*
> (Note these are different from the pair at the top of the page.)

> *It's not raining and it's not snowing.*
> *It's neither raining nor snowing.*

> *Either it's Monday or it's Wednesday.*
> *If it's not Wednesday, then it's Monday.*

> *Every pig is a non-reptile.*
> *No pig is a reptile.*

When two sentences are logically equivalent, they mean the same thing, logically speaking.

Exercise 1.9   *Are these pairs of sentences logically equivalent?*

1.9.1. It's raining or it's Tuesday.
It's raining.

1.9.2. Canada is south of Peru.
Most fish wear eyeglasses.

1.9.3. No pig is purple.
All purple things are non-pigs.

1.9.4. If Fred goes, I'll go.
If I don't go, Fred won't go.

Peculiar Consequences

There are several peculiar consequences that follow from all our definitions. The next exercise points out these peculiar consequences, and asks you to figure out why they follow from the way we have understood things so far.

Exercise 1.10   *Explain why each of these is true.*

1.10.1. Each logically true sentence is logically equivalent to all other logically true sentences.

1.10.2. Every argument which has inconsistent premises is valid.

1.10.3. Every argument which has a logically true conclusion is valid.

1.10.4. Every set of sentences containing one that is logically false is inconsistent.

1.10.5. There are inconsistent sets consisting of just one sentence.

Many students find these consequences very bothersome. A consequences of 1.10.2 above, for example, is that

> *Today is Tuesday.*
> *Today isn't Tuesday.*
> *Pigs can fly.*

is valid. And a consequence of 1.10.3 is that this argument:

> *Brazil is in South America.*
> *It's raining or it isn't.*

is also valid. (Make sure you understand why.) That's weird.

You might remember that in the beginning of this chapter it was stated that an argument was a set of premises that were supposed to support a conclusion; so a good argument would presumably be one in which the premises do this job well. But it seems clear that in both of the cases just above the premises utterly fail to support the conclusion. Before you get too upset by this sort of validity, you should realize that our system isn't totally perverse: we also count as valid all those arguments you always thought were valid. When the premises are consistent, and the conclusion logically indeterminate, then for the argument to be valid, the conclusion has to "follow from" the premises in the ordinary way—has to be "supported by" the premises.

So, for instance,

> *Toodles is a turtle*
> *All turtles are reptiles*
> *Toodles is a reptile*

in which the premises support the conclusion, is still valid under our official definition; and

> *Toodles is a turtle*
> *All turtles are reptiles*
> *It's snowing in Tibet*

in which the premises are irrelevant to the conclusion, is still invalid under our official definition.

But the peculiar cases also fit the our official definition of validity (that it be impossible that the premises be true and the conclusion false). What's happened, then, is that this official definition of validity has replaced the idea of "supporting the conclusion." This idea was too vague. The one we've substituted is, as we'll see, a logically precise and powerful notion. The problem is that it lets in these peculiar cases. But logicians have very good reasons for defining things this way: there isn't any good way (for our purposes) of defining validity that avoids these strange consequences. (Maybe you'd like to try to think of a different definition that doesn't let in these peculiar consequences. But wait till we've seen how this definition works first.) We're not going to try to explain in this book why the definition we use is the best one, despite these peculiar consequences, but maybe you'll get an idea why as we continue.

Sentential Logic

We now begin the branch of deductive logic called **sentential logic**. This is the sort of logic in which sentences are the basic units. (The word *sentential* is the adjective form of the word *sentence*.)

When you connect two sentences with the word *and* you get a third. For example, connecting *It's raining* with *It's Monday* in this way gives you *It's raining and it's Monday*. Similarly, connecting two sentences with *or* gives you a third one.

Or and *and*, when used to join sentences to produce another sentence, are called **sentential connectives** (or **connectives** for short). There are, as we'll see, other connectives.

Sentences generated by joining others with connectives are called **compound sentences**. Basic sentences not formed from others are called **atomic sentences**.

Sometimes the truth value of a compound sentence is wholly determined by the truth values of the two sentences thus joined. For example, when both atomic sentences *It's raining* and *It's Monday* are true, then the compound sentence *It's raining and it's Monday* is also true. When one or both of those atomic sentences are false, then *It's raining and it's Monday* is false. When a connective is used in this way—such that the truth value of the atomic sentences wholly determine the truth value of the compound, it's said to be used **truth-functionally**. We'll see later that some connectives in English sentences are not used truth-functionally.

Atomic Sentences

In our language, capital letters are used for atomic sentences, to abbreviate individual English sentences. Thus we may abbreviate *It's raining* by R. Any other letter can be used, but it's a good idea to use a letter that shows up obviously in the English sentence, so you can easily keep track of what abbreviates what. So then let's abbreviate *It's Monday* by M. Because there are only 26 capital letters, and there are (in theory) an infinite number of different English sentences we might want to abbreviate, additional abbreviations are provided (if needed) by adding numerical subscripts to the capital letters: G_3. L_{95}, etc.

There are five connectives used on atomic sentences to make compound sentences.

Conjunctions

The symbol & will be used for *and* used truth-functionally. Thus we can abbreviate *It's raining and it's Monday* by R & M. The symbol & is called the **ampersand**. A compound sentence formed by connecting two sentences by & is called a **conjunction**. The two sentences thus connected are called **conjuncts**.

As we've seen, when *and* is used truth-functionally, the conjunction formed is true when both conjuncts are true, and false otherwise. We can display this fact in a **truth table**:

M	R	R & M
T	T	T
T	F	F
F	T	F
F	F	F

The four rows below the horizontal line exhibit how the truth value of the compound sentence R & M depends on the truth value of the two conjuncts, the atomic sentences M and R. Each of the four rows gives a different **truth value assignment** to the atomic sentences R and M. The four assignments are all the possibilities there are. The table shows that the compound sentence R & M is true when the atomic sentences M and R are both true, and false otherwise.

One of these rows represents the actual world. For example, if it's a rainy Tuesday, then the third row represents the actual world. The rest of the rows represent possible, non-actual worlds. (Actually, each row represents a whole set of possible worlds. Row 3 for example, represents worlds in which it's a rainy Tuesday and pigs fly, in which it's a rainy Tuesday and pigs don't fly, etc.)

Note that on this truth table, as on every other one we will use, the atomic sentences are listed above the horizontal line and to the left of the vertical line *in alphabetical order*. (In this case, this happens not to be the order they appear in the compound sentence.) We'll use this convention just to make things uniform—to make it a little easier for your overworked and underpaid logic teacher to mark your tests. Another uniform convention for truth tables is the order of giving all possible values for the atomic sentences. When there are two atomic sentences, four rows giving their truth values should have them listed in this order:

T   T
T   F
F   T
F   F

The uniform order will again help in grading, but it will also help you make sure you have all the possibilities listed. Memorize this order.

The relation between the truth value of any conjunction and the truth value of its two conjuncts is the same, whatever those conjuncts are. We can note this fact by producing a truth table which doesn't include letters that stand for particular English sentences, but rather with italic capitals, standing for any letters at all:

P	Q	$P \& Q$
T	T	T
T	F	F
F	T	F
F	F	F

The **&** is a truth-functional connective in our language, and it often translates *and* in English, but not always. Sometimes *and* in English is not truth-functional. To see this, imagine that these two sentences are both true:

I woke up.
I brushed my teeth.

Clearly this sentence:

I woke up and I brushed my teeth.

is true.

But

I brushed my teeth and I woke up.

might be thought of as false, because *and* here may be interpreted to mean *and then*. When *and* means *and then*, the word *and* is not truth-functional, because the truth value of compounds made using *and* with this meaning would not be determined solely by the truth values of the conjuncts. Sometimes two true conjuncts would combine into a true compound, and sometimes into a false one.

Despite some occasions when *and* isn't truth-functional, its main use is truth-functional. We'll take & to be a correct translation of *and* into our language, recognizing, however, that sometimes this won't be exactly right.

Disjunctions

As we've seen, another connective is *or*. This is represented in our language by the symbol ∨, called the **wedge**. A compound sentence constructed by connecting two sentences with ∨ is called a **disjunction**; the two sentences connected are called **disjuncts**.

It's clear that a disjunction is false when both disjuncts are false, and that it's true when one disjunct is true and the other is false.

P	Q	$P \vee Q$
T	T	
T	F	T
F	T	T
F	F	F

But what about when both are true? Suppose, for example, that it's a rainy Monday; then is the compound sentence

It's raining or it's Monday.

true or false? It has seemed to some logicians that there's no clear answer to this in English. But we want there to be a truth-functional connective in our language which does have a clear answer, so logicians have made a more-or-less arbitrary decision to count a disjunction with two true disjuncts as itself true. They recognize that this does not correspond to the rather ambiguous status of *or* in English.

So here's the truth table defining the wedge:

P	Q	$P \vee Q$
T	T	T
T	F	T
F	T	T
F	F	F

The wedge thus represents what's called the **inclusive or** in English. (It's called inclusive because the T values include the case when both disjuncts are T.

The **exclusive or** is false when both connected sentences are true. (It "excludes" that case.) Suppose we used the symbol ∇ to stand for the exclusive or. Its truth table would be:]

P	Q	$P \nabla Q$
T	T	F
T	F	T
F	T	T
F	F	F

But it will turn out that we don't need a separate symbol of the exclusive or, because we can express it in terms of the symbols we already have. We'll see how shortly. So ∇ is not a symbol in our language.

Conditionals

The third connective ⊃ is called the **horseshoe**; $P \supset Q$ translates, very roughly, *If P then Q.* A sentence produced by connecting two with a horseshoe is called a **material conditional** (we'll call it a **conditional** for short). The sentence to the left of the horseshoe is called the **antecedent**; the one to the right is called the **consequent**.

Here is the truth table for the conditional:

P	Q	$P \supset Q$
T	T	T
T	F	F
F	T	T
F	F	T

The conditional, as you can see, is false when the antecedent is true and the consequent false; true otherwise (i.e., whenever the antecedent is false, and whenever the consequent is true.)

We've seen some degree of mismatch between the meaning assigned to the other symbols so far and the logic of the associated English; but this problem is worse for the horseshoe. There's no trouble with the second row of the truth table. In English, it seems, as in our truth table for the ⊃, every conditional statement with a true antecedent and a false consequent is counted as false. Consider, for example,

If bears are mammals, then they breathe with gills.
If Toronto is a big city, then there are fewer than 1000 cars
     there.

But we run into trouble in other cases. Consider conditional sentences in English in which both the antecedent and consequent are true:

If Jupiter has greater mass than the earth, its gravitational pull
     is stronger.
If Jupiter has greater mass than the earth a big red spot often
     appears on its surface.

We'd count the first of these sentences as true; but how about the second? It's true that a big red spot often appears on the surface of Jupiter, but that doesn't have anything to do with the fact that Jupiter is more massive than earth. So maybe the second sentence should be counted as false.

There's a similar problem with both cases in which the antecedent of an English conditional is false. When the consequent is true, the whole sentence in English, it seems, is sometimes counted as true:

If pigs had wings, they (still) couldn't fly.

And sometimes false:

If pigs had wings, they would be sloppy eaters.

Again because in the second example, the consequent has nothing to do with the antecedent. Do you agree that the first sentence is true and the second is false? Maybe it's not really clear what you'd say. The logic of English is rather messy.

Exercise 1.11 *Produce two English conditional sentences in which the antecedent and consequent are both false; but we'd count the first sentence as true and the second as false.*

So it looks pretty clear, anyway, then, that *if...then* is not a truth-functional connective in English. (Do you remember what makes a connective truth-functional?) So our truth-functional ⊃ doesn't translate that very well. But we'll just leave aside the difficulties of finding out what makes *if...then* sentences in English true or false, and just translate it into the ⊃ whenever we see it, realizing that our translation is rather rough and inadequate.

Biconditionals

The next connective is the **triple-bar:** ≡. A sentence constructed by connecting two sentences with a triple-bar is called a **material biconditional** (**biconditional** for short). There is no special name for the two sentences thus connected. The truth table for the biconditional is:

$\mathcal{P}$	Q	$\mathcal{P} \equiv Q$
T	T	T
T	F	F
F	T	F
F	F	T

Roughly speaking, $\mathcal{P} \equiv Q$ translates $\mathcal{P}$ *if and only if* Q. Take a look at its truth table: it shows that $\mathcal{P} \equiv Q$ is true when $\mathcal{P}$ and Q have the same truth value, false when they have different truth values. It means, roughly speaking, you can't have one without the other.

Negations

The last of the five connectives is ~, called the **tilde** (pronounced *TILL-duh*). It's odd to call this a connective, because it does not connect two sentences; it modifies one sentence, creating its **negation**. The negation of a sentence has the opposite truth value of that sentence:

$\mathcal{P}$	~$\mathcal{P}$
T	F
F	T

~$\mathcal{P}$ is the denial of $\mathcal{P}$. So ~$\mathcal{P}$ means *It's not the case that $\mathcal{P}$.* For example, if R means *It's raining*, then ~R means *It's not raining.*

We now have introduced all five of the connectives: &, v, ⊃ , ≡, ~. It will be necessary for you to remember how each of them works—to memorize their truth tables.

Compound Sentences

Each connective creates a compound sentence, and these compound sentences can themselves be connected with (or, in the case of negation, modified by) connectives.

Thus, for example, one can create the conditional

B ⊃ A

and connect this to C by the wedge to get

(B ⊃ A) v C.

Or one can negate B ⊃ A to get ~(B ⊃ A).

Note how the parentheses are necessary to show what has been connected to what. If we just wrote

B ⊃ A v C

That would be ambiguous (and illegal). It might mean a conditional with B as antecedent and A v C as consequent, properly written

B ⊃ (A v C)

or it might instead mean a disjunction with B ⊃ A as one disjunct and C as the other, properly written

(B ⊃ A) v C

The expression

B ⊃ A v C

is **not well-formed**: it needs parentheses to make it unambiguous.

Similarly,

D ≡ E & (F v G)

is not well-formed; it needs more parentheses.

(D ≡ E) & (F v G)

is well formed. So is

D ≡ (E & (F v G)).

A sentence that is not well-formed is illegal in our language—it's just nonsense.

Sometimes parentheses are optional. Both A ≡ B and (A ≡ B) are well-formed, and mean the same thing. Parentheses around an entire sentence are always optional.

~A v B

is well-formed, and means the same thing as

(~A v B)

Other ways of writing the same sentence, inserting optional parentheses, are

~(A) v B
~(A) v (B)
(~A) v (B)
((~A) v (B))

and so on. All these mean the same thing.

~(A v B)

is also well-formed, but it means something different from the previous expressions. The difference in meaning will be made clearer shortly. But for the moment note that

~A v B
(~A v B)
~(A) v B
~(A) v (B)
(~A) v (B)
((~A) v (B))

are all disjunctions, with ~A and B as disjuncts; but

~(A v B)

is the negation of the disjunction

A v B

The expression

~((A v B) & (C & B)

is not well-formed: it has one more left parenthesis than right.

The expression

~((A v B) & (C & B))

is well-formed. It is the negation of the conjunction of

(A v B) and (C & B)

The structure of

~((A v B) & (C & B))

is a little hard to see, because you have to figure out which parentheses pair up. It would make things clearer if you used a different style of parenthesis—square ones—in matched pairs, in addition to matched pairs of round ones:

~([A v B] & [C & B])

Using different styles of parentheses is helpful, but optional. It's correct to use a single style, or both, as long as the left and right parentheses that go together are the same style. That is:

~((A v B) & (C & B))

is okay, and so is

~([A v B] & [C & B])

and

~[[A v B] & (C & B)]

but this isn't:

~[[A v B) & [C & B))

You can tell whether or not a sentence is well-formed by thinking about how that sentence might have been built up out of its elements. Each stage in this construction must be a well-formed sentence in order that the finished product be well-formed. Any two well-formed sentences connected by &, v, ≡, or ⊃ makes a well-formed sentence. Any well-formed sentence negated by ~ makes a well-formed sentence.

For example, consider the sentence

~([A v B] & [C & B])

The basic elements of that sentence are the atomic sentences A, B, and C. These are all well-formed sentences (any capital letter is a well-formed sentence). Then one takes A and B and connects them by v to get the well-formed sentence [A v B]; and one takes C and B and connects them by & to get the well-formed sentence [C & B]. Those two are connected by & to make [A v B] & [C & B]; then finally that whole thing is negated to get ~([A v B] & [C & B]). Everything is well-formed all the way up.

Can you see why the following sentence is not well-formed?

~(A v B & C)

These sentences, however are well-formed:

~([A v B] & C)

~(A v [B & C])

Exercise 1.12 *State whether each of the following sentences is well-formed or not. When a sentence is not well-formed, explain why not.*

1.12.1.   (B ≡ (C & B) v H)

1.12.2.   ((G v H) v ~(H v G)]

1.12.3.   (A v (B & (C ≡ (D ⊃ E))))

1.12.4.   ~ ~ ~A v A

1.12.5.   L$_{14}$ v (m & P)

One further point while we're on this topic. When you're imagining building up compound sentences in the way just described, the last connective added is called the **main connective** of the sentence, and determines what kind of sentence it is. So, for example, to build up the sentence (A ⊃ ~B) ≡ (C v D) the last step would be to connect (A ⊃ ~B) and (C v D) with the ≡; so that ≡ is the main connective of the sentence, and the sentence is a biconditional.

Exercise 1.13 *Circle the main connective in each of the following sentences, and say what kind of sentence it is (that is, conjunction, disjunction, conditional, biconditional, or negation.)*

1.13.1. ~(B ≡ ((C & B) v H))

1.13.2. [(G v H) ⊃ ~(H & G)]

1.13.3. (A v (B & (C ≡ (D ⊃ E)))))

1.13.4. ~ ~ ~A & A

1.13.5. ~ ~ ~(A v A)

Truth Tables for Compound Sentences

Now we'll see how to do truth tables for any sentence. Here's how it's done for the sentence (B ⊃ A) v B. First, draw a horizontal line, and write all the atomic sentences included in this compound sentence (only A and B in this case) in alphabetical order starting from the far left, over this horizontal line; then draw a vertical line, and to the right of that, write the sentence we're doing a truth table of:

A	B	(B ⊃ A) ∨ B

Next, write down the all the combinations of truth values for the contained atomic sentences A and B on the rows underneath them, to the left of the vertical line, in the standard order:

A	B	(B ⊃ A) ∨ B
T	T	
T	F	
F	T	
F	F	

Next, copy the truth values assigned to the atomic sentences in each row, under their sentence letters to the right:

A	B	(B ⊃ A) ∨ B
T	T	T T T
T	F	F T F
F	T	T F T
F	F	F F F

Next, in each row, calculate the truth value of the enclosed sentence (B ⊃ A), as it is determined there by the truth values you've written down for B and A. Write this truth value under the ⊃. For example, in the second row, B is F and A is T, and we know, from the definition of ⊃, that when the antecedent is false and the consequent is true, the whole conditional is true. So T goes under the ⊃ in the second row.

A	B	(B ⊃ A) ∨ B
T	T	T T T
T	F	F **T** T F
F	T	T F T
F	F	F F F

Do this for each row.

A	B	(B ⊃ A) v B
T	T	T **T** T T
T	F	F **T** T F
F	T	T **F** F T
F	F	F **T** F F

Have a close look at the column under the ⊃ in the truth table above. Make sure you understand why the Ts and F in that column are as entered.

Now calculate the truth value in each row, for the whole disjunction. The disjuncts are (B ⊃ A), whose truth value in each row is under the ⊃, and the final B, whose value is under that B on the right. So, for example, in the third row, (B ⊃ A) is F, and B is T. The definition of the wedge tells us that when the first disjunct is false and the second is true, then the whole thing is true. Write that under the v in the third row; similarly calculate the other values:

		↓
A	B	(B ⊃ A) v B
T	T	T T T **T** T
T	F	F T T **T** F
F	T	T F F **T** T
F	F	F T F **T** F

Look carefully and make sure you understand the column under the v before you continue.

The little arrow above the v indicates that this column contains the truth value for the whole compound sentence. The v is the main connective in this sentence. The column under the main connective of a sentence always gives the truth value for the whole sentence, and a little arrow is always drawn on top to point at this column.

(Note, by the way, that, in this case, there is a T in every row of this column. (B ⊃ A) v B is true whatever the truth values of B and A are.)

You'll have noticed that we calculate truth-values of various sub-elements of the sentence in the same order as we would imagine building the sentence up out of its elements, when testing to see if it is well-formed.

Now have a look at the following truth table, for ~(C ≡ D), and make sure you understand everything in here.

C	D	~(C ≡ D)
T	T	F T T T
T	F	T T F F
F	T	T F F T
F	F	F F T F

The arrow ↓ points to the column under ~ in ~(C ≡ D).

Observe how the column under the arrow is the same as in the truth table for the exclusive or—remember that? (Look back a few pages if you don't.) This is a way (as promised) we can express the exclusive or.

Now note carefully the differences between these two truth tables:

G	H	~(G & H)	G	H	(~G & H)
T	T	F T T T	T	T	F T F T
T	F	T T F F	T	F	F T F F
F	T	T F F T	F	T	T F T T
F	F	T F F F	F	F	T F F F

The arrows ↓ point to the ~ in ~(G & H) and to the & in (~G & H).

The little arrow on top is in different places. In the first truth table, it's above the ~; but it's above the & in the second. The last step in building up ~(G & H) from its elements is negating (G & H); so this sentence is a negation, and its main connective is ~. But the last step in building up (~G & H) is connecting ~G and H by the &; so its main connective is the &, and it's a conjunction. Notice how these two have different truth values on some rows. For example, when G is true and H is false, on the second row of both truth tables, ~(G & H) is T, but (~G & H) is F. The difference in parentheses in the two makes all the difference. Be very sure at this point that you understand this sort of thing.

The next truth table is for a compound sentence that contains three atomic sentences.

A	B	C	A	&	(B	v	C)
T	T	T	T	T	T	T	T
T	T	F	T	T	T	T	F
T	F	T	T	T	F	T	T
T	F	F	T	F	F	F	F
F	T	T	F	F	T	T	T
F	T	F	F	F	T	T	F
F	F	T	F	F	F	T	T
F	F	F	F	F	F	F	F

(arrow ↓ points to the & column)

In this case, there are three different atomic sentences, so we need eight rows. (In a truth table with four different atomic sentences, sixteen rows are necessary, and so on; but enormous truth tables are boring and tedious, so we won't be seeing them.)

In the truth table above, you should take careful notice of the standard required arrangement of truth value combinations assigned to the left of the vertical line. If you have trouble memorizing this order, note that the order for the first four rows under the B and the C is the standard one for two-atomic-sentence truth tables, with T under all the As. Then that order for the B and C is repeated, for rows 5 through 8, with F under all the As. Another way of understanding these standard orders is to think of them on the analogy with counting in binary numbers, if you're familiar with that:

000
001
010
011
100   and so on

Exercise 1.14 *Do truth tables for each of the following sentences:*

1.14.1. B ≡ ~(C & B)

1.14.2. (G v H) v ~(H v G)

1.14.3. (M & J) & (C & D)

1.14.4. ~A v B

1.14.5. ~(A v B) (Notice how this has a different truth table from the one for 1.14.4.)

1.14.6. ~(A v ~A)

1.14.7. (A ⊃ B) v (B ⊃ A)

1.14.8. ~((A v B) & (C & B))

Translating

Translating from English into our symbolic language is sometimes tricky, because the "logic" of English is sometimes a very subtle matter. To produce good translations, you'll have to think about what would make English compound sentences true or false. Here are some general guidelines for translation.

- & is often a good translation of the following English expressions: *and, and also, but, however, although, though, yet, nonetheless, moreover.*

- v is often a good translation of *or, either...or* and *or else.*

- *Neither A nor B* can be translated as ~(A v B) or as ~A & ~B. These expressions mean the same thing.

- ~ is often a good translation of *not* and *it is not the case that* and other negative expressions.

- ≡ is often a good translation of *if and only if* and *provided exactly that.*

- A ⊃ B translates the following:
  1. If A then B
  2. B if A
  3. A only if B
  4. Only if B, then A

It's very hard to keep from getting confused when you think about translating various English conditional sentences. To facilitate translations of these English sentences into horseshoe expressions, I suggest you memorize this rule of thumb: in English, *if* (just by itself) comes before the antecedent of the conditional, but *only if* comes before its consequent. Thus in 1 and 2 above, *if* comes before the A, so both of them are translated into a horseshoe sentence in which A is the antecedent. In 3 and 4 above, *only if* comes before the B, so both of them are translated into a horseshoe sentence in which B is the consequent. So all of them have the same translation: A ⊃ B.

> **Exercise 1.15** *Translate:*
>
> 1.15.1. B only if A
>
> 1.15.2. If C then D
>
> 1.15.3. Only if E, then F
>
> 1.15.4. G if H

Even though the guidelines above are often helpful, you can't rely on them always to work. You can't merely translate by looking for English words corresponding to our logical symbols. You have to think about the meanings of the English sentences. The "logic" of English sentences is often a subtle matter; sentences that look like they have the same form sometimes have a different logic. For example, consider this. *Pretzels and beer are on the table* is appropriately translated when we understand it as a conjunction. It means the same as *Pretzels are on the table, and beer is on the table*. And it's appropriately translated (using the obvious sentence letters) as P & B. But *Pretzels and beer are a good combination* is not translated similarly. It is not correctly paraphrased as *Pretzels are a good combination, and beer is a good combination*. They aren't *each* a good combination. So it can't be translated as a conjunction. The best we can do with that sentence is to translate the whole thing by one sentence-letter.

Sometimes English sentences are ambiguous, not telling you clearly where the parentheses should go in their logical translation. Consider the sentence

> *Fred ate apples and bananas or cherries.*

Here's an English paraphrase that means the same thing, but that clearly reveals that what we have here can be understood as a compound of three atomic sentences:

> *Fred ate apples and Fred ate bananas or Fred ate cherries.*

Now, using obvious sentence letters, we can produce this translation:

> A & B v C

But that's not well-formed.

Here are two well-formed sentences:

A & (B v C)
(A & B) v C

These mean different things. Which one is intended by the English? It's not really clear. The English is logically ambiguous.

Sometimes punctuation—commas and semicolons—are used in more careful English writing to remove ambiguities like this. So:

Fred ate apples, and bananas or cherries is clearly A & (B v C)
Fred ate apples and bananas, or cherries is clearly (A & B) v C

In some cases, what might be ambiguity in English doesn't really matter.

Fred ate apples or bananas or cherries

can't be translated A v B v C. That sentence is not well-formed.

Either of these is acceptable:

(A v B) v C
A v (B v C)

And it doesn't matter which one you pick, because they're equivalent in logic: they mean the same thing, logically speaking.

Similarly, A & B & C is not well-formed; parentheses are needed. These:

(A & B) & C
A & (B & C)

are well-formed and equivalent. These:

A ⊃ B ⊃ C
A v B ≡ C

and the like are similarly not well-formed; parentheses are needed. But be careful: it does make a difference where parentheses are inserted in these. For example, (A v B) ≡ C is not equivalent to A v (B ≡ C). If you were asked to translate

Fred ate apples or he ate bananas if and only if he ate cherries

How would you know which translation is the right one? When the English is genuinely ambiguous, as in this case, you'd just have to take your best guess. If the case is genuinely ambiguous, you might be able to persuade your instructor to accept either translation as correct.

Exercise 1.16 *Translate:*

1.16.1. A and B, or C and D

1.16.2. A, and B or C; and D

1.16.3. If A then B, and C; or D

Exercise 1.17 *Translate all the following into our logical language. Use the following abbreviations for the contained atomic sentences:*

> B: Bob is here.
> C: Carol is here.
> T: Ted is here.
> A: Alice is here.

1.17.1.   Bob isn't here.

1.17.2.   Bob is here, but Alice isn't

1.17.3.   Only if Alice is here, then Ted is.

1.17.4.   Alice is here provided exactly that Ted isn't.

1.17.5.   Bob and Alice are both here.

1.17.6.   Neither Alice nor Carol is here.

1.17.7.   Bob and Ted are here, but Alice isn't.

1.17.8.   Bob or Ted is here if Alice isn't

1.17.9.   If and only if Alice isn't here, Bob isn't.

1.17.10.   All four of them are here.

1.17.11.   None of them is here.

1.17.12.   Bob is here only if Ted isn't.

1.17.13.   Bob or Ted, and Carol or Alice, are here.

1.17.14.   It's not the case that Bob is not here.

1.17.15.   Bob is here but Alice and Ted aren't.

1.17.16.   Only if Bob and Ted are here, then Alice is.

1.17.17.   Only Alice is here.

1.17.18.   Bob is here and Alice is here, only if Ted is.

1.17.19.   Bob is here, and Alice is here only if Ted is.

Using Truth Tables

Now we can use truth tables to prove all sorts of things.

Take a look at the truth table for (B ⊃ A) v B:

| | | | ↓ | | | | |
A	B	(B	⊃ A)	v	B
T	T	T T	T	T T
T	F	F T	T	T F
F	T	T F	F	T T
F	F	F T	F	T F

The column under the arrow shows that this sentence is true no matter what truth values the included atomic sentences have. That means that it's necessarily true—it's not possible that it be false. Each row shows us another possible state of affairs regarding the sentences A and B: the four rows show us all possibilities. But in none of these possible states of affairs would the compound sentence be false. Thus we have shown that it's logically true.

The sentence A & (B & ~A) has a F in every row in the column giving its truth value. Thus its truth table proves that it is logically false.

Exercise 1.18 *Do the truth table for* A & (B & ~A). *If you don't get an* F *in every row in the column under the arrow, you've made some mistake.*

On the next truth table, note that instead of filling in all those letters necessary for the step-by-step calculation, I've written in only the last step—the truth values for the compound sentence, under the arrow. I've done the intermediate steps in my head, to save some tedious writing.

| | | ↓ |
C	G	~(C ⊃ G)
T	T	F
T	F	T
F	T	F
F	F	F

This kind of "short form" truth table may be permitted by your instructor—ask! But be careful if you use it that you don't make any careless mistakes. When you're just learning how to use these truth tables, it's probably better to write in everything.

This truth table shows that the sentence ~(C ⊃ G) is true in at least one row (that is, given one truth value assignment to the atomic sentences it includes) and false in at least one other. When a sentence is true on at least one row and false on at least one, the sentence is logically indeterminate.

Since all you need to show that this is indeterminate is one row in which the sentence is true and one in which it is false, you might even just show two rows to prove it, one making the sentence T, and the other making it F, as in this very short short form table:

C	G	↓ ~(C ⊃ G)
T	T	
T	F	T
F	T	F
F	F	

Exercise 1.19 *Go back to those truth tables you did for Exercise 1.14. State, in each case, whether the truth table proves the sentence is logically true, logically false, or logically indeterminate.*

Now take a look at this truth table, again done in short-form.

G	H	↓ ~(G v H)	↓ ~G & ~H
T	T	F	F
T	F	F	F
F	T	F	F
F	F	T	T

This table shows the truth values, on each assignment, for two sentences: ~(G v H) and ~G & ~H. Notice that there are no rows on which the two get different truth values. That is: any row in which one sentence is T, the other is also; and any row in which one sentence is F, the other is also. We've just proven that these two are logically equivalent.

But this truth table:

G	H	↓ ~(G v H)	↓ ~G & H
T	T	F	F
T	F	F	F
F	T	F	T
F	F	T	F

contains at least one row in which the two sentences have different truth values. (In fact, two rows: 3 and 4.) We have proven that these two sentences are not logically equivalent. Actually, to prove this, you'd only have to give a really short short-form table: all you'd need to show is one row on which they have different truth values:

G	H	↓ ~(G v H)	↓ ~G & H
T	T		
T	F		
F	T	F	T
F	F		

Exercise 1.20 *Prove, by means of a truth table, whether the two sentences in each pair are equivalent or not.*

1.20.1.   ~(A & B) , ~(A v B)

1.20.2.   (C ⊃ ~D) , (D ⊃ ~C)

1.20.3.   (A v B) , (B v A)

1.20.4.   (G ⊃ H) , ~(H ⊃ G)

1.20.5.   ~(A & B) , ~A & ~B

1.20.6.   ~(A & B) , ~A v ~B

The next truth table gives values for three sentences:

G	H	↓ ~(G v H)	↓ ~G & ~H	↓ G
T	T	F	F	T
T	F	F	F	T
F	T	F	F	F
F	F	T	T	F

There is no row on which all three sentences are T. We have proven that the set of three sentences is logically inconsistent.

But compare this truth table:

	↓	↓	↓
G H	~(G v H)	~G & ~H	~G
T T	F	F	F
T F	F	F	F
F T	F	F	T
F F	T	T	T

Here there is at least one row in which all three are true (row 4). We've proven these three are consistent.

Since this row suffices to show the set consistent, you might give a really short short-form table just showing this row to prove it:

	↓	↓	↓
G H	~(G v H)	~G & ~H	~G
T T			
T F			
F T			
F F	T	T	T

Exercise 1.21   *For each numbered item, do a truth table showing whether the set of sentences is consistent or inconsistent. Which does it show?*

1.21.1. { A & ~B , A ⊃ B }

1.21.2. { C v (D ≡ E) , C & E }

1.21.3. { A }

1.21.4. { ~(A v ~A) }

Now consider this argument:

J ⊃ K
~K
—————
~J

Remember the definition for validity: this argument is valid if and only if it is impossible for the conclusion to be false if the premises are all true. Now examine the short-form truth table on which we have calculated the truth values for both premises and the conclusion:

| | | ↓ | ↓ | ↓ |
J	K	J ⊃ K	~K	~J
T	T	T	F	F
T	F	F	T	F
F	T	T	F	T
F	F	T	T	T

There is no row on this table on which the premises (J ⊃ K , ~K) are all (both) true and the conclusion (~J) is false. The only row on which the premises are all (that is, *both*) true is row 4; but the conclusion is true on that row. These rows show all possibilities. So it is impossible that the conclusion be false while the premises are true. We have proven it valid.

Compare the truth table for

J ⊃ K
~J
―――――
~K

| | | ↓ | ↓ | ↓ |
J	K	J ⊃ K	~J	~K
T	T	T	F	F
T	F	F	F	T
F	T	T	T	F
F	F	T	T	T

On this one, there is at least one row in which the premises are both true but the conclusion is false—row 3. So this truth table proves this argument invalid.

One can give this shorter-short form table to prove this argument invalid:

| | | ↓ | ↓ | ↓ |
J	K	J ⊃ K	~J	~K
T	T			
T	F			
F	T	T	T	F
F	F			

Exercise 1.22 *Using a truth table, prove each argument valid or invalid.*

1.22.1.   (A ⊃ ~B) , (~A ⊃ B) therefore A ≡ B

1.22.2.   C & D therefore C v D

1.22.3.   B & G , B v G therefore G

1.22.4.   A ⊃ ~A , (B ⊃ A) ⊃ B therefore A ≡ ~B

1.22.5.   G therefore A ⊃ A

1.22.6.   ~(A v ~B) therefore A

1.22.7.   A , ~A therefore B

Did you notice, by the way, that two of the exercises in 1.22 prove examples of the "peculiar consequences" we considered earlier? The arguments in 1.22.5 and 1.22.7 are both valid, even though in both cases the conclusion was irrelevant to the premises. The validity of 1.22.5 resulted from the fact that the conclusion was truth-functionally true; 1.22.7, from the fact that the premises were inconsistent.

Exercise 1.23 *Now go back and have a look at those "peculiar consequences" listed in Exercise 1.10, page 15. Prove examples of each.*

Exercise 1.24 *How many rows, at minimum, on a short-form truth table do you have to show to prove that:*

1.24.1.   A sentence is logically true

1.24.2.   A sentence is logically false

1.24.3.   A sentence is logically indeterminate

1.24.4.   A sentence is not logically true

1.24.5.   A sentence is not logically false

1.24.6.   A sentence is not logically indeterminate

1.24.7.   An argument is valid

1.24.8.   An argument is invalid

1.24.9.   An argument is not valid

1.24.10.   An argument is not invalid

1.24.11.   Two sentences are equivalent

1.24.12.   Two sentences are not equivalent

1.24.13.   A set of sentences is consistent

1.24.14.   A set of sentences is inconsistent

Truth-Functional Logical Properties

Some additional bits of vocabulary we'll be using:

All of the logical properties we have been looking at apply because of the truth-functional characteristics of the sentences. (We shall see later that there is another kind of validity, of consistency, etc.) So the validity we've been looking at is of a special sort, called **truth-functional validity**; the logical truth is **truth-functional truth**, and so on. Using these more specific terms, we can sum up what we have seen so far:

- A sentence is **truth-functionally true** if and only if it is true on every truth value assignment (that is, on every row of its truth table). A sentence is **truth-functionally false** if and only if it is false on every truth value assignment. A sentence is **truth-functionally indeterminate** if and only if it is neither truth-functionally true nor truth-functionally false; that is, if and only if there is at least one truth value assignment on which it is true, and at least one on which it is false.

- Two sentences are **truth-functionally equivalent** if and only if there is no truth value assignment which gives them different truth values.

- A set of sentences is **truth-functionally consistent** if and only if there is at least one truth value assignment on which all the sentences in the set are true. A set is **truth-functionally inconsistent** if and only if the set is not truth-functionally consistent; that is, if and only if there is no truth value assignment on which all the sentences in the set are true.

- An argument is **truth-functionally valid** if and only if there is no truth value assignment on which all the premises are true and the conclusion is false. An argument is **truth-functionally invalid** if and only if it is not truth-functionally valid; that is, if and only if there is at least one truth value assignment on which all the premises are true and the conclusion is false.

Exercise 1.25 *Explain on the basis of these truth table accounts of these concepts why it is that:*

1.25.1. Every argument with a truth-functionally true conclusion is truth-functionally valid.

1.25.2. Every argument with a truth-functionally false premise is truth-functionally valid.

1.25.3. Every set which includes a truth-functionally false sentence is truth-functionally inconsistent.

1.25.4. Every pair of sentences in which both sentences are truth-functionally true is a truth-functionally equivalent pair.

1.25.5. Every pair of sentences in which both sentences are truth-functionally false is a truth-functionally equivalent pair.

Answers to Exercises in Chapter One

EXERCISE 1.1

1.1.1. Pierre Trudeau was the first Prime Minister of Canada. SENTENCE

1.1.2. Never let a dog sense that you are afraid. NOT A SENTENCE. You might be tempted to say that this is true, in a matter of speaking, because it's good advice, but an utterance of advice in the form of an imperative (= do this, don't do that) is really neither true nor false. On the other hand, there are "advice" utterances which are true or false, so they are sentences; for example, you might give advice to somebody who is looking for the bus stop by saying "The bus stop is one block north of here."

1.1.3. Would you like coffee or tea? NOT A SENTENCE

1.1.4. Hooray for the Mooseheads! NOT A SENTENCE

EXERCISE 1.2

1.2.1. You live in Halifax, don't you? SENTENCE. Normally utterances which end with a question-mark aren't sentences; but this one might be an exception. It's probably best interpreted as doing the same thing as the clear sentence "You live in Halifax," true if the person addressed does live in Halifax.

1.2.2. My cousin lives in Moncton. SENTENCE. The complication here is that you might want to say that this sentence is neither really true nor really false, or else maybe both, because it's true when Pierre utters it, and false when Sally utters it. What we're talking about, however, is a particular utterance, by a particular person at a particular time. Each of them is either true or false.

1.2.3. The first human will land on Mars in the year 2049. SENTENCE. We don't know now whether it's true or false, but (according to the view of most philosophers) it now really is true or false. Questions have arisen here, however, because some philosophers argue that the future is "open" in some sense, so that sentences about the future are neither true nor false.

1.2.4. I name this ship the *Joseph Stalin.* PROBABLY NOT A SENTENCE, though it looks like one. This might be interpreted as simply true (if the speaker really is naming the ship that) or false otherwise; but maybe the function of this utterance is not to describe the speaker's action at all, but rather to *do* the action of naming.

1.2.5. I would like some tea. PROBABLY NOT A SENTENCE. Interpreting this as a request for tea, rather than a (true or false) report of what the speaker likes, it's neither true nor false.

1.2.6. This sentence is false. BIG PROBLEM HERE. It looks like a sentence, but it can't be false, because then it would be true; and it can't be true, because then it would be false. Maybe it's neither true nor false, but then it's not a sentence.

1.2.7. (Said while eating chocolate ice cream): "Delicious!" PROBABLY NOT A SENTENCE. It seems rather to be an expression of the speaker's feeling, like "Yippee!" Then it would not be true or false. Although it might be interpreted as a short way of saying the sentence discussed next, which raises problems.

1.2.8. This chocolate ice-cream is delicious! HARD TO SAY. One plausible view is that it's an expression of the speaker's feeling, just like "Yum!" so it's not a sentence. But maybe it's better interpreted as a true or false statement about the ice cream (true if the ice cream really is delicious)— thus a sentence. Or maybe it's really a statement about the speaker (true if the speaker really enjoys the taste of this ice cream.) Think about whether or not it would be appropriate to respond "True" or "False" when somebody said this; and if it's appropriate to give either response, what facts exactly would make this true or false.

EXERCISE 1.3

1.3.1. I'm not going to be at the party tonight because I have logic homework to do. NOT AN ARGUMENT. AN EXPLANATION.

1.3.2. It's likely to be sunny tomorrow, because the weather forecast said so, and they're usually right.

1.3.3. PROBABLY AN ARGUMENT: That's not my car. My car's green. This interpretation takes it that the speaker is trying to convince the hearer that it's not the speaker's car. But maybe not, if the speaker is just commenting on his car's colour.

1.3.4. All Canadians know that Saskatchewan is flat. You won't find any Canadians going to Saskatchewan to ski, because nobody goes to ski to a place they know is flat.

1.3.5. Fred had seventeen beers and consequently passed out. NOT AN ARGUMENT—AN EXPLANATION.

1.3.6. I'm really smart. So I'll surely get an A in logic.

1.3.7. Since I already had lunch, I'm not going to the café with you. NOT AN ARGUMENT—AN EXPLANATION.

1.3.8. People raised in Mexico usually enjoy spicy hot food. I think José will like your cooking. Probably an argument: it's the sort of thing that would be said to convince the hearer that José will like the meal. The words "I think" are not underlined, because the conclusion is not that the speaker thinks something (which is no doubt true, if uttered sincerely) but rather the assertion about José. The "I think" part here merely makes that assertion a little more tentative.

1.3.9. Fred is home tonight, because every night he's always either at the pub or at home, and he's not at the pub.

1.3.10. Fred is home tonight, because the hockey playoffs are on TV. HARD TO SAY whether this is an argument or not. It might be said to convince the hearer that Fred is home tonight. But it might be said to a hearer who already knows that Fred is home tonight, but wants an explanation of why Fred stayed home.

EXERCISE 1.4

1.4.1. If an argument is valid, all its premises are true. FALSE

1.4.2. If an argument has a false conclusion, the argument is invalid. FALSE

1.4.3. If a valid argument has true premises, its conclusion must be true. TRUE

1.4.4. If a valid argument has a true conclusion, all its premises must be true. FALSE

1.4.5. If a valid argument has a false conclusion, all its premises must be false. FALSE

1.4.6. If a valid argument has a false conclusion, its premises can't all be true. TRUE

1.4.7. An invalid argument might have premises that are all true and a true conclusion. TRUE

1.4.8. An invalid argument might have premises that are all true and a false conclusion. TRUE

1.4.9. An invalid argument might have a true conclusion and at least one false premise. TRUE

1.4.10. A sound argument might have a false conclusion. FALSE

EXERCISE 1.5

1.5.1.   If it's raining then the picnic is off.
The picnic is off.
It's raining.

INVALID

1.5.2.   If it's raining then the picnic is off.
The picnic is not off.
It's not raining.

VALID

1.5.3.   No reptiles can fly
Pigs are reptiles
No pigs can fly

VALID

1.5.4.   Every reptile can fly
Pigs are reptiles
Every pig can fly

VALID

1.5.5.   Sally is extremely thirsty
Sally is offered a cold drink of water.
Sally will drink the water

INVALID

1.5.6.   Fred buys Moosehead or Alpine at the liquor store.
Fred bought Moosehead today
Fred didn't buy Alpine today.

INVALID – he might have bought both. (Assuming inclusive *or*)

1.5.7.   All Canadians are happy or handsome
          No Canadian is silly
          All happy people are silly or hardworking.
          All hardworking people are sily or handsome.
          All Canadians are handsome.

          VALID, though this is very hard to see. We'll develop tools later for
          testing and proving validity, which will show that this one is valid.

EXERCISE 1.6

{ Fred is here or in the pub. , Fred isn't here. } CONSISTENT
{ Fred is here or in the pub. , Fred isn't in the pub. } CONSISTENT
{ Fred isn't here. , Fred isn't in the pub. } CONSISTENT

EXERCISE 1.7

1.7.1. { Today is Monday. , It rains here every Monday. , It's raining today. }
       CONSISTENT
1.7.2. { Today is Monday. , It never rains here on Monday. , It's raining
       today. } INCONSISTENT
1.7.3. { Today isn't Monday. , It always rains here on Monday. , It isn't raining
       today.} CONSISTENT
1.7.4. { If it rains tomorrow, we'll go to the movies. , If we go to the movies,
       we'll eat popcorn. , It will rain tomorrow. , We won't eat popcorn
       tomorrow. } INCONSISTENT

EXERCISE 1.8

1.8.1. Turtles can fly. LOGICALLY INDETERMINATE but of course false.
1.8.2. There are more than five coffee trees in Brazil. LOGICALLY
       INDETERMINATE but of course true.
1.8.3. Fred loves Zelda. LOGICALLY INDETERMINATE. Not knowing Fred
       or Zelda, you don't know whether it's true or false, but you do know that
       it's logically indeterminate.
1.8.4. There is a pig which is not a mammal. LOGICALLY
       INDETERMINATE. (You might think, however, that it's definitionally
       false—if pigs are by definition mammals.)
1.8.5. All pigs are mammals, and there is a pig which is not a mammal.
       LOGICALLY FALSE.
1.8.6. All unsupported heavier-than-air things fall toward the ground.
       LOGICALLY INDETERMINATE. This one is, one might suppose, a rather
       basic law of nature, and in that sense might be thought to be "necessary".
       But it's not logically true.

1.8.7. Either something is green or it isn't. LOGICALLY TRUE.

1.8.8. No pig can do algebra, but Porky is a pig and he can do algebra. LOGICALLY FALSE

1.8.9. There exists a machine that runs forever without using any power. INDETERMINATE—contrary to the basic laws of physics, but still logically possible.

1.8.10. If today is Tuesday, then today is not Tuesday. This one probably looks to you like a LOGICALLY FALSE sentence. That's a reasonable answer for you to give at this point—full marks! But you'll find out a little later that, given the logical system we're using, this one turns out to be INDETERMINATE: it's the same as saying *It's not Tuesday*, so it's false every Tuesday, and true every other day.

1.8.11. 7 + 5 = 12 This one is controversial. Most—but not all—philosophers take this to be necessarily true. Of those, some (as was mentioned above) take this to be necessarily true, but neither logically or definitionally true. But some philosophers think that arithmetic is a form of logic. That would make arithmetic truths logically true.

EXERCISE 1.9

1.9.1. It's raining or it's Tuesday. , It's raining. NOT EQUIVALENT. We can imagine it's possible that the first is true, but the second false. Think of a sunny Tuesday. (Make sure you see why this would make the first one true and the second one false.)

1.9.2. Canada is south of Peru. , Most fish wear eyeglasses. NOT EQUIVALENT. Both are obviously actually false, but there is a possible world in which they have different truth values: a world in which the relative positions of Canada and Peru are the familiar ones, but in which most fish do wear eyeglasses. In this possible world, the first sentence is false and the second one is true.

1.9.3. No pig is purple. , All purple things are non-pigs. EQUIVALENT. Try to think of a possible world in which they have different truth values. In each world you think of either there are no purple pigs, in which case both sentences are true, or else there are purple pigs, in which case both are false. There are no possible worlds in which the truth values of these two sentences are different, so they're logically equivalent.

1.9.4. If Fred goes, I'll go. , If I don't go, Fred won't go. EQUIVALENT. You may be able to discover this by thinking about possible worlds; if you can't, wait a bit till we develop the logical tools to prove they're equivalent.

EXERCISE 1.10

1.10.1. Each logically true sentence is logically equivalent to all other logically true sentences. Because they all must be true, it's impossible that one be true and another false; so they must all have the same truth value. In other words: in each possible world, both sentences are true, so in each possible world, one sentence has the same truth value as the other.

1.10.2. Every argument which has inconsistent premises is valid. It's impossible that any argument with inconsistent premises have all true premises; so it's impossible that any such argument have all true premises and a false conclusion. In other words: because the set of premises is inconsistent, there is no possible world in which they're all true. So there is no possible world in which they're all true and the conclusion is false. But that's the definition of validity!

1.10.3. Every argument which has a logically true conclusion is valid. It's impossible that any such argument have true premises and a false conclusion. In other words: the conclusion is logically true, so it's true in each possible world (whatever the truth values of the premises are there). So there is no possible world in which the conclusion is false. So there is no possible world in which the premises are true and the conclusion is false. But that's the definition of validity!

1.10.4. Every set of sentences containing one that is logically false is inconsistent. Because one sentence is logically false, it's impossible that it's true; so it's impossible that all the sentences in this set be true at once. In other words: that sentence is false in all possible worlds; so there is no possible world in which every sentence in that set is true. But that's the definition of inconsistency.

1.10.5. A set containing one logically false sentence is an inconsistent set, because it's impossible that all (one!) of the sentences in that set are true. In other words, there is no possible world in which all (one!) of those sentences are true. We speak, a little peculiarly, about a set containing only one thing, and about "all the members" of that set.

EXERCISE 1.11

There are indefinitely many ways of answering this question, but here are two:
1. If my shoes were on fire, then I'd smell smoke. TRUE
2. If my shoes were on fire, I'd eat them. FALSE

EXERCISE 1.12

1.12.1.   (B ≡ (C & B) v H)

Not well-formed. It's ambiguous: is B connected to [(C&B) v H] by the ≡? Or is [B ≡ (C & B)] connected to H by the v? It's easier to see this sort of problem in a simpler similarly not-well-formed sentence: L ≡ M ⊃ N. An extra pair of brackets is needed here. Either of these two sentences would be well-formed:

(B ≡ [(C & B) v H])

([B ≡ (C & B)] v H)

Note in addition that the outermost parenthesis pair—before the initial B and after the H—isn't necessary, but it isn't wrong either.

1.12.2.   ((G v H) v ~(H v G)]

This one is not well-formed because the initial (and the final] do not match. It would be okay if there were a [to start with instead, or a) at the end.

1.12.3.   (A v (B & (C ≡ (D ⊃ E)))

Not well-formed because the there are four left-brackets but only three right ones. Add a right-bracket at the end to make it well-formed:
(A v (B & (C ≡ (D ⊃ E))))

1.12.4.   ~~~A v A

This one is well-formed. There's nothing wrong with more than one ~. Here's an equivalent way of writing this, also well-formed: ~(~[~A]) v A. You might be tempted to eliminate two of the negations, to turn the sentence into ~A v A. This is in fact logically equivalent to the original sentence (two negations "cancel out" so to speak) but the original sentence was well-formed, and doesn't require any changes.

1.12.5.   L₁₄ v (m & P)

Not well-formed. The L_{14} is okay: an upper-case letter followed by a numerical subscript is a well-formed sentence. But the m is not: lower-case letters are not well-formed sentences.

EXERCISE 1.13

1.13.1.   ⊖(B ≡ ((C & B) v H))
          Negation

1.13.2.   [(G v H)⊖~(H & G)]
          Conditional

1.13.3.   (A⊙(B & (C ≡ (D ⊃ E))))
          Disjunction

1.13.4.   ~~~A⊗A
          Conjunction

1.13.5.   ⊖~~(A v A)
          Negation

EXERCISE 1.14

1.14.1. B ≡ ~(C & B)

B	C	B ≡ ~(C & B)
T	T	T F F T T T
T	F	T T T F F T
F	T	F F T T F F
F	F	F F T F F F

(arrow ↓ points to the ≡ column)

1.14.2. (G v H) v ~(H v G)

G	H	(G v H) v ~(H v G)
T	T	T TT T FTTT
T	F	T TF T FFTT
F	T	F TT T FTTF
F	F	F FF T TFFF

(arrow ↓ points to the middle v column)

1.14.3. (M & J) & (C & D)
Short truth table done here. The important thing to notice is the order of assignments to the four atomic sentences, to the left of the vertical line. (Did you remember to write down the atomic sentences in alphabetical order?)

C	D	J	M	(M & J) & (C & D)
T	T	T	T	T
T	T	T	F	F
T	T	F	T	F
T	T	F	F	F
T	F	T	T	F
T	F	T	F	F
T	F	F	T	F
T	F	F	F	F
F	T	T	T	F
F	T	T	F	F
F	T	F	T	F
F	T	F	F	F
F	F	T	T	F
F	F	T	F	F
F	F	F	T	F
F	F	F	F	F

(arrow ↓ points to the final & column)

1.14.4. ~A v B

A	B	~A v B
		↓
T	T	FT T T
T	F	FT F F
F	T	TF T T
F	F	TF T F

1.14.5. ~(A v B) (Notice how this has a different truth table from the one for 4.)

A	B	~(A v B)
		↓
T	T	F T T T
T	F	F T T F
F	T	F F T T
F	F	T F F F

1.14.6. ~(A v ~A)

A	~(A v ~A)
	↓
T	F T T FT
F	F F T TF

1.14.7. (A ⊃ B) v (B ⊃ A) (Truth table somewhat shortened)

A	B	(A ⊃ B) v (B ⊃ A)
		↓
T	T	T T T
T	F	F T T
F	T	T T F
F	F	T T T

1.14.8. ~((A v B) & (C& B)) (A somewhat shortened table again)

A	B	C	~((A v B) & (C& B))
			↓
T	T	T	F T T T
T	T	F	T T F F
T	F	T	T T F F
T	F	F	T T F F
F	T	T	F T T T
F	T	F	T T F F
F	F	T	T F F F
F	F	F	T F F F

EXERCISE 1.15

1.15.1.	B only if A	B ⊃ A
1.15.2.	If C then D	C ⊃ D
1.15.3.	Only if E, then F	F ⊃ E
1.15.4.	G if H	H ⊃ G

EXERCISE 1.16

1.16.1.   A and B, or C and D
(A & B) v (C & D)

1.16.2.   A, and B or C; and D
[A & (B v C)] & D

1.16.3.   If A then B, and C; or D
[(A ⊃ B) & C] v D

Note how the semicolon is a stronger break in this sentence than the comma. If you were speaking this sort of sentence you might have put a pause where the comma is, and a longer pause where the semicolon is:
"*If* A *then* B ... *and* C .... *or* D."

EXERCISE 1.17

1.17.1.   Bob isn't here.
~B

1.17.2.   Bob is here, but Alice isn't.
B & ~A

1.17.3.   Only if Alice is here, then Ted is.
T ⊃ A

1.17.4.   Alice is here provided exactly that Ted isn't.
A ≡ ~T

1.17.5.   Bob and Alice are both here.
B & A

1.17.6.   Neither Alice nor Carol is here.
~A & ~C
another way, equally correct: ~(A v C)

1.17.7.   Bob and Ted are here, but Alice isn't.
(B & T) & ~A

1.17.8.   Bob or Ted is here if Alice isn't.
~A ⊃ (B v T)

1.17.9. If and only if Alice isn't here, Bob isn't.
~A ≡ ~B

1.17.10. All four of them are here.
(B & C) & (T & A)

1.17.11. None of them is here.
(~B & ~C) & (~T & ~A)
another way equally correct:
~(B ∨ C) & ~(T ∨ A)

1.17.12. Bob is here only if Ted isn't.
B ⊃ ~T

1.17.13. Bob or Ted, and Carol or Alice, are here.
(B ∨ T) & (C ∨ A)

1.17.14. It's not the case that Bob is not here.
~ ~B
(you might be tempted to eliminate the double negative here, and translate this simply as B. This is equivalent to ~ ~B, though ~ ~B is closer to the English. Your instructor may accept any equivalent translation on a test—ask!)

1.17.15. Bob is here but Alice and Ted aren't.
B & (~A & ~T)

1.17.16. Only if Bob and Ted are here, then Alice is.
A ⊃ (B & T)

1.17.17. Only Alice is here.
A & [~B & (~T & ~C)]

1.17.18. Bob is here and Alice is here, only if Ted is.
(B & A) ⊃ T

1.17.19. Bob is here, and Alice is here only if Ted is.
B & (A ⊃ T)

EXERCISE 1.18

A	B	↓ A & (B & ~A)		
T	T	T F	T F	FT
T	F	T F	F F	FT
F	T	F F	T T	TF
F	F	F F	F F	TF

EXERCISE 1.19

1.19.1. LOGICALLY INDETERMINATE
1.19.2. LOGICALLY TRUE
1.19.3. LOGICALLY INDETERMINATE
1.19.4. LOGICALLY INDETERMINATE
1.19.5. LOGICALLY INDETERMINATE
1.19.6. LOGICALLY FALSE
1.19.7. LOGICALLY TRUE
1.19.8. LOGICALLY INDETERMINATE

EXERCISE 1.20

1.20.1. ~(A & B) , ~(A v B) NOT EQUIVALENT

A	B	↓ ~(A & B)	↓ ~(A v B)
T	T	F	F
T	F	T	F
F	T	T	F
F	F	T	T

1.20.2. (C ⊃ ~D) , (D ⊃ ~C) EQUIVALENT

C	D	↓ (C ⊃ ~D)	↓ (D ⊃ ~C)
T	T	F	F
T	F	T	T
F	T	T	T
F	F	T	T

1.20.3. (A v B) , (B v A) EQUIVALENT

A	B	↓ A v B	↓ B v A
T	T	T	T
T	F	T	T
F	T	T	T
F	F	F	F

1.20.4. (G ⊃ H), ~(H ⊃ G) NOT EQUIVALENT. Note that the one row shown is sufficient to prove this.

			↓	↓
G	H		G ⊃ H	~(H ⊃ G)
T	T		T	F
T	F			
F	T			
F	F			

1.20.5. ~(A & B) , ~A & ~B NOT EQUIVALENT. This surprises some people who expect an analogy with "distribution" in arithmetic, where -(x + y) = (-x - y). The one row shown is sufficient to prove non-equivalence.

			↓	↓
A	B		~(A & B)	~A & ~B
T	T			
T	F		T	F
F	T			
F	F			

120.6. ~(A & B) , ~A v ~B EQUIVALENT. This is the way "distribution" works in logic.

			↓	↓
A	B		~(A & B)	~A v ~B
T	T		F	F
T	F		T	T
F	T		T	T
F	F		T	T

EXERCISE 1.21

1.21.1. { A & ~B , A ⊃ B } INCONSISTENT. Note that all rows must be shown.

			↓	↓
A	B		A & ~B	A ⊃ B
T	T		F	T
T	F		T	F
F	T		F	T
F	F		F	T

1.21.2. { C v (D ≡ E) , C & E } CONSISTENT. One row is sufficient.

			↓	↓
C	D	E	C v (D ≡ E)	C & E
T	T	T	T	T
T	T	F		
T	F	T		
T	F	F		
F	T	T		
F	T	F		
F	F	T		
F	F	F		

1.21.3. { A } CONSISTENT: In row 1, all (that is, all one) of the sentences are T.

	↓
A	A
T	T
F	F

1.21.4. { ~(A v ~A) } INCONSISTENT: No row in which all (that is, all one) are T.

	↓
A	~(A v ~A)
T	F T
F	F T

EXERCISE 1.22

1.22.1. (A ⊃ ~B) , (~A ⊃ B) therefore A ≡ B   INVALID: In row 2, both premises are T, and the conclusion is F.

		↓	↓	↓
A	B	(A ⊃ ~B)	(~A ⊃ B)	A ≡ B
T	T	F	T	T
T	F	T	T	F
F	T	T	T	F
F	F	T	F	T

1.22.2. C & D therefore C v D VALID: There is no row in which premise is T
and conclusion is F.

C	D	↓ (C & D)	↓ (C v D)
T	T	T	T
T	F	F	T
F	T	F	T
F	F	F	F

1.22.3. B & G , B v G therefore G VALID: There is no row in which premises
are both T, but conclusion is F.

B	G	↓ (B & G)	↓ B v G	↓ G
T	T	T	T	T
T	F	F	T	F
F	T	F	T	T
F	F	F	F	T

1.22.4. A ⊃ ~A , (B ⊃ A) ⊃ B therefore A ≡ ~B VALID. No row on which all
the premises are T and the conclusion is F.

A	B	↓ A ⊃ ~A	↓ (B ⊃ A) ⊃ B	↓ A ≡ ~B
T	T	F	T	F
T	F	F	F	T
F	T	T	T	T
F	F	T	F	F

1.22.5. G therefore A ⊃ A VALID: No row in which premise is T, conclusion
is F.

A	G	↓ G	↓ A ⊃ A
T	T	T	T
T	F	F	T
F	T	T	T
F	F	F	T

1.22.6. ~(A v ~B) therefore A INVALID, shown by the third row.

A	B	↓ ~(A v ~B)	↓ A
T	T	F	T
T	F	F	T
F	T	T	F
F	F	F	F

1.22.7. A , ~A therefore B VALID.

A	B	↓ A	↓ ~A	↓ B
T	T	T	F	T
T	F	T	F	F
F	T	F	T	T
F	F	F	T	F

EXERCISE 1.23

(1.10.1.) Logically true sentences are equivalent.

A	B	↓ A ⊃ A	↓ (B v ~B)
T	T	T	T
T	F	T	T
F	T	T	T
F	F	T	T

(1.10.4.) Every set of sentences containing one that is logically false is inconsistent.

A	B	↓ A	↓ B	↓ A & ~A
T	T	T	T	F
T	F	T	F	F
F	T	F	T	F
F	F	F	F	F

(1.10.5.)   There are inconsistent sets consisting of just one sentence.

A	↓ A & ~A
T	F
F	F

EXERCISE 1.24

1.24.1. A sentence is logically true ALL OF THEM (all T)
1.24.2. A sentence is logically false ALL OF THEM (all F)
1.24.3. A sentence is logically indeterminate TWO ROWS (one T, one F)
1.24.4. A sentence is not logically true ONE ROW (one F)
1.24.5. A sentence is not logically false ONE ROW (one T)
1.24.6. A sentence is not logically indeterminate ALL OF THEM (either all T or all F)
1.24.7. An argument is valid ALL OF THEM (to show that no row has all T premises and a F conclusion)
1.24.8. An argument is invalid ONE ROW (one with all T premises and a F conclusion)
1.24.9. An argument is not valid ONE ROW (one with all T premises and a F conclusion)
1.24.10. An argument is not invalid ALL OF THEM (to show that no row has all T premises and a F conclusion)
1.24.11. Two sentences are equivalent ALL OF THEM (to show they have the same truth value on each row)
1.24.12. Two sentences are not equivalent ONE ROW (one on which they have different truth values)
1.24.13. A set of sentences is consistent ONE ROW (on which they are all T)
1.24.14. A set of sentences is inconsistent ALL OF THEM (to show that on no row are they all T)

EXERCISE 1.25

1.25.1. Every argument with a truth-functionally true conclusion is truth-functionally valid. The column for the conclusion will have T all the way down, so there will be no row with T premises and F conclusion.
1.25.2. Every argument with a truth-functionally false premise is truth-functionally valid. That column will have F all the way down, so there will be no row with all T premises and F conclusion.
1.25.3. Every set which includes a truth-functionally false sentence is truth-functionally inconsistent. Because the column for that sentence will have F all the way down, so there will be no row in which all the sentences have T.
1.25.4. Every pair of sentences in which both sentences are truth-functionally true is a truth-functionally equivalent pair. Both sentences will have T all the way down, so there will be no row in which they have different truth values.
1.25.5. Every pair of sentences in which both sentences are truth-functionally false is a truth-functionally equivalent pair. Both sentences will have F all the way down, so there will be no row in which they have different truth values.

CHAPTER TWO

SENTENCE DERIVATIONS

Derivations

Truth tables have provided one technique for discovering and proving various truth-functional logical properties: whether a sentence is logically true, false, or indeterminate; whether an argument is valid or invalid; whether a set is consistent or inconsistent; whether a pair of sentences are equivalent. Now we introduce a second technique that can prove many of these things: **derivations**. (In Chapter Three you'll find out why this second technique is necessary.)

Conjunction Rules

First we will look at the use of derivations to prove validity. Consider this valid argument: A & B therefore A. It's valid because if the premise was true, then the conclusion would have to be true. This is a consequence of how the ampersand works. If a conjunction is true, then both of its conjuncts are true. That means that if you assume that the conjunction is true, then you can derive the truth of either of its conjuncts. Reasoning from the conjunction to one of its conjuncts is always allowed: it's a **truth preserving** procedure, meaning that if what you have (the conjunction) is true, then what you get (the first conjunct) will also be true. (Of course, if the conjunction isn't true, then what you get from it using this procedure might be true or false.) If you can get from a premise set to a conclusion using this procedure, then the argument is valid.

We can, then, prove validity by deriving a conclusion from premises using only truth preserving procedures. Deriving one of its conjuncts from a conjunction is one of these allowable procedure—there are others, as we'll see shortly. We can summarize allowable procedure by putting them in the form of rules. We'll call that rule **Conjunction Elimination** abbreviated **&E**. We use this (and other) rules in a process of getting the conclusion from the premise; this process is called a **derivation**. Here is the way this derivation is written:

```
1. | A & B      Ass
2. | A          1, &E
```

There is a vertical line (called a **scope line**) to the left of the whole derivation. The premise is written at the top, on a line numbered 1; it's assumed to get the derivation going. To its right, we write the **justification** of this line, explaining its presence here. It's an assumption, abbreviated **Ass**. (If there are more than one premises in the derivation, they're written down in succeeding lines, numbered 2, 3, etc., also justified as **Ass**.) When the last premise has been written down, a short horizontal line is placed underneath. (In this argument, there's only one premise.)

On the next line (numbered 2) of this derivation, the first conjunct is written; this is derived from line 1 using the rule &E. So its justification names the step it's derived from, followed by a comma, and the name of the rule used: 1, &E.

The derivation we have just seen derives the first conjunct from a conjunction. If a conjunction is true, both conjuncts must be true, so there's a second form of &E, which allows us to use a conjunction to derive the second conjunct. Here's this second form of &E at work in a different derivation:

```
1. | A & B      Ass
2. | B          1, &E
```

Now consider this valid argument:

```
(A & B) & C
A
```

The premise is a conjunction of which (A & B) is the first conjunct. So &E can be used on the premise to get (A & B). But (A & B) is also a conjunction; and &E can be used on this to get its first conjunct, A. Thus, two uses of &E prove that (A & B) & C therefore A is a valid argument:

```
1. | (A & B) & C      Ass
2. | A & B            1, &E
3. | A                2, &E
```

Another 3-step argument would prove (A & B) & C therefore B.

To do a derivation that proves that an argument is valid, then, what you do is list the premise (or premises, if more than one) at the top, as assumptions, with a horizontal line drawn under them. These initial assumptions are called **primary assumptions** of the derivation. (We'll see soon that there can be other assumptions) Then you work your way down till you get to the conclusion as bottom line. (This statement will need a bit of modification later, but will do for now.)

One small bit of symbolism you'll see from now on: the **single-bar turnstile,** ⊢ . This means that the sentences to the right can be derived using the sentences to the left, which are enclosed in the set brackets { } . So, for example, when you're asked to show that

{ A & B } ⊢ B

what you do is a derivation which has A & B as a primary assumption, and B as bottom line.

> *Exercise 2.1.* *Do derivations to prove the following validities. Make sure that everything has exactly the right form: that the lines are in the right place, and that the justifications are exactly as they should be written.*
>
> 2.1.1. { A & (B & C) } ⊢ B.
>
> 2.1.2. { A & [(C & D) & B] } ⊢ C

When there are two (or more) premises to an argument, these are all listed inside the set-brackets, separated by commas. Each premise is a separate primary assumption in the derivation, written above the little horizontal line, and justified by **Ass**. So, for example,

{ A & D , B } ⊢ D

is proven this way:

```
1. | A & D      Ass
2. | B          Ass
   |--------
3. | D          1, &E
```

&E is a rule that tells you what you can do when you already have a conjunction. Now consider what a rule would be like which would be used to *get* a conjunction. If you already knew that both of the conjuncts were true, then you would know that the conjunction is true. In other words, if you already had each of the conjuncts, one on each of two steps in your derivation, then you could get the conjunction—you'd be allowed to write it down as a later step. This rule is called **Conjunction Introduction**, abbreviated **&I**.

Here's this rule in action, in a derivation that proves

{ A , B } ⊢ A & B

1. | A   Ass
2. | B   Ass
   |‾‾‾‾‾‾‾
3. | A & B   1, 2, &I

Two numbers are mentioned in the justification for step 3, because &I needs two steps—one for each conjunct—to derive the conjunction. Note further that the first conjunct needn't come above the second in the derivation.

This is also a correct derivation:

1. | A   Ass
2. | B   Ass
   |‾‾‾‾‾‾‾
3. | B & A   1, 2, &I

And that the order of the numbers in the justification doesn't matter: this is also correct:

1. | A   Ass
2. | B   Ass
   |‾‾‾‾‾‾‾
3. | B & A   2, 1, &I

Remember the comma after each number in the justification.

Here's a longer derivation which uses both &E and &I. It proves that

{ (A & B) & C } ⊢ [C & (B & A)] & B

1. | (A & B) & C   Ass
   |‾‾‾‾‾‾‾‾‾‾‾‾‾‾
2. | A & B   1, &E
3. | A   2, &E
4. | B   2, &E
5. | B & A   3, 4, &I
6. | C   1, &E
7. | C & (B & A)   5, 6, &I
8. | [C & (B & A)] & B   7, 4, &I

Look carefully at each of these steps and its justification, and make sure you understand everything. Notice particularly that the rules can be used not only on atomic sentences but also on compound sentences. Thus, for example, in step 7, &I is used to combine the atomic sentence C with the compound sentence (B & A).

This is the official statement of those two rules:

Conjunction Introduction (&I)

$$\mathcal{P}$$
$$\mathcal{Q}$$
$$\mathcal{P}\,\&\,\mathcal{Q}$$

Conjunction Elimination (&E)

$$\mathcal{P}\,\&\,\mathcal{Q} \qquad \mathcal{P}\,\&\,\mathcal{Q}$$
$$\mathcal{P} \qquad\qquad \mathcal{Q}$$

The italic capitals in these statements stand for any sentences at all, atomic or compound. That means for example, that &E allows us to derive A from (A & B), and it also allows us to derive (C ≡ E) from [(C ≡ E) & (G ⊃ H)].

The rules say what you can get (the bottom line) when you have what's on the line or lines above it. &E has two forms, one for the left conjunct, and one for the right.

Exercise 2.2   *Fill in the proper justifications in these derivations:*

2.2.1
1. | A & (B & C)
2. | B & C
3. | C
4. | A
5. | C & A

2.2.2
1. | (A & B) & (C & D)
2. | E & [(F & G) & (H & I)]
3. | (F & G) & (H & I)
4. | (H & I)
5. | H
6. | I
7. | I & H
8. | C & D
9. | (I & H) & (C & D)
1. | [(I & H) & (C & D)] & H

There are always many correct ways to do every derivation. Compare, for example, these two correct ways of proving that

$\{ (A \& B) \& C \} \vdash B \& C$

1.	(A & B) & C	Ass
2.	A & B	1, &E
3.	B	2, &E
4.	C	1, &E
5.	B & C	3, 4, &I

1.	(A & B) & C	Ass
2.	C	1, &E
3.	A & B	1, &E
4.	B	3, &E
5.	B & C	2, 4, &I

The fact that there are many different correct derivations proving the same thing means that your answer to exercises asking for a derivation may look different from the one given in the answer section at the end of this book, but may be correct also. If you have any doubts about the correctness of your derivation, ask your instructor.

This is even a correct proof of the same validity:

1.	(A & B) & C	Ass
2.	C	1, &E
3.	A & B	1, &E
4.	A	3, &E
5.	B	3, &E
6.	C & B	2, 5, &I
7.	B & C	2, 5, &I

This derivation is a little weird, because it contains steps that don't do any good—that don't advance things toward the aim of the derivation.

Exercise 2.3 *Identify the unnecessary steps in that derivation.*

Even though those steps are unnecessary, they are not wrong—at least as far as following the rules is concerned. They do, however, make your proof less elegant, and they might give someone looking at your proof the idea that you don't exactly know where you're going—what you're doing. Some instructors will subtract credit on an assignment or test when they see unnecessary steps in a derivation; others might give full credit, providing that all the steps are produced correctly in accord with the rules. Ask your instructor how you will be graded!

Can you see how to do this derivation?

$$\{ \sim[(A \lor B) \equiv C] \,\&\, D \} \vdash D$$

Look carefully at it before you read on.

Despite all the complexity of the premise, the derivation is very simple:

```
1. | ~[(A v B) ≡ C] & D     Ass
2. | D                      1, &E
```

The premise, after all, is nothing but a conjunction; its first conjunct is $\sim[(A \lor B) \equiv C]$ and its second is D. So either of these conjuncts can be derived, using &E, as a later step.

Note carefully that you can use &E and &I rules only to eliminate or introduce *conjunctions*. That is to say: &E can be used only when the sentence you're using it on is a conjunction; and it can be used on that sentence only to get one or the other whole conjunct. &I can be used only to combine two whole previous sentences by & to make a new conjunction. What I mean here will be made clearer by the illustrations of mistakes given just below. Mistakes are indicated by the three-thumbs-down sign 👎👎👎 (even worse than a bad movie). Compare these with the other steps, which are correct. Make sure you understand what's wrong with the 👎👎👎 steps.

```
1. | (A v B) & C     Ass
2. | A v B           1, &E
3. | C               1, &E
4. | A               2, &E  👎👎👎
```

Step 2 is not a conjunction, so you can't use &E on it.

```
1. | ~(A & B)        Ass
2. | A               1, &E  👎👎👎
3. | ~A              1, &E  👎👎👎
```

Step 1 is not a conjunction—it's a negation. (Are you having trouble remembering how to tell what kind of sentence something is—a conjunction or something else? This will be reviewed in a moment.)

1. | (A & B) ⊃ C   Ass
2. | A ⊃ C   1, &E ☜☜☜

Line 1 is a conditional, not a conjunction.

You can tell whether a sentence is a conjunction or a disjunction or a material conditional or a negation or a material biconditional by finding the main connective. If the main connective of a sentence is an ampersand, the whole sentence is a conjunction; if the main connective is a wedge, it's a disjunction; and so on. We already talked about this idea back in the last chapter, but in case you've forgotten how to recognize the main connective, here's the explanation again, and a few more exercises on it.

Imagine putting the sentence together, step by step, starting with the atomic sentences (as we did when considering whether sentences are well-formed): the last connective used will be the main connective. For example, consider putting ~[A ⊃ (B v D)] together in this way. First you would take B and D, and join them with the v, getting B v D. Then you would join that to A with the ⊃, getting A ⊃ (B v D). Then you would negate the whole thing, getting the whole sentence. So the ~ in front is the main connective, and the sentence is a negation; thus it can be used in ~E and ~I (we'll get to these rules). Remember where the little arrow goes in truth tables? It goes above the main connective.

So far we've seen the elimination and introduction rules for the &; shortly, we'll get to the elimination and introduction rules for each of the other connectives. The same sorts of restrictions are true for all the other rules. The disjunction rules vE and vI, for example, can be used only to eliminate or introduce whole disjunctions.

Exercise 2.4 Circle the main connective in each of these sentences and say what kind of sentence it is (conjunction, disjunction, conditional, biconditional, or negation):

2.4.1. (A ⊃ (B ≡ (C v D)))

2.4.2. (A ⊃ B) ≡ (C v D)

2.4.3. A ⊃ ((B ≡ C) v D)

2.4.4. ~A ⊃ ((B ≡ C) v D)

2.4.5. ~(A ⊃ ((B ≡ C) v D))

2.4.6. ([~A ⊃ (B v C)] v D)

Look closely at the following derivation and see if you can spot four errors in it.

```
1. │ (A & B) & (C & D)
2. │ A & B              1 &E
3. │ B                  2, &E
4. │ C & D              1, &E
5. │ D                  4, &I
6. │ B & D              3, 5 &I
```

No, no, no, don't read on till you've really tried to spot four.

Okay, here they are:

1. In line 1, the justification **Ass** is missing
2. In line 2, the comma is missing after the numeral 1 in the justification
3. In line 5, the justification should be &E not &I.
4. In line 6, the comma is missing after the numeral 5 in the justification.

No, I'm not fooling around. Yes, I know it's petty to insist on tiny matters of form like this; but that's what's necessary in a formal system like ours. Everything has to be nailed down and precise. (Those of you who have done computer programming will know about this sort of requirement.)

Exercise 2.5. *Give derivations to prove:*

2.5.1. { A & B , C & (D & B) } ⊢ D & (A & C)

2.5.2. { (A & B) & C , D ≡ G } ⊢ (A & C) & (B & [D ≡ G])

Conditional Rules

Here's the elimination rule for the horseshoe:

Conditional Elimination (⊃E)

$$\begin{array}{|l} \mathcal{P} \supset \mathcal{Q} \\ \mathcal{P} \\ \mathcal{Q} \end{array}$$

It tells you that when you have a material conditional as one step, and the antecedent as another, you can get the consequent. Note carefully that it does not say that if you have a conditional and its consequent, you can get the antecedent.

Here's a correct derivation including use of ⊃E:

```
1.│ A ⊃ (B & C)     Ass
2.│ A                Ass
  ├─────
3.│ B & C            1, 2, ⊃E
4.│ B                3, &E
```

Here's another correct derivation:

```
1.│ (A & B) ⊃ (B & C)      Ass
2.│ A & B                  Ass
  ├─────
3.│ B & C                  1, 2, ⊃E
4.│ B                      3, &E
```

This one includes an incorrect use of ⊃E:

```
1.│ (A & B) ⊃ (B & C)     Ass
2.│ B & C                 Ass
  ├─────
3.│ A & B                 1, 2, ⊃E  ♥♥♥
4.│ B                     3, &E
```

Make sure you understand why line 3 is incorrect.

Here's another incorrect use of ⊃E:

```
1.│ (A & B) ⊃ (B & C)     Ass
  ├─────
2.│ B & C                 1, ⊃E  ♥♥♥
```

You need *two* previous steps to use ⊃E: the conditional sentence, and its antecedent. Some students find this hard to remember.

Exercise 2.6 *Prove by doing derivations:*

2.6.1 { (A & B) , (B & A) ⊃ C } ⊢ C

2.6.2. { A , A ⊃ (A ⊃ B) } ⊢   B

The next rule we shall look at is the introduction rule for the horseshoe, ⊃I. It's a different sort of rule. The way it works is that you *assume* the antecedent of the conditional sentence you want to derive, and get the consequent based on this assumption. Once you have done this, you are allowed to get the conditional sentence itself.

Consider this line of reasoning:

> If it's Wednesday, then George is in the pub and Sally is at home. Assume for the moment for the purposes of argument that it is Wednesday. It follows then that George is in the pub and Sally is at home; and from this it follows that George is in the pub. So if it's Wednesday, then George is in the pub.

Here's the way this reasoning looks in a derivation:

```
1. | W ⊃ (G & S)    Ass
2. |  | W            Ass
3. |  | (G & S)      2, 1, ⊃E
4. |  | G            3, &E
5. | W ⊃ G           2-4, ⊃I
```

Step 1 is, as usual, the premise of the argument. What's necessary to introduce the conditional sentence in step 5 is to do a **sub-derivation**, in steps 2 through 4. To begin the sub-derivation, you draw an additional scope line to the right of the original one. On step 2, W, *the antecedent of the conditional sentence you want to introduce*, is written down as an assumption, justified by Ass, and a horizontal line is written underneath it. Then additional steps, in this case, steps 3 and 4, are written down, with the usual sorts of justifications, until you get to *the consequent of the conditional sentence you want to introduce*, which in this case is G. Once this has been accomplished, the subderivation is complete; you end the scope line to its left, which marks the subderivation steps. Now you're allowed to write the conditional you want to introduce, justified by the subderivation with its antecedent as assumption, and its consequent as bottom line. The justification for ⊃I refers to this subderivation by noting the number of its first step, then a dash, then the number of its last step.

Here is the general statement of the rule ⊃I:

Conditional Introduction (⊃I)

```
| | 𝒫
| | Q
| 𝒫 ⊃ Q
```

In the general statement, 𝒫 stands for the antecedent of the conditional you introduce, and Q for its consequent. Note, as always, that these sentences may, in particular uses, be atomic or compound.

Note that you are allowed to introduce as the assumption of a subderivation any sentence you like. But the subderivation can be used for ⊃I only when the assumption of that subderivation is the antecedent of the conditional sentence you're aiming at, and you're going to introduce using ⊃I after the subderivation is closed.

You may be wondering how it can be that you are allowed to introduce any sentence you like as the assumption of a subderivation. Wouldn't this allow all sorts of information into the argument that does not follow from the premises? The reason it does not is that, once the subderivation is ended, no steps inside the subderivation may be used below that in the derivation as justification. The subderivation can itself, as a whole, be used as a justification (as we've seen, in ⊃I, and, as we shall see, in other rules) but not any of the individual steps.

Another way to think about that restriction is this: Suppose you write down step X. Look at the scope line or lines to the left of step X. Any step above X which is immediately to the right of any of these scope lines is available for use as a justification of X. That means, for example, in this proof:

```
1. | W ⊃ (G & S)      Ass
2. |  | W              Ass
3. |  | (G & S)        2, 1, ⊃E
4. |  | G              3, &E
5. | W ⊃ G            2-4, ⊃I
```

to justify step 4 you may refer to step 3 or 2 or 1. (All these are in scopes that make reference possible; but of course not all of them can justify step 4, given our rules.)

But to justify step 5, you may not use step 2 or 3 or 4. Step 1 is available (though not useful); and the whole subderivation, steps 2 through 4, is also available—it's considered to be in the same scope as 5—but the individual steps inside this subderivation are not. ⊃I requires a whole subderivation, and step 5 refers to the whole subderivation 2-4.

In the next sample derivation, an additional step has been added; note that this one, step 6, is illegal:

```
1. | W ⊃ (G & S)     Ass
2. |   | W           Ass
3. |   | (G & S)      2, 1, ⊃E
4. |   | G            3, &E
5. | W ⊃ G           2-4, ⊃I
6. | W & (W ⊃ G)     2, 5, &I  👎👎👎
```

Look very carefully at this derivation, and make sure you understand now why this is illegal. The reason is because it uses step 2, which is not available at that point. This is what's called a **scope error**. Beware of it.

Several subderivations can occur within the same derivations. Look at this:

```
1. | A & B              Ass
2. |   | G              Ass
3. |   | A              1, &E
4  | G ⊃ A             2-3, ⊃I
5. |   | E              Ass
6. |   | A              1, &E
7. | E ⊃ A             5-6, ⊃I
8. | (G ⊃ A) & (E ⊃ A)  4, 7, &I
```

Exercise 2.7   *Find TWO things wrong with the following derivation:*

```
1. | A & B              Ass
2. |   | G              Ass
3. |   | A              1, &E
4  | G ⊃ A             2, 3, ⊃I
5. |   | B              Ass
6. |   | A              1, &E
7. | B ⊃ A             5-6, ⊃I
8. | G & (B ⊃ A)        2, 7, &I
```

Here's a derivation that has one subderivation inside another subderivation:

```
1. | A & B            Ass
2. |  | G             Ass
3. |  |  | H          Ass
4. |  |  | B          1, &E
5. |  | H ⊃ B         3-4, ⊃I
6. | G ⊃ (H ⊃ B)      2-5, ⊃I
```

Examine that last derivation very carefully, and make sure you understand what's going on there.

Note that assumptions of subderivations must be justified by **Ass**. In this derivation:

```
1. | A & B            Ass
2. |  | B             1, &E  👉👉👉
3. |  | A             1, &E
4. | B ⊃ A            2-3, ⊃I
```

the justification for step **2** is mistaken. It's the assumption for that subderivation, so the justification must be **Ass**.

The following derivation does not prove that (A & B) therefore A is valid:

```
1. | A & B            Ass
2. |  | B             Ass
3. |  | A             1, &E
```

To prove that an argument is valid, you have to get the conclusion as the last line *in the main scope of the derivation*–that is, just to the right of the left-most scope line, the one that runs the whole length of the derivation.

It's also a mistake to jump more than one scope line back at the end of a subderivation:

```
1. | A & B            Ass
2. |  | G             Ass
3. |  |  | H          Ass
4. |  |  | B          1, &I
5. | H ⊃ B            3-4, ⊃I  👉👉👉
```

Exercise 2.8. *Prove by doing derivations:*

2.8.1. { G & I } ⊢   H ⊃ G

2.8.2. { A ⊃ [B & (A ⊃ D)] } ⊢   A ⊃ (B & D)

Now we shall introduce more derivation rules.

Disjunction Rules

The disjunction introduction rule comes in two forms:

Disjunction Introduction (∨I)

$$\left|\begin{array}{l}\mathcal{P}\\ \mathcal{P}\vee Q\end{array}\right. \qquad \left|\begin{array}{l}\mathcal{P}\\ Q\vee \mathcal{P}\end{array}\right.$$

It's quite easy: it simply says that to any sentence you can add another of your choice to form a disjunction. Thus from A you can get

A ∨ B
C ∨ A
A ∨ A, etc.

How come this is an acceptable rule? The added disjunct seems to come out of the blue! Our requirement for rules is that they be truth-preserving: if what you use this rule on (the previous sentences referred to in the justification) is true, then the rule must give you true results. Is ∨I truth-preserving? Think about this rule for a moment, and you should see why it is. If some sentence A is true, then it follows that [A ∨ (anything-at-all)] is true. That's simply a consequence of the definition of ∨.

The following derivation, using ∨I, proves that

{ G, (G ∨ B) ⊃ N } ⊢   N

1.	G	Ass
2.	(G ∨ B) ⊃ N	Ass
3.	G ∨ B	1, ∨I
4.	N	2, 4, ⊃E

When using ∨I, you can add any disjunct you like to a sentence. For example, you might have written G ∨ J on line 3, justified by 1, ∨I. This would be correct as far as the application of the rule ∨I is concerned, but it would have been pointless. G v J is of no use in getting where you want to go. You need G v B, the antecedent of the conditional sentence in line 2.

The disjunction elimination rule is the most complicated rule. Here it is:

Disjunction Elimination (vE)

$$
\begin{array}{|l}
\mathcal{P}\text{v } Q \\
\quad \begin{array}{|l} \mathcal{P} \\ \hline \mathcal{R} \end{array} \\
\quad \begin{array}{|l} Q \\ \hline \mathcal{R} \end{array} \\
\mathcal{R}
\end{array}
$$

It gets some sentence $\mathcal{R}$ from a disjunction $\mathcal{P}$ v Q by using two subderivations: one using $\mathcal{P}$ as assumption, the other using Q as assumption, and both arriving at $\mathcal{R}$. Got all that? I didn't think so. Well, look carefully at this derivation which derives C from three premises and uses vE:

1.	A v B	Ass
2.	A ⊃ C	Ass
3.	B ⊃ C	Ass
4.	⎸ A	Ass
5.	⎸ C	4, 2, ⊃E
6.	⎸ B	Ass
7.	⎸ C	6, 3, ⊃E
8.	C	1, 4-5, 6-7, vE

The aim here is getting C by means of using vE on the disjunction A v B. Two subderivations are necessary: one assuming the left disjunct A and deriving C (steps 4-5) and the other one assuming the right disjunct B and deriving C (steps 6-7). Note that the justification for vE on step 8 must include *three* elements: references to the disjunction (in this case, 1), and to both necessary subderivations (in this case, 4-5 and 6-7.)

Exercise 2.9 *Prove by constructing derivations:*

2.9.1 { A & B } ⊢ (A v C) & (D v B)

2.9.2. { E } ⊢ A v (B v [E v F])

2.9.3. { A ∨ B } ⊢ B ∨ A

2.9.4. { (A & C) ∨ (B & A) } ⊢   A

Negation Rules

The two negation rules are:

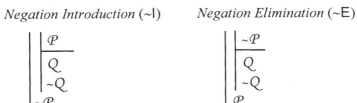

Negation Introduction (~I)   *Negation Elimination (~E)*

Both involve subderivations. The target sentence—what you're trying to get—in ~I is some negation ~𝒫 ; the assumption of the subderivation used to get it must be 𝒫 (that is, the target sentence without a negation). ~E works the other way around: you assume ~𝒫 in the subderivation to get 𝒫. In both cases, the subderivation must include a contradiction, that is, some sentence—any sentence—Q in one step, and the negation of that same sentence, ~Q in another.

Here are a couple of derivations using negation rules:

```
1.|A ⊃ B       Ass
2.|~B & C      Ass
3.|  |A        Ass
4.|  |B        3, 1, ⊃E
5.|  |~B       2, &E
6.|~A          3-5, ~I
```

Step 3 starts a new subderivation with A as assumption, for the purpose of using ~I to wind up with ~A (on step 6.) The contradiction necessary for ~I is steps 4 and 5.

```
1. |~A ⊃ B      Ass
2. |~B & C      Ass
3. |  |~A       Ass
4. |  |B        3, 1, ⊃E
5. |  |~B       2, &E
6. |A           3-5, ~E
```

Step 3 starts a new subderivation with ~A as assumption, for the purpose of using ~E to wind up with A (on step 6.) The contradiction necessary for ~E is steps 4 and 5.

Exercise 2.10 *Prove the following by constructing derivations:*

2.10.1. { A ⊃ (D & ~D) } ⊢   ~A

2.10.2. { ~C ⊃ D , ~D & E } ⊢   C

Biconditional Rules

Biconditional Elimination looks a little like Conditional Elimination, except it allows you to go in both directions:

Biconditional Elimination (≡E)

$$
\begin{array}{|l} \mathcal{P} \equiv \mathcal{Q} \\ \mathcal{P} \\ \mathcal{Q} \end{array}
\qquad
\begin{array}{|l} \mathcal{P} \equiv \mathcal{Q} \\ \mathcal{Q} \\ \mathcal{P} \end{array}
$$

Here's an example using ≡E:

1.	~A ≡ B	Ass
2.	B ≡ C	Ass
3.	B ⊃ ~C	Ass
4.	~A	Ass
5.	B	1, 4, ≡E
6.	C	5, 2, ≡E
7.	~C	5, 3, ⊃E
8.	A	4-7, ~E

The introduction rule for the ≡ involves two subderivations:

Biconditional Introduction (≡I)

$$
\begin{array}{|l}
\quad \begin{array}{|l} \mathcal{P} \\ \hline \mathcal{Q} \end{array} \\
\quad \begin{array}{|l} \mathcal{Q} \\ \hline \mathcal{P} \end{array} \\
\mathcal{P} \equiv \mathcal{Q}
\end{array}
$$

Here's a simple example of ≡I in action:

```
1. | A & B        Ass
2. |  | B         Ass
3. |  | A         1, &E
4. |  | A         Ass
5. |  | B         1, &E
6. | A ≡ B        2-3, 4-5, ≡I
```

Exercise 2.11. *Prove the following by constructing derivations:*

2.11.1. { B ≡ A , A , B ⊃ C } ⊢   C

2.11.2. { C ≡ D } ⊢   D ≡ C

Reiteration

So far we've seen 10 rules: an Introduction and an Elimination rule for each of the five connectives. There's one more rule:

Reiteration (R)

$$\left|\begin{array}{l} \mathcal{P} \\ \mathcal{P} \end{array}\right.$$

This one allows repetition of an earlier step, for example in the following derivation, deriving B ⊃ A from A:

```
1. | A          Ass
2. |  | B        Ass
3. |  | A        1, R
4. | B ⊃ A       2-3, ⊃I
```

Remember that you won't be able to use R when the step you want to repeat is in a scope that makes it unavailable.

Here's a derivation including this mistake:

```
1. | A          Ass
2. |  | B        Ass
3. |  | A        1, R
4. | B ⊃ A       2-3, ⊃I
5. | B          2, R    👎👎👎
```

Another example using R (correctly):

```
1. │ A ⊃ B       Ass
2. │ ~B          Ass
   ├─────
3. │ │ A         Ass
   │ ├───
4. │ │ B         3, 1, ⊃E
5. │ │ ~B        2, R
6. │ ~A          3-5, ~I
```

The next derivation adds step 4 to the previous one, reiterating A ⊃ B inside the subderivation, and referring to this step, not step 1, in the ⊃E step following.

```
1. │ A ⊃ B       Ass
2. │ ~B          Ass
   ├─────
3. │ │ A         Ass
   │ ├───
4. │ │ A ⊃ B     1, R
5. │ │ B         3, 4, ⊃E
6. │ │ ~B        2, R
7. │ ~A          3-6, ~I
```

Step 4 is correct as far as the rules are concerned, but it's unnecessary. Without it, the following step B could have been justified by 3, 1, ⊃E. You don't need to reiterate A ⊃ B inside that subderivation (though it may help you keep track of things). As mentioned earlier, you should check with your instructor about whether you'd be penalized for inserting unnecessary steps.

Exercise 2.12. *Construct a derivation to prove:*

2.12.1. { A } ⊢   A ≡ A

List of All the Rules

Reiteration (R)

$$\mathcal{P}$$
$$\mathcal{P}$$

'&' Rules

Conjunction Introduction (&I)

$$\mathcal{P}$$
$$Q$$
$$\mathcal{P}\,\&\,Q$$

Conjunction Elimination (&E)

$$\mathcal{P}\,\&\,Q$$ $$\mathcal{P}\,\&\,Q$$
$$\mathcal{P}$$ $$Q$$

'⊃' Rules

Conditional Introduction (⊃I)

$$\mathcal{P}$$
$$Q$$
$$\mathcal{P} \supset Q$$

Conditional Elimination (⊃E)

$$\mathcal{P} \supset Q$$
$$\mathcal{P}$$
$$Q$$

'~' Rules

Negation Introduction (~I)

$$\mathcal{P}$$
$$Q$$
$$\sim Q$$
$$\sim \mathcal{P}$$

Negation Elimination (~E)

$$\sim \mathcal{P}$$
$$Q$$
$$\sim Q$$
$$\mathcal{P}$$

'v' Rules

Disjunction Introduction (vI)

$$\mathcal{P}$$ $$\mathcal{P}$$
$$\mathcal{P} \lor Q$$ $$Q \lor \mathcal{P}$$

Disjunction Elimination (vE)

$$\mathcal{P} \lor Q$$
$$\mathcal{P}$$
$$\mathcal{R}$$
$$Q$$
$$\mathcal{R}$$
$$\mathcal{R}$$

'≡' Rules

Biconditional Introduction (≡I)   *Bicondional Elimination* (≡E)

$$
\begin{array}{|l}
\;\;\begin{array}{|l} \mathcal{P} \\ \hline \mathcal{Q} \end{array} \\[4pt]
\;\;\begin{array}{|l} \mathcal{Q} \\ \hline \mathcal{P} \end{array} \\[4pt]
\mathcal{P} \equiv \mathcal{Q}
\end{array}
\qquad
\begin{array}{|l}
\mathcal{P} \equiv \mathcal{Q} \\
\mathcal{P} \\
\mathcal{Q}
\end{array}
\qquad
\begin{array}{|l}
\mathcal{P} \equiv \mathcal{Q} \\
\mathcal{Q} \\
\mathcal{P}
\end{array}
$$

It's very important that you be thoroughly familiar with the eleven rules of our system. If you have a test on derivations, your instructor may provide you with a list of these rules (ask!), but you won't be able to do much with them in a limited time unless you're already quite familiar with them. You should have the rules just about memorized; consult the list just to reassure yourself that you remember a rule.

About This Set of Rules

Why this set of rules in particular? The set just introduced is one you'll find in many other logic textbooks, but it's not the only possible set of rules. In many other textbooks you'll find a different set, excluding some of ours, and including rules such as these:

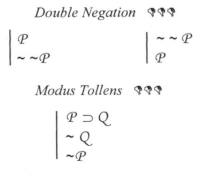

Double Negation ☞☞☞

$$
\begin{array}{|l}
\mathcal{P} \\
\sim\sim\mathcal{P}
\end{array}
\qquad
\begin{array}{|l}
\sim\sim\mathcal{P} \\
\mathcal{P}
\end{array}
$$

Modus Tollens ☞☞☞

$$
\begin{array}{|l}
\mathcal{P} \supset \mathcal{Q} \\
\sim \mathcal{Q} \\
\sim\mathcal{P}
\end{array}
$$

Disjunctive Syllogism ☞☞☞

$$
\begin{array}{|l}
\mathcal{P} \vee \mathcal{Q} \\
\sim \mathcal{P} \\
\mathcal{Q}
\end{array}
\qquad
\begin{array}{|l}
\mathcal{P} \vee \mathcal{Q} \\
\sim \mathcal{Q} \\
\mathcal{P}
\end{array}
$$

Hypothetical Syllogism   ☙☙☙

$$P \supset Q$$
$$Q \supset R$$
$$P \supset R$$

Commutation   ☙☙☙

$$P \vee Q$$
$$Q \vee P$$

$$P \,\&\, Q$$
$$Q \,\&\, P$$

THESE ARE NOT RULES OF OUR SYSTEM!!
DON'T USE THEM!!!!!!!

There's nothing really wrong with the alternative system of rules you'll find elsewhere. Our system, and these others, all meet the basic requirements for this sort of thing: being able to derive the conclusion of any valid argument, and not being able to derive the conclusion of any invalid argument.

None of these rules provides inferences you can't get in our system. You can assure yourself of this by showing that our system can accomplish what each of these rules allows. For example, *Hypothetical Syllogism* will let you get $P \supset R$ immediately when you have $P \supset Q$ and $Q \supset R$. But we can get to the same result in our system, as you can prove by doing the derivation $\{ P \supset Q , Q \supset R \} \vdash P \supset R$, though it will take several steps to do it. (You might try showing the same thing for each of the other ☙☙☙ rules above.)

So logicians have a choice among many different systems. Why choose ours rather than some other one?

In some ways, other systems are nicer than ours. One of the things some logicians look for in a system of derivation is a method for proving logical properties that is somewhat like the logical thought-processes non-logicians actually use; and the five rules above perhaps do this better than the ones in our system. For example, I'm sure you can think of everyday examples of ordinary reasoning in which you use *Disjunctive Syllogism*, but it's much harder to think of a case in which your everyday logical thinking uses ∨E.

One difference between our system of derivation and many others is that ours is small. It gets by with very few rules—only eleven. The system for derivation provided by an all-time best-seller logic book has nineteen. The good news about bigger systems like these is that they often make derivations shorter and easier. The bad news is that you have to become familiar with a larger list of basic rules. One thing that appeals to many logicians about our system is its minimalist elegance. It gives you just exactly what's necessary and no more.

One thing that's very satisfying about our system, from a logician's point of view, is that each rule is "pure" in a sense: the only connective mentioned in any of our rules is the connective that rule introduces or eliminates. (*Disjunctive Syllogism*, for example, by contrast involves both the ∨ and the ~.) This means that each of our rules (except for *Reiteration*) is associated with a single connective, so each pair of I and E rules is associated with one connective, and can be seen, as defining that connective's behaviour in derivations.

Learning the Derivation System

Exercise 2.13. As a review of the functions of our rules, lets begin by filling in the justifications in these derivations

2.13.1.

1. | A
2. | | B
3. | | A
4. | B ⊃ A
5. | (B ⊃ A) & A

2.13.2

1. | (B ∨ A) ≡ C
2. | A ∨ B
3. | | A
4. | | B ∨ A
5. | | C
6. | | B
7. | | B ∨ A
8. | | C
9. | C

2.13.3

1. | A & (B & ~A)
2. | | ~G
3. | | A
4. | | (B & ~A)
5. | | ~A
6. | G

2.13.4

1. | A ⊃ B
2. | ~A ⊃ ~B
3. | | A
4. | | B
5. | | B
6. | | | ~A
7. | | | ~B
8. | | | B
9. | | A
10.| A ≡ B

2.13.5. Would 4,R be a correct justification for step 8 in question 2.13.4? Explain.

But your main job will be to construct your own derivations. This is not a mechanical matter (like constructing truth tables was). It sometimes takes some ingenuity and strategic thought.

Strategies

Here are some hints regarding strategies for constructing derivations.

There are two basic varieties of thought-processes used in constructing derivations: **top-down thinking**, and **bottom-up thinking**. When you use top-down thinking, you look at what you have, and consider what you can get from it using various rules. Often you'll be able to see this by identifying the main connective in the steps you have, and applying the elimination rule for that sort of sentence.

Suppose, for example, you had these two premises:

B ⊃ D
A & B

and you were supposed to derive (B & D) from them. Then top-down thinking might go as follows:

> The first premise is (B ⊃ D). This is a conditional sentence, so ⊃E can be used on this conditional to get D—if I had B. The other premise is (A & B). This premise is a conjunction, so &E can be used on it, to get either A or B.

Bottom-up reasoning looks at what you're trying to get, and considers what it would take to get it. Often it will help here to consider the introduction rule for the sort of sentence you're trying to get. The conclusion you're supposed to derive in our current example is (B & D). You think:

> That's a conjunction which I could get by &I, if I had each of B and D by themselves.

Then you try to see how to get these two lines of reasoning to meet in the middle.

> I've got the B I need from the second premise by &E. That D could come from the first premise plus B, and I can get B from the second premise by &E.

So now you have seen your way through the whole proof. Now you can write it down:

1. | B ⊃ D   Ass
2. | A & B   Ass
3. | B   2, &E
4. | D   1, 4, ⊃E
5. | B & D   3, 4, &I

If you can't think your way through the whole derivation in your head, it might be helpful to use the following technique. Write down a long main scope line (so that you'll have enough room), insert the premises at the top and the conclusion at the bottom:

```
1. | B ⊃ D      Ass
2. | A & B      Ass
   |‾‾‾‾‾‾‾
3. |
   |
   |
   |
   | B & D
```

Begin with top-down thinking. Write down what you can get from those premises, without worrying yet about what you'll need. You should notice that &E can be used on the premise that is a conjunction:

```
1. | B ⊃ D    Ass
2. | A & B    Ass
   |‾‾‾‾‾‾
3. | A        2, &E
4. | B        2, &E
   |
   |
   | B & D
```

If that's all that top-down thinking reveals; try some bottom-up thinking. That conclusion is a conjunction, so what you'll probably need to get it is B and D, separately, which you can combine with &I. You already have a B on line 4. So write D down above the conclusion, without justification, and we'll think in a moment about where we can get it.

```
1. | B ⊃ D     Ass
2. | A & B    Ass
   |‾‾‾‾‾‾
3. | A        2, &E
4. | B        2, &E
   |
   |
   |
   | D         ?
   | B & D    4, ?, &I
```

Now, where could that D come from? There's a D, in the consequent of the first premise. We could get that D by doing ⊃E on the first premise, if we had a **B**. But we do have a **B**, in line **4**. Aha! That's it! Now fill in the justification and line-numbers that are missing:

```
1.| B ⊃ D        Ass
2.| A & B        Ass
  |‾‾‾‾‾‾
3.| A            2, &E
4.| B            2, &E
  |
  |
  |
  |
5.| D            4, 1, ⊃E
6.| B & D        4, 5, &I
```

It turns out that step **3** wasn't necessary in your derivation. Again, check with your instructor about whether credit will be subtracted when you submit derivations with unnecessary steps in them.

Sometimes either the top-down or the bottom-up reasoning will prove much more important; sometimes one of the two will be completely useless.

Consider, for example, the appropriate strategic reasoning in the following derivation:

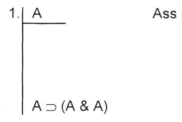

```
1.| A              Ass
  |‾‾‾‾‾
  |
  |
  |
  |
  | A ⊃ (A & A)
```

In this one, top-down reasoning is useless, because the sole premise is just an atomic sentence, without any connectives, and thus it doesn't suggest the use of any elimination rules.

But bottom-up reasoning is much more fruitful: we know how to introduce a conditional sentence, using ⊃I:

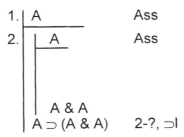

```
1. | A                  Ass
2. |  | A               Ass
   |  |
   |  |
   |  | A & A
   | A ⊃ (A & A)    2-?, ⊃I
```

Now we can get to work on the sub-derivation. Available for justifications on the steps in there are the A, which is the assumption for the subderivation, and the A which is the assumption in the main scope. Again, top-down thinking suggests nothing. What we're trying to get is the last line of the subderivation, A & A. We could get that if we had two As to join together with &I. And we have them! Success! Now fill in the missing line numbers and justification:

```
1. | A                  Ass
2. |  | A               Ass
   |  |
3. |  | A & A           1, 2, &I
4. | A ⊃ (A & A)        2-3, ⊃I
```

Note, by the way, that the two lines necessary for &I don't have to be *different* lines. This justification for line 3 would be equally correct:

```
1. | A                  Ass
2. |  | A               Ass
3. |  | A & A           2, 2, &I
4. | A ⊃ (A & A)        2-3, ⊃I
```

Following is a derivation in which bottom-up thinking is useless, and top-down thinking is all that's necessary in initial stages:

1. | A v B
2. | ~A

B

Bottom-up thinking suggests nothing. Top-down thinking can't get us anything right away, but it does suggest a procedure, because one premise is a disjunction: use **vE**, making the $\mathcal{R}$-sentence mentioned in the general rule for **vE** the conclusion of the argument:

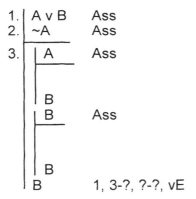

1. | A v B   Ass
2. | ~A   Ass
3. | | A   Ass

      | B
      | B   Ass

      | B
   | B   1, 3-?, ?-?, vE

Examine this and think about it until you understand what's going on. We're going to do a **vE** using step **1**, and the two necessary subderivations, with their first and last steps, have been entered. The strategy here is useful in most cases in which there's a disjunction among the primary assumptions. (This strategy will be discussed again a little later, when you're provided with some "Rules of Thumb" for doing derivations. This one will be called RT2.)

Now the problem becomes completing the two subderivations. The second one is easy: no additional steps need to be inserted. The last line of that subderivation comes directly from its first line, by rule R.

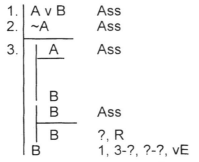

```
1.  A v B      Ass
2.  ~A         Ass
3.      A      Ass

        B
        B      Ass
        B      ?, R
    B          1, 3-?, ?-?, vE
```

But the first subderivation is trickier. This is one of the comparatively rare cases in which neither top-down nor bottom-up thinking really suggests anything to do. There is an important hint in the lines available for justification, however—lines 1, 2, and 3. Notice that one of these lines is the negation of another. This can be used together with one of the negation rules to give us the conclusion to the subderivation we're looking for, like this:

```
1.  A v B       Ass
2.  ~A          Ass
3.    A         Ass
4.      ~B      Ass
5.      A       3, R
6.      ~A      2, R
7.    B         4-6, ~E
8.    B         Ass
9.    B         8, R
10. B           1, 3-7, 8-9, vE
```

The strategy for this derivation is not very obvious; you should study it carefully to see what is done. The strategic techniques here will be applied many times in other un-obvious derivations. We'll see this strategy just below, called RT1.

Rules of Thumb

The derivations we've just been looking at use techniques that are widely applied. These rules of thumb advise you on when they might be useful, and how to use them.

> **RT1.** When the lines available for citation in justifications include a contradiction (some sentence and its negation), then you can get what you want by a negation rule: in a subderivation, assume the opposite of what you want to get, and reiterate the sentence and its negation inside the subderivation. (Here the "opposite" of a sentence is that sentence with a negation added to, or subtracted from, the front.)

Here's an example. Suppose you want to prove { M & A , ~A } ⊢ (G ⊃ Q)

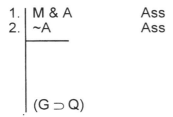

1.	M & A	Ass
2.	~A	Ass
	(G ⊃ Q)	

Examination of the two premises should show you that contradictory sentences, A and ~A, are easily obtainable: the second premise is ~A, and A can be had from the first premise by &E. So what you should do is start a subderivation right away, with the negation of the conclusion as assumption:

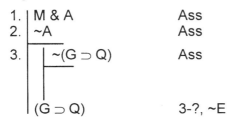

1.	M & A	Ass
2.	~A	Ass
3.	~(G ⊃ Q)	Ass
	(G ⊃ Q)	3-?, ~E

Once the contradictory sentences are inserted inside the subderivation, the conclusion will follow by ~E:

```
1. | M & A              Ass
2. | ~A                 Ass
3. |   | ~(G ⊃ Q)       Ass
4. |   | A              1, &E
5. |   | ~A             2, R
6. | (G ⊃ Q)            2-5, ~E
```

You should keep your eyes open for available contradictory sentences while you're doing derivations. Their availability means you can get anything you want, by assuming its "opposite," in a subderivation which will serve for one of the negation rules.

RT2. When what you have includes a disjunction, it's often a useful technique to start a vE immediately, making the sentence you want to get the 𝑅-sentence.

Example: Suppose you're trying to prove { (A ∨ B) , (B ⊃ A) } ⊢   B.

```
1. | A ∨ B      Ass
2. | A ⊃ B      Ass
   |
   |
   |
   |
   |
   |
   |
   | B
```

This RT suggests that you start a ∨E immediately. The disjunction used is the premise, A ∨ B. Insert two subderivations, one with A as assumption and the other with B as assumption; and both subderivations ending with the "ℛ-sentence" B, which is the conclusion you're aiming for:

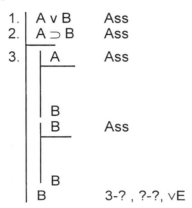

1. │ A ∨ B   Ass
2. │ A ⊃ B   Ass
3. │ ┌ A   Ass

      │ B
      └ B   Ass

      │ B
   B   3-? , ?-? , ∨E

Now filling in the two subderivations:

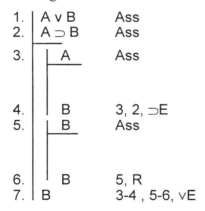

1. │ A ∨ B   Ass
2. │ A ⊃ B   Ass
3. │ ┌ A   Ass

4. │ │ B   3, 2, ⊃E
5. │ └ B   Ass

6. │ │ B   5, R
7. │ B   3-4 , 5-6, ∨E

Here are some other rules of thumb that will often be useful:

RT3. When you want to derive a conclusion which is a conditional sentence, make the overall structure of the derivation a $\supset$I; that is, start a subderivation right after assuming the premises, using the antecedent of the conclusion as assumption, and work your way down inside the subderivation to the consequent of the conclusion; then end the subderivation, and write the conclusion as the next step, justified by $\supset$I.

For example, to prove $\{ A \equiv (B \& C) \} \vdash A \supset B$:

1.| $A \equiv (B \& C)$ Ass

   | $A \supset B$

Because the conclusion is a $\supset$ statement, you should try doing the derivation by a $\supset$I. So insert a subderivation, with the antecedent of the conclusion as assumption, and the consequent of the conclusion as bottom line:

1.| $A \equiv (B \& C)$ Ass
2.| | A   Ass

  | | B
  | $A \supset B$ 2-?, $\supset$I

Now all that's left to do is to finish the subderivation:

1.| $A \equiv (B \& C)$ Ass
2.| | A   Ass
3.| | B & C   1, 2, $\equiv$E
4.| | B   3, &E
5.| $A \supset B$ 2-4, $\supset$I

RT4. When you need a contradiction (inside a ~E or ~I, or, as we shall see, to prove truth-functional falsity or truth-functional inconsistency), and you already have an available step which is a negation, try to derive that step without the initial ~.

For example, suppose you want to prove { ~(A v B) } ⊢ ~A. You start this way:

```
1.| ~(A v B)   Ass
  |
  |
  |
  |
  |
  | ~A
```

Bottom-up strategic thinking suggests that you use ~I to get the conclusion:

```
1. | ~(A v B)    Ass
2. ||  A         Ass
   ||
   ||
   ||
   || ~A         2-?, ~I
```

Now you need a contradiction inside that subderivation. RT4 suggests that since you already have a negation in step 1, you reiterate it inside the subderivation, and try to get that sentence without the negation there:

```
1. | ~(A v B)     Ass
2. ||  A          Ass
3. ||  ~(A v B)    1, R
   ||
   ||
   ||  A v B
   | ~A           2-?, ~I
```

What you need, then, is A ∨ B; this can come from step 2, plus ∨I. All done!

1.	~(A ∨ B)	Ass
2.	A	Ass
3.	~(A ∨ B)	1, R
4.	A ∨ B	2, ∨I
	~A	2-4, ~I

Exercise 2.14. *A mistake has intentionally been made in this last derivation. See if you can find it.*

RT5. When you can't see any way at all to get the conclusion you're after—when all else fails—try a ~E as the overall strategy: assume the negation of what you're trying to get, and then see if you can get a contradiction inside that subderivation. The example for RT4 might be taken as an example of the use of this RT also.

These Rules of Thumb will often be helpful, but not always. Bear them in mind, anyway. The examples given of these RTs in action are fairly simple derivations, and you might wonder why these RTs need to be pointed out at all. You'll find that they will often be helpful in more complicated derivations, in which a successful strategy is not obvious. When we get to a large number of derivation exercises, you'll see them in action in derivations which would not otherwise be obvious.

What Derivations Prove

Before we begin practicing constructing derivations, let's consider what derivations can be used to prove.

So far we have been considering the use of derivations to prove validity of arguments. When an argument is invalid, you will not be able to construct a correct derivation with the conclusion as bottom line. So suppose you don't know whether an argument is valid or not, and you try to construct a derivation, but don't succeed in deriving the conclusion. Maybe it's invalid; or maybe you just haven't found the right way to derive the conclusion. You don't know. This technique can prove that a valid argument is valid, but it can't prove that an invalid argument is invalid.

What else can/can't derivations prove?

Here's what derivations *can* prove:

1. Derivations can prove that a set of sentences is truth-functionally inconsistent. Assume that set of sentences as the primary assumptions of a derivation, and derive a contradiction—that is, get two lines *in the main scope* of the derivation where one is the negation of the other. Here's an example, proving that { A ⊃ B , A & ~B } is an inconsistent set:

```
1. │ A ⊃ B        Ass
2. │ A & ~B       Ass
   ├──────
3. │ A            2, &E
4. │ B            3, 1, ⊃E
5. │ ~B           2, &E
```

The contradiction—the two lines you're after to prove inconsistency— any sentence and its negation—must be in the main scope. The following derivation does not prove inconsistency, because the contradiction is not in the main scope:

```
1. │ A v B            Ass
2. │ C               Ass
   ├──────
3. │ │ ┌ ~C          Ass
   │ │ │
4. │ │ │ C           2, R
5. │ │ │ ~C          3, R
```

Bear in mind when proving inconsistency what exactly constitutes the negation of a sentence. The following derivation does not prove inconsistency; have a close look at it and try to figure out why not, before reading on.

```
1. │ A & B         Ass
2. │ B & ~A        Ass
   ├──────
3. │ ~A            2, &E
4. │ B             2, &E
5. │ ~A & B        3, 4, &I
6. │ A & B         1, R
```

All steps in this derivation are correct; the reason it does not prove inconsistency of the set containing the two assumptions is that a sentence and its negation are nowhere contained. Do you see why step **5** is not the negation of step **6**? The genuine negation of step **6** must negate the whole of it; so ~(A & B) would be its negation, not what's in step **4**. Step **5** is not a negation. It's a conjunction.

> ***Exercise 2.15.*** *Well, while we're thinking about this derivation, why don't you try to produce a correct proof of its inconsistency?*

2. They can prove that a single sentence is truth-functionally false. Assume that one sentence as the primary assumption of a derivation, and derive a contradiction.

Example:

```
1.| A ≡ ~A     Ass
2.|  | A        Ass
   |  |─────
3.|  | A        2, R
4.|  | ~A       3, 1, ≡E
5.|  ~A         2-4, ~I
6.|  A          5, 1, ≡E
```

Again, remind yourself about what constitutes a genuine contradiction (a sentence plus its negation).

So now we have four sorts of situations in which you need to get a contradiction: using ~I, using ~E, proving inconsistency, and proving truth-functional falsity. In some cases it will not be immediately obvious what to do, because just any sentence plus its negation would do: what sentences should you aim at? In almost all cases of this sort, the Rule of Thumb RT4, described a couple of pages back, will help you with this problem. Have a look back at RT4 now, and again when you find yourself puzzled by a derivation when you need a contradiction.

3. They can prove that a single sentence is truth-functionally true. To prove this, you derive the sentence with *no primary assumptions*. An easy derivation of this sort proves that A ⊃ A is truth-functionally true. Start deriving it like this:

```
|
|
|
|
|
| A ⊃ A
```

Notice that there are no primary assumptions (the items that so far have gone above the horizontal line connecting to the main scope line). How do you get something from nothing? Obviously, top-down thinking is no good at all here! But bottom-up thinking works easily. Use ⊃I to get that conclusion:

```
1. |  A        Ass
2. |  A        1, R
3. | A ⊃ A     1-2, ⊃I
```

The fact that logical truths can be derived using no primary assumptions is reflected in the way we symbolize this using the single-bar turnstile:

⊢ A ⊃ A

The single-bar turnstile means, as before, that what's to the right of it can be derived from what's to the left of it; but in this case, there's nothing to its left. Any statement that can be derived from nothing is a logical truth.

4. They can be used to prove that two sentences are truth-functionally equivalent. To prove that two sentences $\mathcal{P}$ and Q are truth-functionally equivalent, you need to do *two* derivations: one proving the argument $\mathcal{P}$ therefore Q is valid, and the other proving the argument Q therefore $\mathcal{P}$ is valid.

A simple case is proving that A and A & A are equivalent:

```
1.| A          Ass          1.| A&A        Ass
2.| A & A      1, 1, &I     2.| A          1, &E
```

Here's what derivations *can't* prove:

1. As already mentioned, they can't prove that an argument is invalid. (They can only prove validity.)

2. They can't prove that a set of sentences is truth-functionally consistent. (They can only prove inconsistency.)

3. They can't prove that a sentence is truth-functionally indeterminate. (They can only prove truth-functional truth and truth-functional falsity.)

4. They can't prove that two sentences are not equivalent. (They can only prove that they are equivalent.)

How to Learn the Skill

Now you've read everything you need to know to do any derivation. But doing derivations is a skill, and takes practice. *You will not be able to do them unless you practice a lot.* Merely reading and understanding what's been said so far usually does not mean that you can do derivations.

IMPORTANT NOTE: *Do not look at the derivation provided in the answer section until you have tried very hard to do the derivation yourself.* Looking at a lot of derivations already done for you will not help you to develop the skill to do them yourself. It's a skill that can be learned only by trying to do it a lot, not by looking at examples someone else has done. Look at the answers after you've worked really hard on a derivation and are still stumped; or after you've got an answer you're confident of. Remember that there are many different correct ways of doing the same derivation, so yours might be right even though it's different from what's in the answers.

Don't skip forward if you're having no trouble with doing the exercises there. Doing a lot of them in an easier category will help you when you get to a more difficult category.

The derivation exercises following are sorted into categories of increasing difficulty; of course, you should try the easy ones first. If you can't do any in the VERY EASY category, read this chapter again, very carefully, doing all the exercises preliminary to this one. If you can do the VERY EASY derivations but run into a lot of trouble in the next category, you might pass a test on derivations, but you won't do well. In the last category, the derivations are VERY DIFFICULT indeed. Some instructors might require you to be able to do very difficult derivations for a very good grade; other might not. If you're worried about this, ask.

Exercise 2.16. Prove all the following using derivations.

GROUP 1: VERY EASY

2.16.1. { A ⊃ B , A } ⊢   B

2.16.2. { C , C ⊃ (D v ~E) } ⊢   D v ~E

2.16.3. { F , G } ⊢   F & G

2.16.4. { H ⊃ I , H } ⊢   H & I

2.16.5. { J & (K & L) } ⊢   J

2.16.6. Prove logically false: M & ~M

2.16.7. { N } ⊢   O ∨ N

2.16.8. { P , Q } ⊢   Q & (Q & P)

2.16.9. { R & S } ⊢   (R & S) ∨ ~T

2.16.10. { U , U ∨ W } ⊢   U & (U ∨ W)

2.16.11. { X ≡ Y , Y } ⊢   X

2.16.12. { A ⊃ B , C ⊃ D , A } ⊢   B

2.16.13. { E & F } ⊢   E ≡ F

2.16.14. { G & (H & I) } ⊢   H

2.16.15. { J & K } ⊢   K & J

2.16.16. Prove inconsistent: { L & M , ~M & L }

2.16.17. Prove inconsistent: { N & ~O , O ≡ N }

2.16.18. Prove logically false: P & ~P

2.16.19. { Q ∨ Q } ⊢   Q

2.16.20. { R } ⊢   S ⊃ R

2.16.21. { T , (T ∨ U) ⊃ W } ⊢   W

2.16.22. Prove logically false: X & (X ⊃ ~X)

2.16.23. { A ⊃ B , B ⊃ C } ⊢   A ⊃ C

2.16.24. { (D & E) ∨ (D & F) } ⊢   D

2.16.25. Prove equivalent: G , G & G

2.16.26. Prove equivalent: (H & I) , (I & H)

2.16.27. ⊢   J ⊃ J

GROUP II: EASY

2.16.28. ⊢   (K ≡ L) ⊃ (K ⊃ L)

2.16.29 { M , N } ⊢   (M ∨ N) & N

2.16.30. { (~O & P) ⊃ (R ∨ ~S) , ~O & P } ⊢   R ∨ ~S

2.16.31. { [T ∨ (U ≡ W)] ⊃ X , X ⊃ Y } ⊢   [T ∨ (U ≡ W)] ⊃ Y

2.16.32. { A ≡ B , B } ⊢   B & (A ∨ C)

2.16.33. { D ⊃ E } ⊢ (D & F) ⊃ E

2.16.34. { (G v H) ⊃ I } ⊢ G ⊃ I

2.16.35. Prove equivalent: J v K , K v J

2.16.36. Prove equivalent: ~L , ~ ~ ~L

2.16.37. { M ⊃ (N & O) } ⊢ M ⊃ O

2.16.38. { (~P & Q) ≡ R , R } ⊢ Q

2.16.39. { S ⊃ T , S ⊃ U } ⊢ S ⊃ (T & U)

2.16.40. { W v X , X ⊃ W } ⊢ W

2.16.41. { Y ⊃ Z , ~Z } ⊢ ~Y

2.16.42. { A ≡ (B v [D & ~A]) } ⊢ C ⊃ (C v C)

2.16.43. { E , (F ⊃ E) ⊃ G } ⊢ G

2.16.44. ⊢ H ≡ H

2.16.45. { I v J , (J v I) ≡ K } ⊢ K

2.16.46. { L ⊃ (L ⊃ M) } ⊢ L ⊃ M

2.16.47. ⊢ (N & ~N) ⊃ O

2.16.48. Prove logically false: P & (P ⊃ ~P)

2.16.49. ⊢ ~(Q & ~Q)

2.16.50. ⊢ R ⊃ (S v R)

2.16.51. { T ⊃ ~U , U } ⊢ ~T

2.16.52. Prove equivalent: W ≡ X , X ≡ W

2.16.53. Prove equivalent: Y , Y v Y

2.16.54. Prove equivalent: A v B , B v A

2.16.55. Prove equivalent: C & C , C v C

2.16.56. Prove inconsistent: { D , D ⊃ ~D }

2.16.57. { E } ⊢ (E v F) & (F ⊃ E)

2.16.58. Prove inconsistent: { G & H , H ≡ ~G }

2.16.59. { ~I ⊃ ~J , J } ⊢ I

2.16.60. { K ⊃ L } ⊢ K ⊃ (K & L)

2.16.61. ⊢ M ⊃ (M v N)

2.16.62. Prove equivalent: (O & P) & R , O & (P & R)

2.16.63. ⊢ (S ≡ T) ⊃ (S ⊃ T)

2.16.64. Prove equivalent: U ≡ W , (U ⊃ W) & (W ⊃ U)

2.16.65. { X ⊃ Y , Y ⊃ Z } ⊢ X ⊃ Z

2.16.66. { (A & B) v (C & B) } ⊢ B

2.16.67. { D ⊃ E , F ⊃ G , D } ⊢ E v G

GROUP III: MEDIUM DIFFICULTY

2.16.68. { (H & I) ⊃ J , J ⊃ K , I & H } ⊢ K

2.16.69. { L ⊃ M , M ⊃ N } ⊢ ~N ⊃ ~L

2.16.70. { O ⊃ ~P , ~ ~P } ⊢ ~O

2.16.71. ⊢ Q ⊃ (R ⊃ Q)

2.16.72. { (S v T) ⊃ ~U , U } ⊢ ~S

2.16.73. { W ⊃ X , W ⊃ ~X } ⊢ ~W

2.16.74. ⊢ ~Y ⊃ (Y ⊃ Z)

2.16.75. { A ≡ B , B ≡ C) } ⊢ A ⊃ (D v C)

2.16.76. { (E v F) ⊃ (G & H) , (I v J) ⊃ (E v F) , I } ⊢ H

2.16.77. { K & ~L } ⊢ ~(K ⊃ L)

2.16.78. { (M v N) ⊃ O , (O v P) ⊃ (R v ~M) } ⊢ M ⊃ R

2.16.79. { ~S ⊃ ~T , (T & U) & W } ⊢ S

2.16.80. { A v B , A ⊃ C , B ⊃ D } ⊢ C v D

2.16.81. { E v F } ⊢ (E ⊃ F) ⊃ F

2.16.82. { G v H , ~G } ⊢ H

2.16.83. { I ⊃ J , I v K , ~K } ⊢ L ⊃ J

2.16.84. ⊢ [(M v M) & (M ⊃ N)] ⊃ N

2.16.85. { O ⊃ (P ⊃ R) } ⊢ P ⊃ (O ⊃ R)

2.16.86. { S ⊃ (~T v U) , S & T } ⊢ U

2.16.87. { W ⊃ X , ~X ≡ W } ⊢ ~W

2.16.88. Prove inconsistent: { Y v Z , ~Y & ~Z }

2.16.89. Prove logically false: A ≡ ~A

2.16.90. Prove logically false: ~(B ⊃ ~ ~B)

2.16.91. Prove inconsistent: { C & D , ~(C ≡ D) }

2.16.92. ⊢ (E & ~E) ⊃ F

2.16.93. ⊢ (G & H) ⊃ ~(G ⊃ ~H)

2.16.94. { I , ~I ≡ ~J } ⊢ J

2.16.95. Prove equivalent: K ≡ L , (K ⊃ L) & (~K ⊃ ~L)

2.16.96. Prove equivalent: M ⊃ N , ~N ⊃ ~M

2.16.97. { ~O v P } ⊢ O ⊃ P

2.16.98. ⊢ ~Q ⊃ (Q ⊃ R)

2.16.99. { S ⊃ T , U ≡ T } ⊢ (S v U) ⊃ T

2.16.100. { W ≡ X , Y } ⊢ (W & Y) ≡ (Y ⊃ X)

2.16.101. { A ⊃ (B ⊃ ~A) } ⊢ B ⊃ ~A

2.16.102. { C v D , D ⊃ E } ⊢ ~C ⊃ E

2.16.103. Prove inconsistent: { F ≡ G , ~F ≡ G }

2.16.104. ⊢ H ≡ ~ ~H

GROUP IV: DIFFICULT

2.16.105. { I v J , I ≡ (~I v J) } ⊢ J

2.16.106. { K & L } ⊢ ~(~L v ~K)

2.16.107. Prove inconsistent: { M ⊃ ~M , ~M ⊃ M }

2.16.108. Prove logically false: N ≡ ~N

2.16.109. Prove logically false: ~(O v ~O)

2.16.110. Prove inconsistent: { ~(P ⊃ Q) , (P v R) ⊃ Q }

2.16.111. { ~(S ⊃ T) } ⊢ S & ~T

2.16.112. { T ≡ S } ⊢ (T & S) v (~T & ~S)

2.16.113. Prove equivalent: ~(U & W) , ~U v ~W

2.16.114. { ~X ⊃ Y } ⊢ X v Y

2.16.115. ⊢ (A ⊃ B) v (B ⊃ A)

2.16.116. ⊢   C v ~C

2.16.117. { D ⊃ E } ⊢   ~D v E

2.16.118. { (F ⊃ G) ⊃ G } ⊢   F v G

Answers to Exercises in Chapter Two

EXERCISE 2.1

2.1.1. { A & (B & C) } ⊢   B

1.	A & (B & C)	Ass
2.	B & C	1, &E
3.	B	2, &E

2.1.2. { A & [(C & D) & B] } ⊢   C

1.	A & [(C & D) & B]	Ass
2.	(C & D) & B	1, &E
3.	C & D	2, &E
4.	C	3, &E

EXERCISE 2.2

2.2.1.

1.	A & (B & C)	Ass
2.	B & C	1, &E
3.	C	2, &E
4.	A	1, &E
5.	C & A	3, 4, &I

2.2.2.

1.	(A & B) & (C & D)	Ass
2.	E & [(F & G) & (H & I)]	Ass
3.	(F & G) & (H & I)	2, &E
4.	(H & I)	3, &E
5.	H	4, &E
6.	I	4, &E
7.	I & H	5, 6, &I
8.	C & D	1, &E
9.	(I & H) & (C & D)	7, 8, &I
10.	[(I & H) & (C & D)] & H	9, 5, &I

EXERCISE 2.3 Unnecessary steps are indicated with the thumbs-down sign: 👎👎👎

1.	(A & B) & C	Ass	
2.	C	1, &E	
3.	A & B	1, &E	
4.	A	3, &E	👎👎👎
5.	B	3, &E	
6.	C & B	2, 5, &I	👎👎👎
7.	B & C	2, 5, &I	

EXERCISE 2.4

2.4.1. (A ⊖ (B ≡ (C v D))) Conditional

2.4.2. (A ⊃ B) ⊜ (C v D) Biconditional

2.4.3. A ⊖ ((B ≡ C) v D) Conditional

2.4.4. ~A ⊖ ((B ≡ C) v D) Conditional

2.4.5. ⊖(A ⊃ ((B ≡ C) v D)) Negation

2.4.6. ([~A ⊃ (B v C)] ⓥ D) Disjunction

EXERCISE 2.5

2.5.1. { A & B , C & (D & B) } ⊢ D & (A & C)

1.	A & B	Ass
2.	C & (D & B)	Ass
3.	D & B	2, &E
4.	D	3, &E
5.	A	1, &E
6.	C	2, &E
7.	A & C	5, 6, &I
8.	D & (A & C)	4, 7, &I

NOTE: There are several correct ways to do this (and every other) derivation. For example, things can be done in this order:

1.	A & B	Ass
2.	C & (D & B)	Ass
3.	C	2, &E
4.	A	1, &E
5.	A & C	3, 4, &I
6.	D & B	2, &E
7.	D	6, &E
8.	D & (A & C)	5, 7, &I

2.5.2. { (A & B) & C , D ≡ G } ⊢ (A & C) & (B & [D ≡ G])

1.	(A & B) & C	Ass
2.	D ≡ G	Ass
3.	A & B	1, &E
4.	A	3, &E
5.	C	1, &E
6.	A & C	4, 5, &I
7.	B	3, &E
8.	B & [D ≡ G]	7, 2, &I
9.	(A & C) & (B & [D ≡ G])	6, 9, &I

EXERCISE 2.6.

2.6.1. { (A & B) , (B & A) ⊃ C } ⊢ C

1.	A & B	Ass
2.	(B & A) ⊃ C	Ass
3.	A	1, &E
4.	B	1, &E
5.	B & A	3, 4, &I
6.	C	5, 2, ⊃E

2.6.2. { A , A ⊃ (A ⊃ B) } ⊢ B

1.	A	Ass
2.	A ⊃ (A ⊃ B)	Ass
3.	A ⊃ B	1, 2, ⊃E
4.	B	1, 3, ⊃E

EXERCISE 2.7

1.	A & B	Ass	
2.	G	Ass	
3.	A	1, &E	
4	G ⊃ A	2, 3, ⊃I	👉👉👉
5.	B	Ass	
6.	A	1, &E	
7.	B ⊃ A	5-6, ⊃I	
8.	G & (B ⊃ A)	2, 7, &I	👉👉👉

a. The justification for line 4 is wrong; should be 2-3, ⊃I.

b. Line 8 commits a scope error. Line 2 is not available there. In this case, there is no correct way to get line 8.

EXERCISE 2.8

2.8.1. { G & I } ⊢ H ⊃ G

1.	G & I	Ass
2.	H	Ass
3.	G	1, &E
4.	H ⊃ G	2-3, ⊃I

2.8.2. { A ⊃ [B & (A ⊃ D)] } ⊢ A ⊃ (B & D)

1.	A ⊃ [B & (A ⊃ D)]	Ass
2.	A	Ass
3.	B & (A ⊃ D)	1, 2, ⊃E
4.	B	3, &E
5.	A ⊃ D	3, &E
6.	D	2, 5, ⊃E
7.	B & D	4, 6, &I
8.	A ⊃ (B & D)	2-7, ⊃I

EXERCISE 2.9

2.9.1 { A & B } ⊢ (A v C) & (D v B)

1.	A & B	Ass
2.	A	1, &E
3.	A v C	2, vI
4.	B	1, &E
5.	D v B	4, vI
6.	(A v C) & (D v B)	3, 5, &I

2.9.2. { E } ⊢ A v (B v [E v F])

1.	E	Ass
2.	E v F	1, vI
3.	B v [E v F]	2, vI
4.	A v (B v [E v F])	3, vI

2.9.3 { A v B } ⊢ B v A

1.	A v B	Ass
2.	A	Ass
3.	B v A	2, vI
4.	B	Ass
5.	B v A	4, vI
6.	B v A	1, 2-3, 4-5, vE

2.9.4. { (A & C) v (B & A) } ⊢ A

1.	(A & C) v (B & A)	Ass
2.	A & C	Ass
3.	A	2, &E
4.	B & A	Ass
5.	A	4, &E
6.	A	1, 2-3, 4-5, vE

EXERCISE 2.10

2.10.1. { A ⊃ (D & ~D) } ⊢ ~A

1.	A ⊃ (D & ~D)	Ass
2.	A	Ass
3.	D & ~D	1, 2, ⊃E
4.	D	3, &E
5.	~D	3, &E
6.	~A	2-5, ~I

2.10.2. { ~C ⊃ D , ~D & E } ⊢ C

1.	~C ⊃ D	Ass
2.	~D & E	Ass
3.	~C	Ass
4.	D	3, 1, ⊃E
5.	~D	2, &E
6.	C	3-5, ~E

EXERCISE 2.11

2.11.1. { B ≡ A , A , B ⊃ C } ⊢ C

1.	B ≡ A	Ass
2.	A	Ass
3.	B ⊃ C	Ass
4.	B	2, 1, ≡E
5.	C	4, 3, ⊃E

2.11.2. $\{ C \equiv D \} \vdash D \equiv C$

1.	C ≡ D	Ass
2.	D	Ass
3.	C	2, 1, ≡E
4.	C	Ass
5.	D	4, 1, ≡E
6.	D ≡ C	2-3, 4-5, ≡I

EXERCISE 2.12

2.12.1. $\{ A \} \vdash A \equiv A$

1.	A	Ass
2.	A	Ass
3.	A	2, R
4.	A	Ass
5.	A	4, R
6.	A ≡ A	2-3, 4-5, ≡I

NOTE: Can you see another correct justification for step 3? It's 1, R. Similarly, step 5 might be justified by 1, R. How about this justification for step 5: 2, R? ❡❡❡! That's a scope error.

EXERCISE 2.13

2.13.1.

1.	A	Ass
2.	B	Ass
3.	A	1, R
4.	B ⊃ A	2-3, ⊃I
5.	(B ⊃ A) & A	4,1, &I

2.13.2.

1.	(B v A) ≡ C	Ass
2.	A v B	Ass
3.	A	Ass
4.	B v A	3, vI
5.	C	4, 1, ≡E
6.	B	Ass
7.	B v A	6, vI
8.	C	7, 1, ≡E
9.	C	2, 3-5, 6-8, vE

2.13.3.

1.	A & (B & ~A)	Ass
2.	~G	Ass
3.	A	1, &E
4.	(B & ~A)	1, &E
5.	~A	4, &E
6.	G	2-5, ~E

2.13.4.

1.	A ⊃ B	Ass
2.	~A ⊃ ~B	Ass
3.	A	Ass
4.	B	3, 1, ⊃E
5.	B	Ass
6.	~A	Ass
7.	~B	2, 6, ⊃E
8.	B	5, R
9.	A	6-8, ~E
10	A ≡ B	3-4, 5-9, ≡I

2.13.5. 4, R would not be a correct justification. It's a scope error.

EXERCISE 2.14

The mistake is that the line number has been omitted from the last line. Yes, we do have to be that ridiculously picky.

EXERCISE 2.15

1.	A & B	Ass
2.	B & ~A	Ass
3.	~A	2, &E
4.	A	1, &E

EXERCISE 2.16

2.16.1. { A ⊃ B , A } ⊢ B

1.	A ⊃ B	Ass
2.	A	Ass
3.	B	1, 2, ⊃E

2.16.2. { C , C ⊃ (D v ~E) } ⊢ D v ~E

1.	C	Ass
2.	C ⊃ (D v ~E)	Ass
3.	D v ~E	1, 2, ⊃E

2.16.3. { F , G } ⊢ F & G

1.	F	Ass
2.	G	Ass
3.	F & G	1, 2, &I

2.16.4. { H ⊃ I , H } ⊢ H & I

1.	H ⊃ I	Ass
2.	H	Ass
3.	I	1, 2, ⊃E
4.	H & I	2, 3, &I

2.16.5. { J & (K & L) } ⊢ J

1.	J & (K & L)	Ass
2.	J	1, &E

2.16.6. Prove logically false: M & ~M

1.	M & ~M	Ass
2.	M	1, &E
3.	~M	1, &E

2.16.7. { N } ⊢ O v N

1.	N	Ass
2.	O v N	1, vI

2.16.8. { P , Q } ⊢ Q & (Q & P)

1.	P	Ass
2.	Q	Ass
3.	Q & P	1, 2, &I
4.	Q & (Q & P)	2, 3, &I

2.16.9. { R & S } ⊢ (R & S) v ~T

1.	R & S	Ass
2.	(R & S) v ~T	1, vI

2.16.10. { U , U v W } ⊢ U & (U v W)

1.	U	Ass
2.	U v W	Ass
3.	U & (U v W)	1, 2, &I

2.16.11. { X ≡ Y , Y } ⊢ X

1.	X ≡ Y	Ass
2.	Y	Ass
3.	X	1, 2, ≡E

2.16.12. { A ⊃ B , C ⊃ D , A } ⊢ B

1.	A ⊃ B	Ass
2.	C ⊃ D	Ass
3.	A	Ass
4.	B	3, 1, ⊃E

2.16.13. { E & F } ⊢ E ≡ F

1. | E & F   Ass
2. | | E   Ass
3. | | F   1, &E
4. | | F   Ass
5. | | E   1, &E
6. | E ≡ F   2-3, 4-5, ≡I

2.16.14. { G & (H & I) } ⊢ H

1. | G & (H & I)   Ass
2. | H & I   1, &E
3. | H   2, &E

2.16.15. { J & K } ⊢ K & J

1. | J & K   Ass
2. | J   1, &E
3. | K   1, &E
4. | K & J   2, 3, &I

2.16.16. Prove inconsistent: { L & M , ~M & L }

1. | L & M   Ass
2. | ~M & L   Ass
3. | M   1, &E
4. | ~M   2, &E

2.16.17. Prove inconsistent: { N & ~O , O ≡ N }

1. | N & ~O   Ass
2. | O ≡ N   Ass
3. | N   1, &E
4. | O   2, 3, ≡E
5. | ~O   1, &E

2.16.18. Prove logically false: P & ~P

1.	P & ~P	Ass
2.	P	1, &E
3.	~P	1, &E

2.16.19. { Q v Q } ⊢ Q

1.	Q v Q	Ass
2.	Q	Ass
3.	Q	2, R
4.	Q	Ass
5.	Q	4, R
6.	Q	1, 2-3, 4-5, vE

And, incidentally, here's another correct way of doing this derivation you might examine:

1.	Q v Q	Ass
2.	Q	Ass
3.	Q	2, R
4.	Q	1, 2-3, 2-3, vE

2.16.20. { R } ⊢ S ⊃ R

1.	R	Ass
2.	S	Ass
3.	R	1, R
4.	S ⊃ R	2-3, ⊃I

2.16.21. { T , (T v U) ⊃ W } ⊢ W

1.	T	Ass
2.	(T v U) ⊃ W	Ass
3.	T v U	1, vI
4.	W	2, 3, ⊃E

2.16.22. Prove logically false: X & (X ⊃ ~X)

```
1. | X & (X ⊃ ~X)     Ass
2. | X                1, &E
3. | X ⊃ ~X           1, &E
4. | ~X               2, 3, ⊃E
```

2.16.23. { A ⊃ B , B ⊃ C } ⊢ A ⊃ C

```
1. | A ⊃ B    Ass
2. | B ⊃ C    Ass

3. |  | A      Ass
4. |  | B      3, 1, ⊃E
5. |  | C      4, 2, ⊃E
6. | A ⊃ C    3-5, ⊃I
```

2.16.24. { (D & E) v (D & F) } ⊢ D

```
1. | (D & E) v (D & F)     Ass

2. |  | D & E             Ass
3. |  | D                 2, &E
4. |  | D & F             Ass

5. |  | D                 4, &E
6. | D                    1, 2-3, 4-5, vE
```

2.16.25. Prove equivalent: G , G & G

```
1. | G          Ass
2. | G          1, R
3. | G & G      1, 2, &I
```

```
1. | G & G      Ass
2. | G          1, &E
```

And, by the way, you might note that the first of these two derivations can also be done correctly like this:

```
1. | G          Ass
2. | G & G  1, 1, &I
```

2.16.26. Prove equivalent: H & I , I & H

1.	H & I	Ass
2.	I	1, &E
3.	H	1, &E
4.	I & H	2, 3, &I

1.	I & H	Ass
2.	H	1, &E
3.	I	1, &E
4.	H & I	2, 3, &I

2.16.27. ⊢ J ⊃ J

1.	J	Ass
2.	J	1, R
3.	J ⊃ J	1-2, ⊃I

2.16.28. ⊢ (K ≡ L) ⊃ (K ⊃ L)

1.	K ≡ L	Ass
2.	K	Ass
3.	L	2, 1, ≡E
4.	K ⊃ L	2-3, ⊃I
5.	(K ≡ L) ⊃ (K ⊃ L)	1-4, ⊃I

2.16.29 { M , N } ⊢ (M v N) & N

1.	M	Ass
2.	N	Ass
3.	M v N	1, vI
4.	(M v N) & N	2, 3, &I

2.16.30. { (~O & P) ⊃ (R v ~S) , ~O & P } ⊢ R v ~S

1.	(~O & P) ⊃ (R v ~S)	Ass
2.	~O & P	Ass
3.	R v ~S	1, 2, ⊃E

2.16.31. { [T v (U ≡ W)] ⊃ X , X ⊃ Y } ⊢   [T v (U ≡ W)] ⊃ Y

1.	[T v (U ≡ W)] ⊃ X	Ass
2.	X ⊃ Y	Ass
3.	T v (U ≡ W)	Ass
4.	X	3, 1, ⊃E
5.	Y	2, 4, ⊃E
6.	[T v (U ≡ W)] ⊃ Y	3-5, ⊃I

2.16.32. { A ≡ B , B } ⊢   B & (A v C)

1.	A ≡ B	Ass
2.	B	Ass
3.	A	1, 2, ≡E
4.	A v C	3, vI
5.	B & (A v C)	2, 4, &I

2.16.33. { D ⊃ E } ⊢   (D & F) ⊃ E

1.	D ⊃ E	Ass
2.	D & F	Ass
3.	D	2, &E
4.	E	3, 1, ⊃E
5.	(D & F) ⊃ E	2-4 ⊃I

2.16.34. { (G v H) ⊃ I } ⊢   G ⊃ I

1.	(G v H) ⊃ I	Ass
2.	G	Ass
3.	G v H	2, vI
4.	I	3, 1, ⊃E
5.	G ⊃ I	2-4, ⊃I

2.16.35. Prove equivalent: J v K , K v J

1.	J v K		Ass
2.		J	Ass
3.		K v J	2, vI
4.		K	Ass
5.		K v J	4, vI
6.	K v J		1, 2-3, 4-5, vE

1.	K v J		Ass
2.		K	Ass
3.		J v K	2, vI
4.		J	Ass
5.		J v K	4, vI
6.	J v K		1, 2-3, 4-5, vE

2.16.36. Prove equivalent: ~L , ~ ~ ~L

1.	~L		Ass
2.		~ ~L	Ass
3.		~L	1, R
4.		~ ~L	2, R
5.	~ ~ ~L		2-4, ~I

1.	~ ~ ~L		Ass
2.		~ ~L	Ass
3.		~ ~ ~L	1, R
4.		~ ~L	2, R
5.	~L		2-4, ~E

And by the way, an equally correct and shorter way to do both derivations would be to eliminate step 4 in each; the contradiction needed would be in steps 2 and 3.

2.16.37. { M ⊃ (N & O) } ⊢   M ⊃ O

1.	M ⊃ (N & O)	Ass
2.	M	Ass
3.	N & O	2, 1, ⊃E
4.	O	3, &E
5.	M ⊃ O	2-4, ⊃I

2.16.38. { (~P & Q) ≡ R , R } ⊢   Q

1.	(~P & Q) ≡ R	Ass
2.	R	Ass
3.	~P & Q	2, 1, ≡E
4.	Q	3, &E

2.16.39. { S ⊃ T , S ⊃ U } ⊢   S ⊃ (T & U)

1.	S ⊃ T	Ass
2.	S ⊃ U	Ass
3.	S	Ass
4.	T	3, 1, ⊃E
5.	U	3, 2, ⊃E
6.	T & U	4, 5, &I
7.	S ⊃ (T & U)	3-6, ⊃I

2.16.40. { W v X , X ⊃ W } ⊢   W

1.	W v X	Ass
2.	X ⊃ W	Ass
3.	W	Ass
4.	W	3, R
5.	X	Ass
6.	W	5, 2, ⊃E
7.	W	1, 3-4, 5-6, vE

2.16.41. { Y ⊃ Z , ~Z } ⊢ ~Y

1.	Y ⊃ Z	Ass
2.	~Z	Ass
3.	Y	Ass
4.	Z	3, 1, ⊃E
5.	~Z	2, R
6.	~Y	3-5, ~I

2.16.42. { A ≡ (B ∨ [D & ~A]) } ⊢ C ⊃ (C ∨ C)

1.	A ≡ (B ∨ [D & ~A])	Ass
2.	C	Ass
3.	C ∨ C	2, ∨I
4.	C ⊃ (C ∨ C)	2-3, ⊃I

2.16.43. { E , (F ⊃ E) ⊃ G } ⊢ G

1.	E	Ass
2.	(F ⊃ E) ⊃ G	Ass
3.	F	Ass
4.	E	1, R
5.	F ⊃ E	3-4, ⊃I
6.	G	5, 2, ⊃E

2.16.44. ⊢ H ≡ H

1.	H	Ass
2.	H	1, R
3.	H	Ass
4.	H	3, R
5.	H ≡ H	1-2, 3-4, ≡I

And an equally correct and shorter way to do that last one is:

1.	H	Ass
2.	H	1, R
3.	H ≡ H	1-2, 1-2, ≡I

2.16.45. { I v J , (J v I) ≡ K } ⊢ K

1.	I v J	Ass
2.	(J v I) ≡ K	Ass
3.	I	Ass
4.	J v I	3, vI
5.	J	Ass
6.	J v I	5, vI
7.	J v I	1, 3-4, 5-6, vI
8.	K	7, 2, ≡E

2.16.46. { L ⊃ (L ⊃ M) } ⊢ L ⊃ M

1.	L ⊃ (L ⊃ M)	Ass
2.	L	Ass
3.	L ⊃ M	2, 1, ⊃E
4.	M	2, 3, ⊃E
5.	L ⊃ M	2-4, ⊃I

2.16.47. ⊢ (N & ~N) ⊃ O

1.	N & ~N	Ass
2.	~O	Ass
3.	N	1, &E
4.	~N	1, &E
5.	O	2-4, ~E
6.	(N & ~N) ⊃ O	1-5, ⊃I

2.16.48. Prove logically false: P & (P ⊃ ~P)

1.	P & (P ⊃ ~P)	Ass
2.	P	1, &E
3.	P ⊃ ~P	1, &E
4.	~P	2, 3, ⊃E

2.16.49. ⊢ ~(Q & ~Q)

1.	Q & ~Q	Ass
2.	Q	1, &E
3.	~Q	1, &E
4.	~(Q & ~Q)	1-3, ~I

2.16.50. ⊢ R ⊃ (S v R)

1.	R	Ass
2.	S v R	1, vI
3.	R ⊃ (S v R)	2-3, ⊃I

2.16.51. { T ⊃ ~U , U } ⊢ ~T

1.	T ⊃ ~U	Ass
2.	U	Ass
3.	T	Ass
4.	~U	3, 1, ⊃E
5.	U	2, R
6.	~T	3-5, ~I

2.16.52. Prove equivalent: W ≡ X , X ≡ W

1.	W ≡ X	Ass
2.	X	Ass
3.	W	2, 1, ≡E
4.	W	Ass
5.	X	4, 1, ≡E
6.	X ≡ W	2-3, 4,5, ≡I

1.	X ≡ W	Ass
2.	W	Ass
3.	X	2, 1, ≡E
4.	X	Ass
5.	W	4, 1, ≡E
6.	W ≡ X	2-3, 4,5, ≡I

2.16.53. Prove equivalent: Y , Y v Y

1.	Y	Ass
2.	Y v Y	1, vI

1.	Y v Y	Ass
2.	Y	Ass
3.	Y	2, R
4.	Y	Ass
5.	Y	4, R
6.	Y	1, 2-3, 4-5, vE

2.16.54. Prove equivalent: A v B , B v A

1.	A v B	Ass
2.	A	Ass
3.	B v A	2, vI
4.	B	Ass
5.	B v A	4, vI
6.	B v A	1, 2-3, 4-5, vE

1.	B v A	Ass
2.	B	Ass
3.	A v B	2, vI
4.	A	Ass
5.	A v B	4, vI
6.	A v B	1, 2-3, 4-5, vE

2.16.55. Prove equivalent: C & C , C v C

1.	C & C	Ass
2.	C	1, &E
3.	C v C	2, vI

```
1. │ C v C      Ass
2. │ ┌ C        Ass
3. │ │ C        2, R
4. │ │ C        Ass
5. │ │ C        4, R
6. │ C          1, 2-3, 4-5, vE
7. │ C          1, 2-3, 4-5, vE
8. │ C & C      6, 7, &I
```

Here, by the way, is a much shorter version, equally correct, of the second derivation:

```
1. │ C v C      Ass
2. │ │ C        Ass
3. │ │ C        2, R
4. │ C          1, 2-3, 2-3, vE
5. │ C & C      4, 4, &I
```

2.16.56. Prove inconsistent: { D , D ⊃ ~D)

```
1. │ D          Ass
2. │ D ⊃ ~D     Ass
3. │ ~D         1, 2, ⊃E
4. │ D          1, R
```

An equally correct, shorter proof would leave out step 4 (since there already was a contradiction in steps 3 and 1).

2.16.57. { E } ⊢ (E v F) & (F ⊃ E)

```
1. │ E                    Ass
2. │ E v F                1, vI
3. │ │ F                  Ass
4. │ │ E                  1, R
5. │ F ⊃ E                3-4, ⊃I
6. │ (E v F) & (F ⊃ E)    2, 5, &I
```

2.16.58. Prove inconsistent: { G & H , H ≡ ~G }

1.	G & H	Ass
2.	H ≡ ~G	Ass
3.	G	1, &E
4.	H	1, &E
5.	~G	4, 2, ≡E

2.16.59. { ~I ⊃ ~J , J } ⊢ I

1.	~I ⊃ ~J	Ass
2.	J	Ass
3.	~I	Ass
4.	~J	1, 3, ⊃E
5.	J	2, R
6.	I	3-5, ~E

2.16.60. { K ⊃ L } ⊢ K ⊃ (K & L)

1.	K ⊃ L	Ass
2.	K	Ass
3.	L	2, 1, ⊃E
4.	K & L	2, 3, &I
5.	K ⊃ (K & L)	2-4, ⊃I

2.16.61. ⊢ M ⊃ (M v N)

1.	M	Ass
2.	M v N	1, vI
3.	M ⊃ (M v N)	1-2, ⊃I

2.16.62. Prove equivalent: (O & P) & R , O & (P & R)

1.	(O & P) & R	Ass
2.	O & P	1, &E
3.	O	2, &E
4.	P	2, &E
5.	R	1, &E
6.	P & R	4, 5, &I
7.	O & (P & R)	3, 6, &I

1.	O & (P & R)	Ass
2.	P & R	1, &E
3.	P	2, &E
4.	R	2, &E
5.	O	1, &E
6.	O & P	3, 5, &I
7.	(O & P) & R	6, 4, &I

2.16.63. ⊢ (S ≡ T) ⊃ (S ⊃ T)

1.	S ≡ T	Ass
2.	S	Ass
3.	T	2, 1, ≡E
4.	S ⊃ T	2-3, ⊃I
5.	(S ≡ T) ⊃ (S ⊃ T)	1-4, ⊃I

2.16.64. Prove equivalent: U ≡ W , (U ⊃ W) & (W ⊃ U)

1.	U ≡ W	Ass
2.	U	Ass
3.	W	1, 2, ≡E
4.	U ⊃ W	2-3, ⊃I
5.	W	Ass
6.	U	5, 1, ≡E
7.	W ⊃ U	5-6, ⊃I
8	(U ⊃ W) & (W ⊃ U)	4, 7, &I

1.	(U ⊃ W) & (W ⊃ U)	Ass
2.	U	Ass
3.	U ⊃ W	1, &E
4.	W	2, 3, ⊃E
5.	W	Ass
6.	W ⊃ U	1, &E
7.	U	5, 6, ⊃E
8.	U ≡ W	2-4, 5-7, ≡I

2.16.65. { X ⊃ Y , Y ⊃ Z } ⊢ X ⊃ Z

1.	X ⊃ Y	Ass
2.	Y ⊃ Z	Ass
3.	X	Ass
4.	Y	3, 1, ⊃E
5.	Z	4, 2, ⊃E
6.	X ⊃ Z	3-5, ⊃I

2.16.66. { (A & B) v (C & B) } ⊢ B

1.	(A & B) v (C & B)	Ass
2.	A & B	Ass
3.	B	2, &E
4.	C & B	Ass
5.	B	4, &E
6.	B	1, 2-3, 4-5, vE

2.16.67. { D ⊃ E , F ⊃ G , D } ⊢ E v G

1.	D ⊃ E	Ass
2.	F ⊃ G	Ass
3.	D	Ass
4.	E	3, 1, ⊃E
5.	E v G	4, vI

2.16.68. { (H & I) ⊃ J , J ⊃ K , I & H } ⊢ K

1.	(H & I) ⊃ J	Ass
2.	J ⊃ K	Ass
3.	I & H	Ass
4.	I	3, &E
5.	H	3, &E
6.	H & I	4, 5, &I
7.	J	6, 1, ⊃E
8.	K	7, 2, ⊃E

2.16.69. { L ⊃ M , M ⊃ N } ⊢ ~N ⊃ ~L

1.	L ⊃ M	Ass
2.	M ⊃ N	Ass
3.	~N	Ass
4.	L	Ass
5.	M	4, 1, ⊃E
6.	N	5, 2, ⊃E
7.	~N	3, R
8.	~L	4-7, ~I
9.	~N ⊃ ~L	3-8, ⊃I

2.16.70. { O ⊃ ~P , ~ ~P } ⊢ ~O

1.	O ⊃ ~P	Ass
2.	~ ~P	Ass
3.	O	Ass
4.	~P	3, 1, ⊃E
5.	~ ~P	2, R
6.	~O	3-5, ~I

2.16.71. ⊢ Q ⊃ (R ⊃ Q)

1.	Q	Ass
2.	R	Ass
3.	Q	1, R
4.	R ⊃ Q	2-3, ⊃I
5.	Q ⊃ (R ⊃ Q)	1-4, ⊃I

2.16.72. { (S v T) ⊃ ~U , U } ⊢ ~S

1.	(S v T) ⊃ ~U	Ass
2.	U	Ass
3.	S	Ass
4.	S v T	3, vI
5.	~U	4, 1, ⊃E
6.	U	2, R
7.	~S	3-6, ~I

2.16.73. { W ⊃ X , W ⊃ ~X } ⊢   ~W

1.	W ⊃ X	Ass	
2.	W ⊃ ~X	Ass	
3.	│ W	Ass	
4.	│ X	3, 1, ⊃E	
5.	│ ~X	3, 2, ⊃E	
6.	~W	3-5, ~I	

2.16.74. ⊢   ~Y ⊃ (Y ⊃ Z)

1.	│ │ ~Y	Ass
2.	│ │ Y	Ass
3.	│ │ │ ~Z	Ass
4.	│ │ │ Y	2, R
5.	│ │ │ ~Y	1, R
6.	│ │ Z	3-5, ~E
7.	│ Y ⊃ Z	2-6, ⊃I
8.	Y ⊃ (Y ⊃ Z)	1-7, ⊃I

2.16.75. { A ≡ B , B ≡ C) } ⊢   A ⊃ (D v C)

1.	A ≡ B	Ass
2.	B ≡ C	Ass
3.	│ A	Ass
4.	│ B	3, 1, ≡E
5.	│ C	4, 2, ≡E
6.	│ D v C	5, vI
7.	A ⊃ (D v C)	3-6, ⊃I

2.16.76. { (E v F) ⊃ (G & H) , (I v J) ⊃ (E v F) , I } ⊢   H

1.	(E v F) ⊃ (G & H)	Ass
2.	(I v J) ⊃ (E v F)	Ass
3.	I	Ass
4.	I v J	3, vI
5.	E v F	4, 2, ⊃E
6.	G & H	5, 1, ⊃E
7.	H	6, &E

2.16.77. { K & ~L } ⊢ ~(K ⊃ L)

1.	K & ~L	Ass
2.	K ⊃ L	Ass
3.	K	1, &E
4.	L	3, 2, ⊃E
5.	~L	1, &E
6.	~(K ⊃ L)	2-5, ~I

2.16.78. { (M v N) ⊃ O , (O v P) ⊃ (R v ~M) } ⊢ M ⊃ R

1.	(M v N) ⊃ O	Ass
2.	(O v P) ⊃ (R v ~M)	Ass
3.	M	Ass
4.	M v N	3, vI
5.	O	4, 1, ⊃E
6.	O v P	5, vI
7.	R v ~M	6, 2, ⊃E
8.	R	Ass
9.	R	8, R
10.	~M	Ass
11.	~R	Ass
12.	~M	10, R
13.	M	3, R
14.	R	11-13, ~E
15.	R	7, 8-9, 10-14, vE
16.	M ⊃ R	3-15, ⊃I

2.16.79. { ~S ⊃ ~T , (T & U) & W } ⊢ S

1.	~S ⊃ ~T	Ass
2.	(T & U) & W	Ass
3.	T & U	2, &E
4.	~S	Ass
5.	~T	4, 1, ⊃E
6.	T	3, &E
7.	S	4-6, ~E

2.16.80. { A v B , A ⊃ C , B ⊃ D } ⊢ C v D

```
1. | A v B          Ass
2. | A ⊃ C          Ass
3. | B ⊃ D          Ass
4. |  | A           Ass
5. |  | C           4, 2, ⊃E
6. |  | C v D        5, vI
7. |  | B           Ass
8. |  | D           7, 3, ⊃E
9. |  | C v D        8, vI
10.| C v D          1, 4-6, 7-9, vE
```

2.16.81. { E v F } ⊢ (E ⊃ F) ⊃ F

```
1. | E v F            Ass
2. |  | E ⊃ F         Ass
3. |  |  | E          Ass
4. |  |  | F          3, 2, ⊃E
5. |  |  | F          Ass
6. |  |  | F          5, R
7. |  | F             1, 3-4, 5-6, vE
8. | (E ⊃ F) ⊃ F      2-7, ⊃I
```

2.16.82. { G v H , ~G } ⊢ H

```
1. | G v H           Ass
2. | ~G              Ass
3. |  | G            Ass
4  |  |  | ~H        Ass
5. |  |  | G         3, R
6. |  |  | ~G        2, R
7. |  | H            4-6, ~E
8. |  | H            Ass
9. |  | H            8, R
10.| H               1, 3-7, 8-9, vE
```

2.16.83. { I ⊃ J , I v K , ~K } ⊢   L ⊃ J

1.	I ⊃ J		Ass
2.	I v K		Ass
3.	~K		Ass
4.		L	Ass
5.		I	Ass
6.		J	5, 1, ⊃E
7.		K	Ass
8.		~J	Ass
9.		K	7, R
10.		~K	3, R
11.		J	8-10, ~E
12.		J	2, 5-6, 7-11, vE
13.	L ⊃ J		4-12, ⊃I

2.16.84. ⊢   [(M v M) & (M ⊃ N)] ⊃ N

1.	(M v M) & (M ⊃ N)	Ass
2.	M v M	1, &E
3.	M	Ass
4.	M	3, R
5.	M	Ass
6.	M	5, R
7.	M	2, 3-4, 5-6, vE
8.	M ⊃ N	1, &E
9.	N	7, 8, ⊃E
10.	[(M v M) & (M ⊃ N)] ⊃ N	1-10, ⊃I

2.16.85. { O ⊃ (P ⊃ R) } ⊢   P ⊃ (O ⊃ R)

1.	O ⊃ (P ⊃ R)	Ass
2.	P	Ass
3.	O	Ass
4.	P ⊃ R	3, 1, ⊃E
5.	R	2, 4, ⊃E
6.	O ⊃ R	3-5, ⊃I
7.	P ⊃ (O ⊃ R)	2-6, ⊃I

2.16.86. { S ⊃ (~T v U) , S & T } ⊢   U

1.	S ⊃ (~T v U)		Ass
2.	S & T		Ass
3.	S		2, &E
4.	~T v U		3, 1, ⊃E
5.	~T		Ass
6.		~U	Ass
7.		T	2, &E
8.		~T	5, R
9.	U		6-8, ~E
10.	U		Ass
11.	U		10, R
12.	U		4, 5-9, 10-11, vE

2.16.87. { W ⊃ X , ~X ≡ W } ⊢   ~W

1.	W ⊃ X	Ass
2.	~X ≡ W	Ass
3.	W	Ass
4.	X	3, 1, ⊃E
5.	~X	3, 2, ≡E
6.	~W	3-5, ~I

2.16.88. Prove inconsistent: { Y v Z , ~Y & ~Z }

1.	Y v Z		Ass
2.	~Y & ~Z		Ass
3.	Y		Ass
4.	Y		3, R
5.	Z		Ass
6.		~Y	Ass
7.		Z	5, R
8.		~Z	2, &E
9.	Y		6-8, ~E
10.	Y		1, 3-4, 5-9, vE
11.	~Y		2, &E

2.16.89. Prove logically false: A ≡ ~A

```
1.| A ≡ ~A      Ass
2.|  | A        Ass
3.|  | A        2, R
4.|  | ~A       3, 1, ≡E
5.| ~A          2-4, ~I
6.| A           5, 1, ≡E
```

2.16.90. Prove logically false: ~(B ⊃ ~ ~B)

```
1.| ~(B ⊃ ~ ~B)    Ass
2.|  | B            Ass
3.|  |  | ~B        Ass
4.|  |  | B         2, R
5.|  |  | ~B        3, R
6.|  | ~ ~B         3-5, ~I
7.| B ⊃ ~ ~B        2-6, ⊃I
8.| ~(B ⊃ ~ ~B)     1, R
```

(Line 8 isn't really necessary: the contradiction needed is already on lines 7 and 1. Similarly, line 5 isn't really necessary. But both lines make what's going on a lot clearer.)

2.16.91. Prove inconsistent: { C & D , ~(C ≡ D) }

```
1.| C & D       Ass
2.| ~(C ≡ D)    Ass
3.|  | C        Ass
4.|  | D        1, &E
5.|  | D        Ass
6.|  | C        1, &E
7.| C ≡ D       3-4, 5-6, ≡I
8.| ~(C ≡ D)    2, R
```

2.16.92. ⊢ (E & ~E) ⊃ F

1.	E & ~E	Ass
2.	~F	Ass
3.	E	1, &E
4.	~E	1, &E
5.	F	2-4, ~E
6.	(E & ~E) ⊃ F	1-5, ⊃I

2.16.93. ⊢ (G & H) ⊃ ~(G ⊃ ~H)

1.	G & H	Ass
2.	G ⊃ ~H	Ass
3.	G	1, &E
4.	~H	2, 3, ⊃E
5.	H	1, &E
6.	~(G ⊃ ~H)	2-5, ~I
7.	(G & H) ⊃ ~(G ⊃ ~H)	1-6, ⊃I

2.16.94. { I , ~I ≡ ~J } ⊢ J

1.	I	Ass
2.	~I ≡ ~J	Ass
3.	~J	Ass
4.	~I	3, 2, ≡E
5.	I	1, R
6.	J	3-5, ~E

2.16.95. Prove equivalent: K ≡ L , (K ⊃ L) & (~K ⊃ ~L)

1.	K ≡ L	Ass
2.	K	Ass
3.	L	2, 1, ≡E
4.	K ⊃ L	2-3, ⊃I
5.	~K	Ass
6.	L	Ass
7.	K	6, 1, ≡E
8.	~K	5, R
9.	~L	6-8, ~I
10.	~K ⊃ ~L	5-9, ⊃I
11.	(K ⊃ L) & (~K ⊃ ~L)	4, 10, &I

1.	(K ⊃ L) & (~K ⊃ ~L)	Ass
2.	K	Ass
3.	K ⊃ L	1, &E
4.	L	2, 3, ⊃E
5.	L	Ass
6.	~K	Ass
7.	~K ⊃ ~L	1, &E
8.	~L	6, 7, ⊃E
9.	L	5, R
10.	K	6-9, ~E
11.	K ≡ L	2-4, 5-10, ≡I

2.16.96. Prove equivalent: M ⊃ N , ~N ⊃ ~M

1.	M ⊃ N	Ass
2.	~N	Ass
3.	M	Ass
4.	N	3, 1, ⊃E
5.	~N	2, R
6.	~M	3-5, ~I
7.	~N ⊃ ~M	2-6, ⊃I

1.	~N ⊃ ~M	Ass
2.	M	Ass
3.	~N	Ass
4.	~M	3, 1, ⊃E
5.	M	2, R
6.	N	3-5, ~E
7.	M ⊃ N	2-6, ⊃I

2.16.97. { ~O v P } ⊢ O ⊃ P

1.	~O v P	Ass
2.	O	Ass
3.	~O	Ass
4.	~P	Ass
5.	O	2, R
6.	~O	3, R
7.	P	4-6, ~E
8.	P	Ass
9.	P	8, R
10.	P	1, 3-7, 8-9, vE
11.	O ⊃ P	2-10, ⊃I

2.16.98. ⊢ ~Q ⊃ (Q ⊃ R)

1.	~Q	Ass
2.	Q	Ass
3.	~R	Ass
4.	~Q	1, R
5.	Q	2, R
6.	R	3-5, ~E
7.	Q ⊃ R	2-6, ⊃I
8.	~Q ⊃ (Q ⊃ R)	1-7, ⊃I

2.16.99. { S ⊃ T , U ≡ T } ⊢ (S v U) ⊃ T

1.	S ⊃ T	Ass
2.	U ≡ T	Ass
3.	S v U	Ass
4.	S	Ass
5.	T	4, 1, ⊃E
6.	U	Ass
7.	T	6, 2, ≡E
8.	T	3, 4-5, 6-7, vE
9.	(S v U) ⊃ T	3-8, ⊃I

2.16.100. { W ≡ X , Y } ⊢ (W & Y) ≡ (Y ⊃ X)

1.	W ≡ X	Ass
2.	Y	Ass
3.	W & Y	Ass
4.	Y	Ass
5.	W	3, &E
6.	X	5, 1, ≡E
7.	Y ⊃ X	4-6, ⊃I
8.	Y ⊃ X	Ass
9.	X	2, 8, ⊃E
10.	W	9, 1, ≡E
11.	W & Y	2, 10, &I
12.	(W & Y) ≡ (Y ⊃ X)	3-7, 8-11, ≡I

2.16.101. { A ⊃ (B ⊃ ~A) } ⊢ B ⊃ ~A

1.	A ⊃ (B ⊃ ~A)	Ass
2.	B	Ass
3.	A	Ass
4.	B ⊃ ~A	3, 1, ⊃E
5.	~A	2, 4, ⊃E
6.	A	3, R
7.	~A	3-6, ~I
8.	B ⊃ ~A	2-7, ⊃I

2.16.102. { C v D , D ⊃ E } ⊢ ~C ⊃ E

1.	C v D	Ass
2.	D ⊃ E	Ass
3.	~C	Ass
4.	C	Ass
5.	~E	Ass
6.	C	4, R
7.	~C	3, R
8.	E	5-7, ~E
9.	D	Ass
10.	E	2, 9, ⊃E
11.	E	1, 4-8, 9-10, vE
12.	~C ⊃ E	3-11, ⊃I

2.16.103. Prove inconsistent: { F ≡ G , ~F ≡ G }

1.	F ≡ G	Ass
2.	~F ≡ G	Ass
3.	F	Ass
4.	G	3, 1, ≡E
5.	~F	4, 2, ≡E
6.	F	3, R
7.	~F	3-6, ~I
8.	G	7, 2, ≡E
9.	F	8, 1, ≡E

2.16.104. ⊢   H ≡ ~ ~H

1.	H	Ass
2.	~H	Ass
3.	H	1, R
4.	~H	2, R
5.	~ ~H	2-4, ~I
6.	~ ~H	Ass
7.	~H	Ass
8.	~ ~H	6, R
9.	~H	7, R
10	H	7-9, ~E
11	H ≡ ~ ~H	1-5, 6-10, ≡I

2.16.105. { I v J , I ≡ (~I v J) } ⊢   J

1.	I v J	Ass
2.	I ≡ (~I v J)	Ass
3.	I	Ass
4.	~I v J	3, 2, ≡E
5.	~I	Ass
6.	~J	Ass
7.	I	3, R
8.	~I	5, R
9.	J	6-8, ~E
10.	J	Ass
11.	J	10, R
12.	J	4, 5-9, 10-11, vE
13.	J	Ass
14.	J	13, R
15.	J	1, 3-12, 13-14, vE

2.16.106. { K & L } ⊢ ~(~L v ~K)

1.	K & L	Ass
2.	~L v ~K	Ass
3.	~L	Ass
4.	~L	3, R
5.	~K	Ass
6.	L	Ass
7.	~K	5, R
8.	K	1, &E
9.	~L	6-8, ~I
10	~L	2, 3-4, 5-9, vE
11	L	1, &E
12	~(~L v ~K)	2-11, ~I

2.16.107. Prove inconsistent: { M ⊃ ~M , ~M ⊃ M }

1.	M ⊃ ~M	Ass
2.	~M ⊃ M	Ass
3.	M	Ass
4.	~M	3, 1, ⊃E
5.	M	3, R
6.	~M	3-5, ~I
7.	M	6, 2, ⊃E

2.16.108. Prove logically false: N ≡ ~N

1.	N ≡ ~N	Ass
2.	N	Ass
3.	~N	1, 2, ≡E
4.	N	2, R
5.	~N	2-4, ~I
6.	N	5, 1, ≡E

2.16.109. Prove logically false: ~(O v ~O)

1.	~(O v ~O)	Ass
2.	~O	Ass
3.	O v ~O	2, vI
4.	~(O v ~O)	1, R
5.	O	2-4, ~E
6.	O v ~O	5, vI
7.	~(O v ~O)	1, R

2.16.110. Prove inconsistent: { ~(P ⊃ Q) , (P v R) ⊃ Q }

1.	~(P ⊃ Q)	Ass
2.	(P v R) ⊃ Q	Ass
3.	P	Ass
4.	P v R	3, vI
5.	Q	4, 2, ⊃E
6.	P ⊃ Q	3-5, ⊃I
7.	~(P ⊃ Q)	1, R

2.16.111. { ~(S ⊃ T) } ⊢ S & ~T

1.	~(S ⊃ T)	Ass
2.	~S	Ass
3.	S	Ass
4.	~T	Ass
5.	S	3, R
6.	~S	2, R
7.	T	4-6, ~E
8.	S ⊃ T	3-7, ⊃I
9.	~(S ⊃ T)	1, R
10	S	2-9, ~E
11.	T	Ass
12.	S	Ass
13.	T	11, R
14.	S ⊃ T	12-13, ⊃I
15.	~(S ⊃ T)	1, R
16.	~T	11-15, ~I
17.	S & ~T	10, 16, &I

2.16.112. { T ≡ S } ⊢   (T & S) v (~T & ~S)

```
1.  | T ≡ S                              Ass
2.  |  | ~[(T & S) v (~T & ~S)]         Ass
3.  |  |  | T                            Ass
4.  |  |  | S                            3, 1, ≡E
5.  |  |  | T & S                        3, 4, &I
6.  |  |  | (T & S) v (~T & ~S)          5, vI
7.  |  |  | ~[(T & S) v (~T & ~S)]       2, R
8   |  | ~T                              3-7, ~I
9.  |  |  | S                            Ass
10  |  |  | T                            9, 1, ≡E
11  |  |  | ~T                           8, R
12  |  | ~S                              9-11, ~I
13  |  | ~T & ~S                         8, 12, &I
14  |  | (T & S) v (~T & ~S)             13, vI
15  |  | ~[(T & S) v (~T & ~S)]          2, R
16  | (T & S) v (~T & ~S)                2-15, ~E
```

The difficulty in this derivation is that vI cannot be used as the last step, to get that final disjunction. The reason is that you can't get either disjunct all by itself, then use vI on it. Neither disjunct by itself follows from the premise. The technique used instead is a very subtle and un-obvious one, and rather difficult to see. Look at this derivation carefully; you'll notice an analogous procedure used in several of the more difficult derivations in which a disjunction is derived.

2.16.113. Prove equivalent: ~(U & W) , ~U v ~W

1.	~(U & W)	Ass
2.	~(~U v ~W)	Ass
3.	~U	Ass
4.	~U v ~W	3, vI
5.	~(~U v ~W)	2, R
6.	U	3-5, ~E
7.	~W	Ass
8.	~U v ~W	7, vI
9.	~(~U v ~W)	2, R
10.	W	7-9, ~E
11.	U & W	6, 10, &I
12.	~(U & W)	1, R
13.	~U v ~W	2-12, ~E

1.	~U v ~W	Ass
2.	~U	Ass
3.	U & W	Ass
4.	U	3, &E
5.	~U	2, R
6.	~(U & W)	3-5, ~I
7.	~W	Ass
8.	U & W	Ass
9.	W	8, &E
10.	~W	7, R
11.	~(U & W)	8-10, ~I
12.	~(U & W)	1, 2-6, 7-11, vE

2.16.114. { ~X ⊃ Y } ⊢ X v Y

1.	~X ⊃ Y	Ass
2.	~(X v Y)	Ass
3.	X	Ass
4.	X v Y	3, vI
5.	~(X v Y)	2, R
6.	~X	3-5, ~I
7.	Y	6, 1, ⊃E
8.	X v Y	7, vI
9.	~(X v Y)	2, R
10.	X v Y	2-9, ~E

2.16.115. ⊢   (A ⊃ B) v (B ⊃ A)

1.	~[(A ⊃ B) v (B ⊃ A)]	Ass
2.	B	Ass
3.	A	Ass
4.	B	2, R
5.	A ⊃ B	3-4, ⊃I
6.	(A ⊃ B) v (B ⊃ A)	5, vI
7.	~[(A ⊃ B) v (B ⊃ A)]	1, R
8.	~B	2-7, ~I
9.	B	Ass
10	~A	Ass
11.	B	9, R
12.	~B	8, R
13.	A	10-12, ~E
14.	B ⊃ A	9-13, ⊃I
15.	(A ⊃ B) v (B ⊃ A)	14, vI
16.	~[(A ⊃ B) v (B ⊃ A)]	1, R
17.	(A ⊃ B) v (B ⊃ A)	1-16, ~E

Incidentally, that's an odd logical truth, isn't it? It means that given any two sentences X and Y, it *has* to be the case that either X ⊃ Y or Y ⊃ X. If you think about it, you'll see that this is a consequence of the truth table defining the horseshoe. X has to be T or F. If it's T, then Y ⊃ X is true. If it's F, then X ⊃ Y is true. Here's another similar logical truth that might even seem odder: (A ⊃ B) v (C ⊃ A). You might try to derive that one too.

2.16.116. ⊢   C v ~C

1.		~(C v ~C)	Ass
2.		C	Ass
3.		C v ~C	2, vI
4.		~(C v ~C)	1, R
5.		~C	2-4, ~I
6.	C v ~C	5, vI
7.	~(C v ~C)	1, R
8.	C v ~C	1-7, ~E

2.16.117. { D ⊃ E } ⊢   ~D v E

1.	D ⊃ E	Ass
2.	~(~D v E)	Ass
3.	~D	Ass
4.	~D v E	3, vI
5.	~(~D v E)	2, R
6.	D	3-5, ~E
7.	E	6, 1, ⊃E
8.	~D v E	7, vI
9.	~(~D v E)	2, R
10.	~D v E	2-9, ~E

2.8.118. { (F ⊃ G) ⊃ G } ⊢ F v G

1.	(F ⊃ G) ⊃ G	Ass
2.	~(F v G)	Ass
3.	F	Ass
4.	F v G	3, vI
5.	~(F v G)	2, R
6.	~F	3-5, ~I
7.	F	Ass
8.	~G	Ass
9	F	7, R
10.	~F	6, R
11.	G	8-10, ~E
12.	F ⊃ G	7-11, ⊃I
13.	G	12, 1, ⊃E
14.	F v G	13, vI
15.	~(F v G)	2, R
16.	F v G	2-15, ~E

CHAPTER THREE

QUANTIFIER LOGIC

Predicates and Constants

There are logical properties that are not the result of sentential connectives. For example, the argument

> *Seymour is a reptile*
> *No reptiles fly*
> *Seymour doesn't fly*

is valid. The best job we can do so far to symbolize this argument is:

> S
> R
> ~F

But this is truth-functionally invalid.

Another example of the limitations of what we've done so far: The sentence *No pigs are pigs* is logically false. But the best job we can do so far to symbolize that sentence is P; and this is truth-functionally indeterminate.

To accommodate the logic of sentences like these, we need ways of translating sentences into logic that do not treat them as merely atomic sentences, or truth-functional combinations of these. We need to go *inside* sentences and analyze and symbolize their logical structure. Here's how this is done.

First we add to our logical language **individual constants**. These are all the lower-case letters between a and u. These stand, in our logical language, for particular things (or people).

So we might want to define:

f: Fred
b: the book on my table
c: Cleveland, Ohio
r: my right shoe
g: George Bush

and so on. (In case we need more individual constants, we can also put subscripts on them: g_3, h_{95}, etc.)

Now we need a way of saying something about these individuals. So we add **predicates** to our language. These are all the capital letters, except for V (because V would confuse things, since it looks like the wedge). Consider these predicates:

Bx: x is blue
Px: x is a pig
Rx   x is a reptile
Sx: x went to the store
Lx: I love x

In all of these formulas the x marks a place into which we can stick an individual constant, and get a sentence. (x is not an individual constant; remember that individual constants are the lower-case letters between, and including, a and u. More about w, x, y, and z shortly.) Substituting names of things in the general formulas Sx gets you sentences.

Sg means *George Bush went to the store*;
Sf means *Fred went to the store*
Sc means *Cleveland, Ohio went to the store* (which is clearly false).

As always, if we need more predicate letters than the alphabet supplies, we can use numerical subscripts, for example, A_1b , $G_{48}m_{63}$.

If you're familiar with the notion of a predicate from studying grammar, don't get confused. The notion of a predicate in logic is related to this, but not exactly the same. Predicates in logic can be thought of as incomplete sentences—sentences with holes in them; when the holes get filled with individual constants, complete sentences results. So you can think of the predicate Sx as the incomplete sentence

___ *went to the store.*

When you fill that blank with the name of something, you get a sentence—either true or false.

Went to the store is what's called in grammar the predicate of the sentence *George went to the store*. But other logic predicates do not correspond to grammatical predicates. Consider Lx: I love x. *I love* is not the grammatical predicate in the sentence *I love beer.*

The predicates we've looked at so far are **one place predicates**. This means that they each are sentences with one hole in them; supplying one individual constant makes them into sentences.

But we can also have **two place predicates**. These have two holes in them. Examples might be :

Sxy: x is smarter than y
Mxy: Millicent prefers x to y
Kxy: x kicked y

Putting constants in here gives sentences:

Kmr means *Marvin kicked my right shoe.*
Mbr means *Millicent prefers the book on the table to Cleveland, Ohio.*

And so on. Notice that the order that we insert these constants makes a difference.

Lrg means *My right shoe is smarter than George Bush*
Lgr means *George Bush is smarter than my right shoe.*

I'll leave it to you to decide which of these is true.

We can also have three-place predicates, for example,

Bxyz: x *is between* y *and* z
Pxyz: x *prefers* y *to* z

So, for example, Pgrc means *George Bush prefers my right shoe to Cleveland, Ohio.* We can have predicates with as many places as you need.

In the definition of a predicate (for example, Lxy: x *is larger than* y) we use **individual variables**, the letters w, x, y, and z (plus subscripts if necessary). Individual constants stand for particular individuals, but variables can stand for any individuals. (We'll see the much more important use for variables shortly.) The definitions of predicates tell you how many places each predicate has. You can unambiguously use the same capital letter for two different predicates if they have a different number of places. For example, in the same translation scheme, you can have Bx mean x *is blue*, and Bxy mean x *is bigger than* y. If both of these predicates have been introduced, you can tell which one is meant by seeing how many places it has. So Bab must mean a *is bigger than* b.

Notice that we have the possibility of translating the same sentence in a variety of ways. Suppose I wanted to translate *Fred prefers Cleveland, Ohio to San Francisco*. I might do this with a one-place predicate:

Px: x *prefers Cleveland, Ohio to San Francisco*

Insert the individual constant f in the hole in this and you get Pf, meaning *Fred prefers Cleveland, Ohio to San Francisco*. Or else, I might create a different predicate

Fx: *Fred prefers* x *to San Francisco*

Now, assigning the individual constant c to Cleveland, Ohio, I can write Fc, meaning *Fred prefers Cleveland, Ohio to San Francisco*.

Another possibility is to use the two place predicate

Fxy: *Fred prefers* x *to* y

Now the sentence can be symbolized Fcs (with the constant s for San Francisco.)

Or we might create a three-place predicate,

Pxyz: x *prefers* y *to* z

and translate the sentence Pfcs.

For that matter, you might remember that we already have a way left over from sentential logic for translating sentences, merely by assigning them a sentence-letter. So we might translate that sentence as merely A.

All of these are okay as translations, but only the one using a three-place predicate reveals all the logical structure of the sentence. There are (as we'll see later) logical matters that can't be dealt with if we fail to reveal all the logical structure of sentences. The best translation reveals all the logical structure of the sentence.

Exercise 3.1.

Using the following symbolization key:

Sx: x is a student
Lxy: x lives in y
Pxyz: x prefers y to z
Hxy   x hates y
a: Arnold
n: Nancy
d: Darlene
s: San Francisco
c: Cleveland, Ohio

Translate the following sentences:

3.1.1. Arnold and Darlene live in Cleveland, Ohio.

3.1.2. Nancy prefers San Francisco to Cleveland, Ohio, but Darlene doesn't.

3.1.3. If Nancy is a student who lives in Cleveland, Ohio, then Darlene is too.

3.1.4. Arnold hates himself.

3.1.5. Nancy and Darlene hate San Francisco and Cleveland, Ohio.

3.1.6. None of the three hates Darlene.

3.1.7. Nancy hates Cleveland, Ohio if she hates San Francisco too.

3.1.8. Nancy hates Arnold or Darlene.

So far, the only way we've seen to create sentences using predicates is to fill all places with individual constants. A predicate with unfilled places, or with variables in its places, or with too many constants, is not well-formed.

So if we define Lxy (thus establishing it as a two-place predicate), and the constants a, b, and c, then these are well-formed sentences:

Lab
Lac
Laa

but these are not well-formed sentences:

La ☜☜☜
Ly ☜☜☜
Lxy ☜☜☜
Lax ☜☜☜
Lww ☜☜☜
Labc ☜☜☜

Well-formed sentences created out of predicates and constants can be used in exactly the same ways as the atomic sentences we have used earlier. Thus these are well-formed sentences:

~Lab ⊃ Laa
~[M v (Laa & Lbb)]

You can do truth tables for these compound sentences, and use them in derivations, and so on.

The Universal Quantifier

But we still are not able to handle sentences or arguments involving the logical words *some*, *all*, *none*, etc. These sorts of things are exactly what the logic we are now presenting was designed for. Here's how that works.

Given this definition:

Px: x is a pig

we symbolize the (false!) sentence

Everything is a pig

as this:

(∀x)Px

That upside-down A is called the **universal quantifier**. It means, roughly speaking, *all*. In this sentence, it is said to **bind** the variable x. (We'll see the significance of the notion of a bound / unbound variable later.) You can understand this sentence as saying:

For all (or each) x, Px

thus

Everything is a pig.

Think of the universal quantifier as giving you instructions how to understand the formula that follows. It says, remove the quantifier part of the sentence, (∀x), and replace the variable x in what's left of that sentence with constants naming (in turn) each thing in the universe: Pa, Pb, Pc, and so on. These resulting sentences are called **substitution instances** of the quantified sentence. In Pa, the constant a is the **instantiating constant**. In Pb, the instantiating constant is b. The universally quantified sentence (∀x)Px is true if and only if every one of these resulting substitution instances is true—if and only if (Pa & Pb) & Pc .... In other words, that quantified sentence is true if and only if everything is a pig. You only need one false substitution instance to make the universally quantified statement false. Because Goofy (who is a dog) is not a pig, Pg is false, so (∀x)Px is false.

How can we make a quantified sentence that is true? Well, consider one built out of these predicates:

Px: x is a pig
Mx: x is a mammal

The sentence is

(∀x)(Px ⊃ Mx).

Consider what that sentence says: remove the quantifier part (∀x) and replace the x in turn with constants naming each thing in the universe. Let's consider some of these.

- Pp ⊃ Mp The instantiating constant p here, let's suppose, stands for Porky, who is a pig (and also, of course, a mammal). Thus this substitution instance says:

  If Porky is a pig, then Porky is a mammal.

  In this case the antecedent and the consequent are both true, so this substitution instance is true.

- Ps ⊃ Ms The instantiating constant s here, let's suppose, stands for Sammy, who is a snake and not a mammal. So this means:

  If Sammy is a pig, then Sammy is a mammal.

  The antecedent and the consequent are both false, so this substitution instance is true. (Please try to remember how the horseshoe works, even though we learned it so long ago: whenever the antecedent is false, the whole conditional is true.)

- **Pg ⊃ Mg** The instantiating constant **g** here, let's suppose, stands for Goofy, who is a dog, not a pig, and is a mammal. So this means

  If Goofy is a pig, then Goofy is a mammal.

  The antecedent is false and the consequent true, so this substitution instance is true.

All those three substitution instances are true. What would it take for there to be a substitution instance which is false? There would have to be an instantiating constant which would make the antecedent true and the consequent false. (Remember this about the conditional?) Thus, this individual would have to be a pig but not a mammal. As a matter of fact, there aren't any such things; so there is no substitution instance that is in fact false. Every one of them is in fact true, so the quantified sentence is in fact true. The quantified sentence says, in effect, all pigs are mammals. This is true because each thing is either not a pig (like Goofy) or else, if a pig, then also a mammal (like Porky). In other words, no matter what real substitution instance we consider, either the antecedent is false (that is, the thing isn't a pig) or else the consequent is true (that is, the thing is a mammal) or both. You can't find a real substitution instance in which the antecedent is true (it's a pig) but the consequent is false (it's not a mammal). That's because all pigs are mammals! The universally quantified horseshoe sentence is the way of translating *all Ps are Qs* for any predicates *P* and *Q*.

Exercise 3.2.

Consider these sentences:

3.2.1. (∀x)(Ax v Bx)

3.2.2. (∀x)(Ax ≡ Bx)

3.2.3. (∀x)[Ax ⊃ (Bx v Cx)]

In each case, make up a set of definitions for the predicates that makes the sentence true; then make up another set of definitions that makes the sentence false. Given this second set of definitions, produce a definition for a constant that gives a false substitution instance.

The Existential Quantifier

There are two quantifiers. The other one is ∃, the **existential quantifier**. (The word *existential* is just a fancy adjective derived from the noun *existence*. As used in logic, it has nothing to do with existentialism.) The existential quantifier is read, roughly, as *some* x or *there exists an* x or *there is at least one* x. (∃x)Px means that there exists at least one pig, a clearly true sentence. It tells us, as before, to consider substitution instances Pa, Pb, Pc, and so on; but the existentially quantified sentence is true just in case one or more of these substitution instances are true— that is, if and only if (Pa v Pb) v Pc... . So if Px means x *is a pig*, then it's obvious that (∃x)Px is true, because it's easy to find a true substitution instance: Porky. Pp is true, so (∃x)Px is true.

The translation of all of these:

> *Some pig is a mammal*
> *At least one pig is a mammal*
> *There exists a pig which is a mammal*

is (∃x)(Px & Mx). This is of course true also. What it takes for any existentially quantified sentence to be true is at least one true substitution instance. For this sentence, (∃x)(Px & Mx), Porky provides a true substitution instance, because he's a pig and a mammal. So we have an example of a true substitution instance: Pp & Mp, and that's all that's needed to show that the existentially quantified sentence (∃x)(Px & Mx) is true.

How would you say *No pig is a reptile*? There are several ways, but for the moment let's just consider one: ~(∃x)(Px & Rx). This says, reading it very literally, *it's false that there exists something that is both a pig and a reptile*.

Exercise 3.3.

Consider these sentences:

3.3.1. (∃x)(Ax v Bx)

3.3.2. (∃x)(Ax ≡ Bx)

3.3.3. (∃x)[Ax & (Bx v Cx)]

In each case, make up definitions for the predicates which makes the sentence true; then make up another set of definitions which makes the sentence false. Given the first set of definitions, produce a definition for a constant that gives a true substitution instance.

Exercise 3.4

Using the following translation key:

Tx: x is a turtle
Fx: x is funny
Sx: x is sad

translate these sentences into logic:

3.4.1. All turtles are funny.

3.4.2. Some turtles are funny.

3.4.3. No turtles are funny.

3.4.4. Some turtles are funny or sad.

3.4.5. Some funny things are sad.

3.4.6. Nothing is both funny and sad.

3.4.7. Everything is either funny or sad.

3.4.8. Things are funny if and only if they're not sad.

Well-Formed Quantified Sentences

Adding quantifiers, variables, and constants to Sentential Logic creates a larger, more powerful system called Quantifier Logic. Before we go any further, we should consider formation rules—the rules that define what counts as a well-formed sentence and what doesn't—in Quantifier Logic.

First, we need to understand the notion of the **scope of a quantifier**. (Don't get confused: this not related to scope lines in derivations.) In a sentence with a quantifier in it, the scope of that quantifier (loosely speaking) extends across the expression immediately to its right. So in the sentence (∃x)Bxa, the scope of the existential quantifier extends over the expression Bxa. In the sentence (∃x)Bxa ∨ Gb, the scope of the existential quantifier similarly extends over the expression Bxa. But in the sentence (∃x)(Bxa ∨ Gb), the "expression immediately to the right" of the existential quantifier is determined by those parentheses, so its scope is Bxa ∨ Gb.

Every variable needs to be **bound** by a quantifier. The expression Ax means nothing at all—it is not well formed, and is not a legitimate sentence; in this expression, the variable x is **unbound**. (The only place an unbound variable shows up legitimately is in a definition.) To bind this variable, it has to be inside the scope of a quantifier—modified by a quantifier, so to speak.

These sentences:

$(\forall x)(Ax)$
$(\exists x)(Ax)$

are well-formed sentences: in both cases, the variable is bound by a quantifier.

The second set of parentheses in these sentences is unnecessary. The scope of the quantifier is (informally speaking) what's to the right of it. So we can also correctly write

$(\forall x)Ax$
$(\exists x)Ax$

When we have two instances of the same variable in the scope of the same quantifier, parentheses are necessary. Thus we have to write, for instance,

$(\forall x)(Ax \supset Bx)$
$(\exists x)(Ax \ \& \ Bx)$

In both these sentences, the two instances of the variable x are inside the scope of the sentence's quantifier. But in

$(\forall x)Ax \supset Bx$ ✨✨✨

the scope of the quantifier just extends over the Ax. The variable in Bx is unbound, and this makes the whole sentence not well-formed, a piece of nonsense. Note however that

$(\forall x)Ax \supset Ba$

is a well-formed sentence. It's a conditional: the horseshoe connects two legitimate sentences,

$(\forall x)Ax$
Ba

This is also a well-formed sentence:

$(\forall x)(Ax \supset Ba)$

(All of this holds for the existential quantifier also.)

Which variable you use doesn't have any significance.

$(\forall x)(Ax)$

means exactly the same thing as

$(\forall w)Aw$
$(\forall y)(Ay)$
$(\forall z)Az$
$(\forall x_3)(Ax_3)$

and so on.

This is not a well-formed sentence:

$(\forall x)Ay$ ❦❦❦

The quantifier would bind xs inside its scope (that's the significance of the x next to the ∀), but the y is unbound.

Similarly,

$(\forall y)(Ax)$ ❦❦❦

is not well-formed.

This is not a well-formed sentence:

$(\forall x)(Ax \supset By)$ ❦❦❦

The quantifier has as its scope the whole expression in parentheses that follows it; but it binds only the xs. (That's the significance of the x next to the ∀.) So the y is unbound.

In

$(\forall y)(Ax \supset By)$ ❦❦❦

the x is unbound, so this is another expression that's not well-formed.

This is not a well-formed sentence:

$(\exists g)(Lg)$ ❦❦❦

Only variables can be quantified, and g is not a variable. (Did you remember that a − u are constants, and w − z are variables?)

Lg

all by itself is a well-formed sentence, and so is

$(\forall z)(Hz \equiv Lg)$.

Look through the following lists of sentences, and make sure you understand why...

- These are well-formed sentences:

  (∃z)(Az ⊃ Bz)
  (∃x)Ax
  (∃x)[Ax v (Ba ≡ Cbdx)]
  (∃z)Az v (∃x)Bx
  (∃z)Az v (∃z)Bz
  (∃x)Ax & [(∀x)Bx v (∀x)Cx]
  (∃x)(G & Baxad)
  (∃x)Ax & Bg
  (∃x)(Ag & Bx)

- But these expressions are not well-formed:

  (∃x)Ax ⊃ Bx   ☹☹☹
  (∃y)[Ay v (Bz & Cy)]   ☹☹☹
  (∃x)Ax ⊃ (∀y)(Ax v By)   ☹☹☹
  (∃x)(Ax ≡ [Bx v Cx]   ☹☹☹
  ((∀y)(Ay v By)) ⊃ Cy)   ☹☹☹

Because Quantifier Logic accepts everything we had in Sentential Logic, those atomic sentences, and compound sentences using them, are still acceptable. So these are well-formed sentences in Quantifier Logic:

A & (B ≡ C)
(∃x)(Ax) ⊃ B
(∃x)(Ax ⊃ B)

Exercise 3.5 *For each numbered formula, say whether it's well-formed or not; if not, explain why.*

3.5.1.   (∃z)(Gz ⊃ Haz)

3.5 2.   (∃x)Jx v G

3.5 3.   (∃x)[Mx ≡ (Ba v N) & Cbdx]

3.5.4.   (∀z)Lz ⊃ (∃x)Pxz

3.5.5.   (∃x)Rx & Sx

3.5.6.   (∀y)[May v (Taz & Uby)]

3.5.7.   (∃x)Ax ⊃ (∀y)(Rx ≡ By)

3.5.8.   (∀a)Ja ⊃ La

3.5.9.   (∃z)Wz v (∃z)Wz

3.5.10. (∀x)Ax & [(∀x)Bx & (∃x)Cx]

3.5.11. (∃xy)(G & Baxy)

3.5.12. (∀z)Az & Bx

3.5.13. (∃x)(Ag & Bx)

3.5.14. (∃x)(Ag & K ⊃ Bx)

3.5.15. (∃x)(Ax & [L ≡ M])

3.5.16. (∃x)Ax & [L ≡ M]

3.5.17. (∃x)(Ax & [L ≡ M]

Understanding Quantified Sentences

Suppose that

Gx: x is green.

Now what's the difference between these two sentences:

~(∀z)Gz   and   (∀z)~Gz   ?

Think about this until you think you have the answer.

The answer is that the first one is the negation of (∀z)Gz; it says that it's false that everything is green. This is not the same as saying that *nothing* is green. This is the same as saying there is at least one thing that isn't green. This sentence is true.

The second one, on the other hand, is not a negation. It says that everything is not-green. This *is* the same as saying that nothing is green. I happen to know that this sentence is false. I saw something green just yesterday.

Now consider this. We've already seen that

~(∃x)(Px & Rx)

means *No pig is a reptile.*

It's the negation of

(∃x)(Px & Rx)

so it says: *It's false that (there exists at least one thing which is both a pig and a reptile).* Think about this until you see that this means *no pig is a reptile.*

Now think about

$(\forall x)(Px \supset {\sim}Rx)$

This says, reading it very literally, *For each thing: if it's a pig then it's not a reptile.* Think about this until you understand that this also means *No pig is a reptile.*

These two are both correct translations of the sentence *No pig is a reptile;* so of course they are logically equivalent, and we'll be able to prove their logical equivalence later.

How would you say, *Not all pigs are reptiles*? Before we consider translations, think about this sentence in English. It doesn't say *No pigs are reptiles.* Neither does it say *All pigs are non-reptiles.* It allows the possibility that there are a few reptile pigs. What is says is merely that they're not *all* reptiles; that is, that it's false that they're all reptiles; in other words, that at least one of them is not a reptile.

Here, then, are two translations of that sentence:

${\sim}(\forall x)(Px \supset Rx)$

This says *it's false that all pigs are reptiles.* And

$(\exists x)(Px \mathbin{\&} {\sim}Rx)$

says that *at least one thing is a pig and a non-reptile.*

Think about these two until you can see that both of them translate *Not all pigs are reptiles.* These two, both correct translations, are logically equivalent.

This is a confusing matter because sometimes English doesn't make a clear distinction between two different things that might be said. Consider this sentence: *All tests in logic are not easy.* What exactly is that supposed to mean? Does it mean that all of the logic tests are non-easy—that is, that they're all hard? Or does it mean that they're not *all* easy—that is, that at least some of them are hard? The first interpretation of that English sentence is unambiguously expressed in logic (given the obvious translation of the predicates) by

$(\forall x)(Tx \supset {\sim}Ex)$

This means they're all non-easy—they're all hard—none of them are easy. The second interpretation of the English is unambiguously represented in logic by

$\sim(\forall x)(Tx \supset Ex)$

This means that it's false that they're all easy—that at least some of them are hard.

You can see that it makes a difference where you put the tilde. Consider, for example, the difference in meaning between these two sentences:

$\sim(\forall x)(Px \supset Rx)$

As we've seen, this says that it's false that all pigs are reptiles, that is, that at least one pig isn't a reptile. This is clearly true. It understates things (because they're all non-reptiles—not just at least one of them) but it's true.

But:

$(\forall x)\sim(Px \supset Rx)$

says something quite different. It says that everything has this characteristic: that it's false that (if it's a pig then it's a reptile). What in the world does this mean? It's easier to see the meaning of this when we realise that

$\sim(A \supset B)$

is equivalent to

$(A \And \sim B)$

So this quantified sentence is equivalent to:

$(\forall x)(Px \And \sim Rx)$

Thus it says: each thing in the universe is a pig, and it's also a non-reptile. It's surely false. All that's needed to show that it's false is one thing that's not a pig, or else one thing that's a reptile.

Now consider that sort of sentence in general. Could you ever have two predicates Ax and Bx which would make the sentence

$(\forall x)\sim(Ax \supset Bx)$

true? What you'd need was a meaning for Ax such that that predicate would be true of *everything* in the universe; and a meaning for Bx such that that predicate would be true of *nothing* in the universe. Predicates of either sort are very hard to find. Just try. Ordinary predicates are true of some things and false of others. That means that any universal statement of this form with almost any translation would be false.

For the same sort of reason, ordinary English sentences are almost never correctly translated into sentences of the form

$$(\forall x)(Px \,\&\, Qx)$$

It would take two very extraordinary predicates—both true of *everything*—to make this sentence true; so every sentence of this form using ordinary predicates (true of some things and false of others) would be false. And similarly, ordinary English sentences would almost never be correctly translated into sentences of the form

$$(\exists x)(Px \supset Qx)$$

That's because it would take two very extraordinary predicates to make this false: the first (Px) true of everything, and the second (Qx) true of nothing. You should consider various meanings for the predicates Px and Qx, and see why this sentence is automatically true with any of them. For example, consider Px meaning x *is a pig*; and Qx meaning x *is a reptile*. Or consider Px meaning x *is a pig*, and Qx meaning x *is a mammal*. Stop now and make sure you understand why both of these meanings make that sentence true.

Consider now the ordinary way we translate English sentences of the form *All Fs are Rs*:

$$(\forall x)(Fx \supset Rx)$$

What this means, as we have seen, is that every substitution instance of this

Fa ⊃ Ra
Fb ⊃ Rb
and so on

is true.

In other words,

$$(\forall x)(Fx \supset Rx)$$

will be true just in case there is no substitution instance of it that makes it false. But what if *nothing* has predicate F? For example, suppose that Fx means x *is a flying pig*. Because there aren't any of these, whatever individual constant you substitute in that expression will make the antecedent false; so the conditional will always be true. In other words, *If x is a flying pig, then x is (whatever)*, is true for all existing things. That means, when nothing has the predicate in the antecedent, the universal statement is true. Work your way carefully through this paragraph again to convince yourself that this is true. The upshot of this is the following: We translate *All unicorns are happy* as

$(\forall x)(Ux \supset Hx)$

But because there are no unicorns, this is *true*. But how about *All unicorns are sad*:

$(\forall x)(Ux \supset Sx)$

That's true too. So is *No unicorns are sad*, interpreted as

$(\forall x)(Ux \supset {\sim}Sx)$

In fact, everything you say about unicorns as a whole is true—because there aren't any! (Well, just about everything. *Unicorns exist*—$(\exists x)Ux$— is false.) This peculiar consequence of our logical model is called **vacuous truth**. (If you don't like it, try to think of a way around it.)

Some translations from English into Logic involve subtleties and complications. The best way for you to find out how to do them is to attempt the next set of exercises, and to check carefully with the answers afterwards.

Exercise 3.6

Assuming this translation key:

Px:	x is a pig
Lxy:	x lives in y
Hx:	x is happy
s:	Sally
a:	Arnold
c:	Cleveland, Ohio

Translate the following sentences:

3.6.1.   Every pig is happy.

3.6.2.   No pig is unhappy.

3.6.3.   Arnold, Sally, and some pigs are happy.

3.6.4.   Either each pig is happy or none is.

3.6.5.   Either each pig is happy or at least one isn't.

3.6.6.   If Sally is happy, every pig is.

3.6.7.   Sally is happy only if all pigs are.

3.6.8.   If any pig is happy, Sally is.

3.6.9.   Sally lives in Cleveland, Ohio, but no pigs do.

3.6.10.   Every pig who lives in Cleveland, Ohio is happy.

3.6.11.   Some pigs are not happy.

3.6.12.   If a pig isn't happy, then it doesn't live in Cleveland, Ohio.

3.6.13.   If a pig lives in Cleveland, Ohio, it's happy.

3.6.14.   If some pigs live in Cleveland, Ohio, Sally is happy.

3.6.15.   Arnold doesn't live anywhere.

3.6.16.   Pigs are happy.

Multiple Quantification

How would you translate *Some pigs are happy and some live in Cleveland, Ohio*? How about this:

$(\exists x)[Px \,\&\, (Hx \,\&\, Lxc)]$?

Before you read on, see if you can understand why this is not the correct translation.

I hope you figured out that this is not correct because it says that there exists at least one thing which is a happy pig living in Cleveland, Ohio. That's not exactly what the sentence said. It said that there exists at least one happy pig, and that there exists at least one pig that lives in Cleveland, Ohio, though not necessarily the same pig. That sentence would be true even if all the Cleveland, Ohio pigs were sad, and all the happy pigs lived in San Francisco.

Here's a correct translation of that sentence:

$(\exists x)(Px \,\&\, Hx) \,\&\, (\exists x)(Px \,\&\, Lxc)$

This is just a conjunction of two quantified statements. The first quantifier binds the first two xs in this sentence—they're inside its scope. The second quantifier binds the third and fourth xs, those inside its scope. Notice that the use of the same variable in both conjuncts doesn't indicate that we're talking about the same individual thing. Thus we're not saying that any pig both is happy and lives in Cleveland, Ohio. We're saying that some pig (one or more) is happy, and some pig (one or more, possibly different ones) lives in Cleveland, Ohio. We could as well have used a different variable in the second conjunct:

$(\exists x)(Px \mathbin{\&} Hx) \mathbin{\&} (\exists y)(Py \mathbin{\&} Lyc)$

But notice carefully that, just as using the same variable in both conjuncts doesn't mean it's the same thing we're talking about, using a different one doesn't mean it's a different thing. The two versions of this sentence are logically equivalent. Both would be made true if there's one happy pig who lives in Cleveland, Ohio. Both would be made true if there's no happy pig living in Cleveland, Ohio, but if there's an unhappy pig living in Cleveland, Ohio, and one (or more) happy pig living in San Francisco.

When two or more of the same variable are bound by one quantifier, then they do refer to the same thing.

Thus in

$(\exists x)(Px \mathbin{\&} Hx)$

both xs are bound by the same quantifier, so this says that there exists at least one thing such that *that thing* is both a pig and happy.

In

$(\forall x)(Px \supset Hx)$

we're saying of each thing that if it is a pig, then it (the same thing) is happy. If we want to say *There's at least one thing such that that thing is a happy pig living in Cleveland, Ohio*, we have to put the same variable three times inside the scope of one existential quantifier:

$(\exists x)[(Px \mathbin{\&} Hx) \mathbin{\&} Lxc]$

The translation of *Every pig knows Arnold* is

$(\forall x)(Px \supset Kxa)$

(Obviously, Kxy means x *knows* y.) Now how do we say *Every pig knows every dog*? We need the additional predicate Dx: x is a dog.

Here's how it's translated:

$(\forall x)[Px \supset (\forall y)(Dy \supset Kxy)]$

Here for the first time we have **multiple quantification**—that is, a sentence with one quantifier inside the scope of another. Notice that the scope of the $(\forall x)$ extends over the area in square brackets—right to the end, including the scope of the second quantifier $(\forall y)$, which is what is inside the round parentheses only: $(Dy \supset Kxy)$.

Let's look at several common sorts of examples of multiple quantification.

$$(\forall x)[Px \supset (\exists y)(Dy \ \& \ Kxy)]$$

means:

Every pig knows at least one dog

alternatively:

Each pig knows a dog

Be careful here. These sentences do not say that there is a particular dog that is known by every pig, though that would make them true. What would also make these sentences true is if there is no single dog that every pig knows, but each pig knows some dog (or other). (For example: Porky Pig knows Fido; Petunia Pig doesn't know Fido, but she knows Rover; etc.) A translation of that logical statement into stilted English close to its logical structure is: For each x, if x is a pig, then there is a dog which x knows.

If we want to say, by contrast that there's a particular (very popular) dog who is known by all pigs, then we have to do things in different order:

$$(\exists x)[Dx \ \& \ (\forall y)(Py \supset Kyx)]$$

This sentence:

$$(\exists x)[Px \ \& \ (\exists y)(Dy \ \& \ Kxy)]$$

means: *At least one pig knows at least one dog.*

Now look at some multiple quantification sentences involving negations:

$$\sim(\forall x)[Px \supset (\forall y)(Dy \supset Kxy)].$$

This is the negation of the first multiple quantification sentence we looked at; so it means: It's false that each pig knows each dog. In other words, it says that there's a pig who doesn't know each dog.

So you can see that this sentence is logically equivalent to it:

$$(\exists x)[Px \ \& \ \sim(\forall y)(Dy \supset Kxy)]$$

which says that there's at least one pig who doesn't know every dog. And this one is logically equivalent to those two:

$$(\exists x)[Px \ \& \ (\exists y)(Dy \ \& \ \sim Kxy)]$$

This says that there exists at least one pig such that there exists at least one dog whom that pig doesn't know;

And here's another equivalent one:

(∃x)[Dx & (∃y)(Py & ~Kyx)]

This says that there exists at least one dog such that there exists at least one pig who doesn't know that dog.

You should go over all four of the sentences just presented very carefully, thinking about what each one means, until you are satisfied that they all mean the same thing. Yes, I know, it's hard to keep all this straight. Go away and do something else for a while, then come back and read this last bit over again.

Now consider various translations of: *No pig knows any dog*:

~(∃x)[Px & (∃y)(Dy & Kxy)]
(∀x)[Px ⊃ (∀y)(Dy ⊃ ~Kxy)]
(∀x)[Dx ⊃ ~(∃y)(Py & Kyx)]

Again, think about all these until you can see that they all mean the same as that English sentence.

Now consider various translations of: *There's a particular dog whom no pig knows*.

(∃x)[Dx & (∀y)(Py ⊃ ~Kyx)]
(∃x)[Dx & ~(∃y)(Py & Kyx)]

We've been considering alternative logical expressions that have the same meaning. These will, of course be logically equivalent. We don't have ways of proving logical equivalence in Quantifier Logic yet, but it may help you at this point to have a list of the forms of logical equivalence that are often involved here:

~(∀x)$P$$x$ is equivalent to (∃x)~$P$$x$

~(∃x)$P$$x$ is equivalent to (∀x)~$P$$x$

and you'll remember this equivalence from Sentence Logic:

~(P ⊃ Q) is equivalent to (P & ~Q)

Exercise 3.7.

Assuming this translation key:

Px: x is a pig
Mx: x is a mammal
Ixy: x is in y
c: Canada

consider the meaning of all these sentences; say whether each is (in reality, actually, just plain) true or false, and explain.

3.7.1. (∀x)(Px ⊃ Ixc)

3.7.2. (∀x)[Px ⊃ (Ixc v ~Ixc)]

3.7.3. (∀x)[Ixc ⊃ (Mx v ~Mx)]

3.7.4. (∃x)[Px & (Ixc & ~Ixc)]

3.7.5. (∃x)(Px ⊃ ~Mx)

3.7.6. (∀x)[Px ⊃ (Mx ≡ Ixc)]

A reminder that the particular variables used don't make any difference. The following two sentences are logically equivalent:

(∃x)[Dx & ~(∃y)(Py & Kyx)]
(∃w)[Dw & ~(∃x)(Px & Kxw)]

If one quantifier is inside the scope of another, you must use different variables. The following is not well formed:

(∃x)[Dx & ~(∃x)(Px & Kxx)]   ❧❧❧

Note that the following has an unbound variable (so it is not well formed):

(∃x)(Dx) & ~(∃y)(Py & Kyx)   ❧❧❧

Exercise 3.8.

Using this translation key:

     Cx: x is a cat
     Mx: x is a mouse
     Lxy: x likes y

Translate the following:

3.8.1. Every cat likes some mouse or other.

3.8.2. There's a mouse that's liked by all cats.

3.8.3. No mouse likes any cat.

3.8.4. No mouse likes every cat.

3.8.5. Some cats like some mice.

3.8.6. Each cat doesn't like some mice.

3.8.7. Mice don't like cats.

3.8.8. Some cats don't like any mice.

You've noticed that each English sentence has a variety of equivalent translations into logic. There are all sorts of equivalent variations of sorts we haven't looked at yet.

For example, one might translate

Some cat likes some mouse

as

     (∃x)[Cx & (∃y)(My & Lxy)]

or by this equivalent sentence:

     (∃x)(∃y)[(Cx & My) & Lxy]

You are not advised to try to symbolize things this way, by piling the quantifiers up in front. Sometimes it's extremely confusing this way: moving embedded quantifiers out front like this does not always produce an equivalent sentence, and most people find sentences with quantifiers stacked out front very difficult to understand. The way we have been doing things is confusing enough: don't give yourself more trouble than you need to.

But you will, no doubt, be delighted to hear that we do have to complicate things just a little more. Take a look at these translations (using the obvious symbol meanings):

1. *No dog likes any cat or mouse.*

   ~(∃x)[Dx & (∃y)[(Cy v My) & Lxy]]

2. *Any dog that Arnold likes, likes some cat.*

   (∀x)[(Dx & Lax) ⊃ (∃y)(Cy & Lxy)]

3. *Mice don't like cats and dogs.*

   (∀x)[Mx ⊃ (∀y)[(Cy v Dy) ⊃ ~ Lxy]]

Note on this one that despite the fact that the English says "*cats and dogs*" the logic uses a v between Cy and My. To see why, consider what this means, with an ampersand there instead:

   (∀x)[Mx ⊃ (∀y)[(Cy & Dy) ⊃ ~ Lxy]]

This one says that if x is a mouse, then if y is *both a cat and a dog*, x doesn't like y. That's not what's meant by 3, right? The one with the v in it says that if x is a mouse, then if y is *a cat or a dog*, then x doesn't like y. That's more like it.

4. *Mice like dogs.*

   (∀x)[Mx ⊃ (∀y)(Dy ⊃ Lxy)]

The English here is slightly ambiguous. Does the speaker mean *all* mice? Or only *some*? I think that it's more likely that what's meant is *all* mice. Similarly, I think this is saying, about each mouse, that it likes *all* dogs (not just *some*).

5. *Mice like dogs and only dogs.*

Here are three equivalent ways to translate this:

   (∀x)[Mx ⊃ (∀y)(Dy ≡ Lxy)]
   (∀x)(Mx ⊃ (∀y)[(Dy ⊃ Lxy) & (Lxy ⊃ Dy)])
   (∀x)[Mx ⊃ (∀y)(Dy ⊃ Lxy)] & (∀x)[Mx ⊃ (∀y)(Lxy ⊃ Dy)]

6. *If a mouse doesn't like any dogs, it doesn't like any cats.*

   (∀x)(Mx ⊃ [~(∃y)(Dy & Lxy) ⊃ ~(∃y)(Cy & Lxy)])

The odd thing here is that we translate *a mouse* here with the ∀, not the ∃. Think about the English: it's not talking about a particular mouse—it's talking about any mice—all mice.

7. *If a mouse doesn't like any dogs, it doesn't like a cat.*

$(\forall x)(Mx \supset [(\exists y)(Dy \ \& \sim\! Lxy) \supset (\exists y)(Cy \ \& \sim\! Lxy)]$

Think carefully about the two English sentences, to see why their logic is different, and make sure you see why this explains the difference in the two quantified sentences. (English expresses logical relations in very complicated ways!)

8. *Sally likes dogs, cats, and mice.*

$(\forall x)([(Dx \ v \ Cx) \ v \ Mx] \supset Lsx)$

Again, I interpret this to be to mean that Sally likes all dogs, all cats, and all mice, not that there are some particular ones she likes. That's why the $\forall$ is in here, rather than the $\exists$. Again, what she likes is anything that's a cat, dog, *or* mouse; not anything that's all three at once; so there are vs in here, not &s.

But let's add the predicate Oxy, meaning x *owns* y; and consider the translation of:

9. *Sally owns dogs, cats, and mice.*

In this case I thinks it's clear that it wouldn't reasonably be said that Sally owns all the dogs, cats, and mice in the world. It no doubt means she owns at least one of each. So it's not translated:

$(\forall x)([(Dx \ v \ Cx) \ v \ Mx] \supset Osx)$

Instead, it should be translated:

$[(\exists x)(Dx \ \& \ Osx) \ \& \ (\exists x)(Cx \ \& \ Osx)] \ \& \ (\exists x)(Mx \ \& \ Osx)$

See if you can see why both of these are incorrect:

$(\exists x)([(Dx \ \& \ Cx) \ \& \ Mx] \ \& \ Osx)$ ๑๑๑
$(\exists x)([(Dx \ v \ Cx) \ v \ Mx] \ \& \ Osx)$ ๑๑๑

Exercise 3.9 *Using the following translation key:*

Cx: x is a cat
Dx: x is a dog
Mx: x is a mammal
Lxy: x likes y
Oxy: x owns y
Sxy: x is the sister of y
a: Arthur
b: Beth

translate each of the following:

3.9.1.   Arthur likes cats and dogs.

3.9.2.   Beth owns cats and dogs.

3.9.3.   Cats and dogs like Beth.

3.9.4.   Not all mammals are cats or dogs.

3.9.5.   Not all mammals owned by Beth are cats or dogs.

3.9.6.   If it's a dog, then Beth likes it.

3.9.7.   If Arthur owns a dog, he doesn't own any cats.

3.9.8.   If Arthur owns a dog, he likes it.

3.9.9.   No cats or dogs like Arthur.

3.9.10.   Arthur doesn't like anything he owns.

3.9.11.   Any cat owned by Beth doesn't like Arthur.

3.9.12.   Beth likes her sister.

3.9.13.   Beth and her sister like each other.

3.9.14.   Beth likes her sister's dog.

3.9.15.   Beth likes whatever Arthur owns.

3.9.16.   Beth and Arthur are co-owners of a dog.

Now, using the following translation key:

Lxyz: x likes y at z
Tx: x is a time
Px: x is a person
a: Arthur
b: Beth

translate each of the following:

3.9.17. Arthur likes Beth sometimes.

3.9.18. Nobody likes Arthur ever.

3.9.19. Beth never likes anyone.

3.9.20. Everybody likes somebody sometime.

Quantificational Logical Properties

We have been talking throughout this book about a variety of logical properties:

- Validity and invalidity

- Consistency and inconsistency

- Logical truth, falsity, and indeterminacy

- Equivalence and non-equivalence

In Chapter One, we saw how these sometimes resulted from the truth-functional connectives in sentences. When they did, we called them *truth-functional validity*, *truth-functional invalidity*, *truth-functional consistency*, and so on.

In this chapter, we've been looking at the quantificational structure of sentences. Logical properties are sometimes the result of the quantificational structure of sentences, not their truth-functional structure.

For example, the argument

All pigs can fly
Porky is a pig
Porky can't fly

is valid, but not because of its truth-functional structure. We should say that this argument is truth-functionally invalid, but **quantificationally valid**. All those other logical properties can also be the result of the quantificational structure of sentences, so we can have **quantificational invalidity**, **quantificational consistency**, and so on.

Proving Quantificational Logical Properties

Way back when we were doing Sentential Logic, we studied the truth table method for proving truth-functional logical properties (truth-functional validity/invalidity, truth-functional truth, etc.). Remember? The truth-table method gave us a way of proving all these things because it permitted examination of all possible worlds. But we don't have a truth-table method for proving quantificational logical properties. But we do have a somewhat analogous, somewhat weaker method that will be introduced shortly. First, a few words about why the truth table method is unavailable here.

Consider the simple invalid argument

(A ∨ B) therefore A

Here's its truth table:

A	B	A ∨ B ↓	A ↓
T	T	T	T
T	F	T	T
F	T	T	F
F	F	F	F

Consider why this truth table, in particular row 3 of the table, proves the argument invalid. Its four rows show what things are like in every possible world—what things are like, that is, with regard to the atomic and compound sentences we're interested in. And it turns out that in one variety of possible world—where A is false and B is true, the premise of that argument is true, and its conclusion is false; so the argument is invalid.

But we can't do this for Quantifier Logic. The reason is that there are too many relevant possible worlds to list.

Consider this clearly invalid argument:

$(\forall x)(Mx \supset Nx)$
$(\exists x)Mx$
$\sim(\exists x)Nx$

What would we have to do to make a list of every possible world? Consider some individual a: in some possible worlds **Ma** is true, and in some false. In some possible worlds **Na** is true, and in some false. Okay, so that's four possible worlds to consider:

Ma	Na	$(\forall x)(Mx \supset Nx)$	$(\exists x)Nx$	$\sim(\exists x)Nx$
T	T			
T	F			
F	T			
F	F			

But we can't fill in the values to the right, because we haven't considered the other individuals. We don't know, for example, whether to write T or F under $(\forall x)(Mx \supset Nx)$ in the first row. All we're given there is that **Ma** and **Na** are both true, but we aren't told about other individuals, so we don't know if it's true or false that all Ms are Ns. To construct a truth table for these two predicates and two individuals (**a** and **b**) would need sixteen rows. Here are the first few of them:

Ma	Na	Mb	Nb	$(\forall x)(Mx \supset Nx)$	$(\exists x)Nx$	$(\exists x)Nx$
T	T	T	T			
T	T	T	F			
T	T	F	T			

and so on. There's no point in filling the rest of these in, because it's clear that to include every individual, we'd need an impossibly long truth table. (How long? If there were an infinite number of individuals, the truth table would have to be infinitely long.)

Exercise 3.10

Are there in fact an infinite number of individuals?

In any case, it's clear that a large or infinite number of individuals makes even a partial truth table out of the question here. But there is another approach we can take.

Consider this sentential truth table again:

A	B	A v B	A
		↓	↓
T	T	T	T
T	F	T	T
F	T	T	F
F	F	F	F

For the argument to be valid, it can't be the case that the premise A v B is true and the conclusion A is false, no matter what the truth value of the atomic sentences A and B happen to be. Those atomic sentences will each have a particular truth value, depending on what sentences it translates. Given this translation:

A: Fish live under water
B: Jupiter is bigger than the Earth

then A is true and B is true, and the real world is represented by row 1. But when we're considering the validity or invalidity of that argument, we don't care about what particular meaning those atomic sentence letters have, or what the facts about the world are. The argument is valid if there is no possibility of a true premise and a false conclusion no matter what those sentences mean. So we can show that the argument is invalid by showing that, were those sentences given meanings that made A false and B true, as shown in row 3, then the premise would be true and the conclusion false. So an alternative way of proving invalidity would be to invent a translation into English for A and B which (given the facts) would make A false and B true. It's easy to come up with one:

A: The moon is made of cheese
B: Fish live under water

Given this translation, the premise of the argument:

The moon is made of cheese or fish live under water

is true, and the conclusion

The moon is made of cheese

is false. (This, in effect, produces row 3 of the truth table.) That shows that the argument is invalid. Okay, we've just discovered a new way of proving invalidity, which we can call **Finding an Interpretation**. An interpretation is a translation-scheme for a set of sentences in logic. If you can find an interpretation under which (given the facts of the real world) the premise(s) of the argument is (are) true, and the conclusion is false, then that shows the argument is invalid. This will work for Quantifier Logic as well. We'll try this out in a moment.

But first, consider why we didn't use the method of Finding an Interpretation to prove logical characteristics in Sentential Logic. The reason is that we had a perfectly good method to do this already: truth tables. And the Truth Table Method was better than Finding an Interpretation because it was able to prove all of those logical properties, but Finding an Interpretation is able to prove only some. Here's why. We can prove that an argument is invalid by finding an interpretation that gives true premise(s) and a false conclusion. If the argument is valid, however, there will be no such interpretation. But how can you prove that? You can try to find an interpretation like that for a while, but failing to find one doesn't prove there isn't any. Similarly for other logical properties. Test yourself on your grasp of things by doing the following exercise:

Exercise 3.11.

For each of the following logical matters, say whether or not Finding an Interpretation can prove it.When it can, say how. (Examples: This method can prove invalidity by finding an interpretation which gives true premises and a false conclusion. Validity means that there is no such interpretation, so this method can't prove that.)

3.11.1. Logical truth/falsity/indeterminacy

3.11.2. Consistency/inconsistency

3.11.3. Equivalence/non-equivalence

Try to recall now what the Derivation Method can and can't prove. If you can, you might notice that the Derivation Method and the Method of Finding an Interpretation complement each other: each can prove exactly what the other can't. In Chapter 2, I said that you'd find out later why derivations were necessary despite the fact that truth-tables told you all the logical facts you needed to know about. Now you know. Truth tables don't work for Quantifier Logic; Finding an Interpretation works for some logical matters only; derivations are necessary for proving the rest.

Okay, let's try the Method of Finding an Interpretation on Quantifier Logic Sentences.

Here's the clearly invalid argument we considered above:

$(\forall x)(Mx \supset Nx)$
$(\exists x)Mx$
$\overline{\sim(\exists x)Nx}$

To prove this invalid, we need an interpretation which would make the premises true and the conclusion false. An interpretation in this case gives a translation for the predicates Mx and Nx. The first premise means that all Ms are Ns, so to make that true, let's try

Mx: x is a pig
Nx: x is a mammal

Under that interpretation,

$(\forall x)(Mx \supset Nx)$

means *All pigs are mammals*, which is true. Under this interpretation the second premise

$(\exists x)Mx$

means *There exists at least one pig*, which is also true. And the conclusion

$\sim(\exists x)Nx$

means *No mammals exist* which is false. There, we've done it!

Doing this example was easy. There was no problem finding an interpretation to make the first premise true, and we were lucky that this interpretation made the second premise true, and the conclusion false.

Other cases will not be so easy. Let's try this invalid argument:

$(\forall x)(Ax \supset Bx)$
$(\forall x)(Ax \supset Cx)$
$\overline{(\forall x)(Bx \supset Cx)}$

Okay, suppose we try this translation scheme:

Ax: x is a pig
Bx: x is a mammal

Right, that makes the first premise true.

Now to make the second premise true, let's try

Cx: x is an animal

So the first premise says *all pigs are mammals*, and the second one says *all pigs are animals*, so they're both true; so far so good. But this interpretation makes the conclusion mean *all mammals are animals*, which is also true. No good! We needed an interpretation on which the conclusion was false.

Consider this one instead:

Ax: x is a pig
Bx: x is an animal
Cx: x is a mammal

This interpretation makes the argument mean this:

All pigs are animals (true)
All pigs are mammals (true)
All animals are mammals (false)

That does it. You can see that it's sometimes going to take some ingenuity, or trial-and-error, to use this method.

As we've seen, an interpretation gives a translation for each predicate letter; but when sentences also contain individual constants, the interpretation needs to define these, by identifying the individual to which each constant refers.

So for instance, to show this argument invalid:

$(\forall x)(Ax \supset Bx)$
Ag
~Bg

This interpretation will do:

Ax: x is a city in the USA
Bx: x is located north of Brazil
g: Chicago

Now look at this invalid argument:

$(\forall x)(Ax \supset Bx)$
$\sim(\exists x)Ax$
$\sim(\exists x)Bx$

To prove this invalid, we'll need a translation for Ax that will make

$\sim(\exists x)Ax$

true. So the predicate Ax will have to apply, in fact, to nothing. What predicate is true of nothing? Here's one:

Ax: x is a unicorn

Good, now let's continue trying to do this one. The first premise also needs to be true. Please remember—or review, if you can't remember (pp. 166-7)—what was said earlier in this chapter about vacuous truth. That makes it easy: given that no unicorns exist, any old translation for Bx would make the first premise true. But remember that we need to make the conclusion false, so we need a translation such that there are some Bs. So

Bx: x is blue

will do the trick. Now the first premise says

All unicorns are blue (true—vacuously)

the second one says

No unicorns exist (true)

and the conclusion says

Nothing blue exists (false).

Okay, now let's prove the invalidity of this argument:

$(\exists x)(Ax \mathbin{\&} Bx)$
$(\forall x)Ax$
$\overline{(\forall x)Bx}$

To do this you'll need a translation for Ax that makes the second premise true. This will have to be a predicate that's true of everything. This is not easy to come by! Here's one:

Ax: x is something

$(\forall x)Ax$ is true—everything is something!

Exercise 3.12   *Prove the following arguments are invalid by Finding an Interpretation*

3.12.1. $(\forall x)(Ax \supset Bx)$
             $(\forall x)(\sim Ax)$
             $\overline{(\forall x)(\sim Bx)}$

3.12.2. $(\forall x)[Ax \supset (Bx \lor Cx)]$
             $Ag \mathbin{\&} \sim Bg$
             $\overline{\sim Cg}$

3.12.3. $(\forall x)[Ax \supset (Bx \lor Cx)]$
             $Ag \mathbin{\&} Bg$
             $\overline{Cg}$

3.12.4. $(\forall x)[(Ax \lor Bx) \supset Cx]$
            $\underline{(\exists x)Ax}$
            $(\exists x)Bx$

3.12.5. $(\exists x)(Ax \lor Bx)$
            $\overline{(\exists x)(Ax \ \& \ Bx)}$

3.12.6. $\underline{(\forall x)(Ax \supset Bgx)}$
            $Ag \ \& \ {\sim}Bgg$

3.12.7. Ag
            $\underline{(\forall x)[Ax \supset (\exists y)(Ay \ \& Bxy)]}$
            $(\exists x)(Ax \ \& \ Bgx)$

3.12.8. $\underline{(\forall x)(Ax \supset Bx)}$
            $(\exists x)(Ax \ \& \ Bx)$

3.12.9. $(\forall x)(Ax \supset Bx)$
            $\underline{(\forall x)(Cx \supset Bx)}$
            $(\exists x)(Bx \ \& \ Cx)$

3.12.10. $(\exists x)(Ax \ \& \ Bx)$
            $\underline{(\exists x)(Ax \ \& \ Cx)}$
            $(\exists x)(Bx \ \& \ Cx)$

3.12.11. $(\forall x)(Axa \supset Axb)$
            $\underline{(\forall x)(Axc \supset Axb)}$
            $(\forall x)(Axa \supset Axc)$

3.12.12. $(\exists x)(Ax \ \& \ Bx)$
            $(\forall x)(Ax \supset Cx)$
            $\overline{{\sim}(\exists x)(Bx \ \& \ {\sim}Cx)}$

Here is a summary of what Finding an Interpretation can and cannot do; and how it does what it can.

- It can prove arguments quantificationally invalid, by producing an interpretation which makes the premises true and the conclusion false. It cannot prove quantificational validity.

- It can prove a set of sentences is quantificationally consistent, by producing an interpretation which makes all the sentences in the set true. It cannot prove a set is quantificationally inconsistent.

- It can prove that a sentence is quantificationally indeterminate by producing an interpretation which makes the sentence true, and another interpretation which makes the sentence false. It cannot prove either that a sentence is quantificationally true or quantificationally false.

- It can prove that a pair of sentences are not quantificationally equivalent by producing an interpretation which makes one sentence true and the other false. It cannot prove that a pair of sentences are quantificationally equivalent.

Exercise 3.13   *Prove the following sets of sentences are consistent by Finding an Interpretation.*

3.13.1. { (∀x)(Ax ⊃ Bx) , (∃x)Ax , (∃x)~Bx }

3.13.2. { (∃x)(Ax & Bxg) , ~(∃x)(Ax & Bgx) }

3.13.3. { (∀x)[Ax ⊃ (∃y)(Ay & Bxy)] , Ag & Bgg }

3.13.4. { (∀x)(Ax ⊃ Bx) , (∀x)(Ax ⊃ ~Bx) }

Exercise 3.14   *Prove the following sentences are logically indeterminate by Finding Interpretations:*

3.14.1. (∃x)(Ax & Bx)

3.14.2. (∀x)[Ax ⊃ (Bx v Cx)]

3.14.3. (∀x)[Ax ⊃ (∃y)(By & Cxy)]

3.14.4. (∃x)[Ax & Bxg]

Exercise 3.15   *Prove the following pairs of sentences are not logically equivalent by Finding an Interpretation:*

3.15.1. (∃x)Axb , (∃x)Abx

3.15.2. ~(∃x)Ax , (∃x)~Ax

3.15.3. (∃x)(∀y)Axy , (∀y)(∃x)Axy

3.15.4. (∃x)(Ax ⊃ Bx) , (∃x)(Ax & Bx)

Answers to Exercises in Chapter Three

EXERCISE 3.1

3.1.1. Arnold and Darlene live in Cleveland, Ohio.
Lac & Ldc

3.1.2. Nancy prefers San Francisco to Cleveland, Ohio, but Darlene doesn't.   Pnsc & ~Pdsc

3.1.3. If Nancy is a student who lives in Cleveland, Ohio, then Darlene is too.   (Sn & Lnc) ⊃ (Sd & Ldc)

3.1.4. Arnold hates himself.   Haa

3.1.5. Nancy and Darlene hate San Francisco and Cleveland, Ohio.
(Hnc & Hns) & (Hdc & Hds)

3.1.6. None of the three hates Darlene.   (~Had & ~Hnd) & ~Hdd

3.1.7. Nancy hates Cleveland, Ohio if she hates San Francisco too.
Hns ⊃ Hnc

3.1.8. Nancy hates Arnold or Darlene. Hna v Hnd.

EXERCISE 3.2.

3.2.1. (∀x)(Ax v Bx)

TRUE: Ax: x is an apple
         Bx: x isn't an apple

FALSE: Ax: x is a pig
       Bx: x is a goat

For individual s: Sammy the snake,
The substitution instance (As v Bs) is FALSE.

3.2.2. $(\forall x)(Ax \equiv Bx)$

TRUE: Ax: x is an even number
          Bx: x is evenly divisible by 2

FALSE: Ax: x is an even number
          Bx: x is larger than 10

For individual e: 8
The substitution instance $(Ae \equiv Be)$ is false.

3.2.3. $(\forall x)[Ax \supset (Bx \lor Cx)]$

TRUE: Ax: x is an even number
          Bx: x is evenly divisible by 2
          Cx: x is bigger than 8.

FALSE: Ax: x is an even number
          Bx: x is larger than 10
          Cx: x is smaller than 4

For individual s: 6
The substitution instance $[As \supset (Bs \lor Cs)]$ is false.

EXERCISE 3.3.

3.3.1. $(\exists x)(Ax \lor Bx)$

TRUE: Ax: x is an even number
          Bx: x is bigger than 5

For individual s: 11
The substitution instance $(As \lor Bs)$ is true.

FALSE: Ax: x is a unicorn
          Bx: x is a flying pig

3.3.2. $(\exists x)(Ax \equiv Bx)$

TRUE: Ax: x is an even number
        Bx: x is bigger than 5

For individual **s**: 3
The substitution instance $(As \equiv Bs)$ is true.

FALSE: Ax: x is red
        Bx: x isn't red
(No matter what thing x you pick, it would give Ax and Bx different truth values. So there isn't anything that satisfies this interpretation, and it's false.

3.3.3. $(\exists x)[Ax \& (Bx \lor Cx)]$

TRUE: Ax: x is an even number
        Bx: x is bigger than 5
        Cx: x is smaller than 3

For individual t: 2
The substitution instance At & (Bt v Ct) is true.

FALSE: Ax: x is a unicorn
        Bx: x flies
        Cx: x lives in Brazil

EXERCISE 3.4

3.4.1. All turtles are funny.
    $(\forall x)(Tx \supset Fx)$

3.4.2. Some turtles are funny.
    $(\exists x)(Tx \& Fx)$

3.4.3. No turtles are funny.
    $\sim(\exists x)(Tx \& Fx)$

3.4.4. Some turtles are funny or sad.
    $(\exists x)[Tx \& (Fx \lor Sx)]$

3.4.5.Some funny things are sad.
    $(\exists x)(Fx \& Sx)$

3.4.6. Nothing is both funny and sad.
    $\sim(\exists x)(Fx \& Sx)$

3.4.7. Everything is either funny or sad.
    $(\forall x)(Fx \lor Sx)$

3.4.8. Things are funny if and only if they're not sad.
   $(\forall x)(Fx \equiv \sim Sx)$

EXERCISE 3.5

3.5.1. $(\exists z)(Gz \supset Haz)$ Well-formed

3.5.2. $(\exists x)Jx \lor G$ Well-formed

3.5.3. $(\exists x)[Mx \equiv (Ba \lor N) \& Cbdx]$ ☜☜☜ Not well-formed. The variables are all bound, but inside the square brackets the expression needs another pair of parentheses.

3.5.4. $(\forall z)Lz \supset (\exists x)Pxz$ ☜☜☜ Not well-formed. The z at the end is unbound.

3.5.5. $(\exists x)Rx \& Sx$ ☜☜☜ Not well-formed. The x in Sx is unbound.

3.5.6. $(\forall y)[May \lor (Taz \& Uby)]$ ☜☜☜ Not well-formed. The z is unbound.

3.5.7. $(\exists x)Ax \supset (\forall y)(Rx \equiv By)$ ☜☜☜ Not well-formed. The second x is unbound.

3.5.8. $(\forall a)Ja \supset La$ ☜☜☜ Not well-formed. $(\forall a)$ doesn't make sense— you can't quantify a constant.

3.5.9. $(\exists z)Wz \lor (\exists z)Wz$ Well-formed

3.5.10. $(\forall x)Ax \& [(\forall x)Bx \& (\exists x)Cx]$ Well-formed.

3.5.11. $(\exists xy)(G \& Baxy)$ ☜☜☜ Not well-formed. $(\exists xy)$ doesn't make sense: one variable only per quantifier.

3.5.12. $(\forall z)Az \& Bx$ ☜☜☜ Not well-formed. The x is unbound.

3.5.13. $(\exists x)(Ag \& Bx)$ Well-formed.

3.5.14. $(\exists x)(Ag \& K \supset Bx)$ ☜☜☜ Not well-formed. Needs an extra pair of parentheses, as for example: $(\exists x)(Ag \& [K \supset Bx])$.

3.5.15. $(\exists x)(Ax \& [L \equiv M])$ Well-formed.

3.5.16. $(\exists x)Ax \& [L \equiv M]$ Well-formed.

3.5.17. $(\exists x)(Ax \& [L \equiv M]$ ☜☜☜ Not well-formed. Needs) at the end.

EXERCISE 3.6

3.6.1. Every pig is happy.
   $(\forall x)(Px \supset Hx)$

3.6.2. No pig is unhappy. This can by symbolized the same way as 1:
$(\forall x)(Px \supset Hx)$.
Alternatively, what is equivalent:
$\sim(\exists x)(Px \;\&\; \sim Hx)$.

3.6.3. Arnold, Sally, and some pigs are happy.
$(Ha \;\&\; Hs) \;\&\; (\exists x)(Px \;\&\; Hx)$

3.6.4. Either each pig is happy or none is.
$(\forall x)(Px \supset Hx) \lor \sim(\exists x)(Px \;\&\; Hx)$

3.6.5. Either each pig is happy or at least one isn't.
$(\forall x)(Px \supset Hx) \lor (\exists x)(Px \;\&\; \sim Hx)$.
This is a logical truth; we'll prove it later. In the meantime, it will look more like a logical truth if it is symbolized in this way, equivalent to the first:
$(\forall x)(Px \supset Hx) \lor \sim(\forall x)(Px \supset Hx)$

3.6.6. If Sally is happy, every pig is.
$Hs \supset (\forall x)(Px \supset Hx)$

3.6.7. Sally is happy only if all pigs are.
$Hs \supset (\forall x)(Px \supset Hx)$ (I hope you haven't forgotten about how to understand "only if" already.)

3.6.8 If any pig is happy, Sally is.
$(\exists x)(Px \;\&\; Hx) \supset Hs$

3.6.9. Sally lives in Cleveland, Ohio, but no pigs do.
$Lsc \;\&\; \sim(\exists x)(Px \;\&\; Lxc)$

3.6.10 Every pig who lives in Cleveland, Ohio, is happy.
$(\forall x)[(Px \;\&\; Lxc) \supset Hx]$ or else
$(\forall x)[Px \supset (Lxc \supset Hx)]$

3.6.11 Some pigs are not happy.
$(\exists x)(Px \;\&\; \sim Hx)$
or else this equivalent version:
$\sim(\forall x)(Px \supset Hx)$

3.6.12. If a pig isn't happy, then it doesn't live in Cleveland, Ohio.
$(\forall x)[(Px \;\&\; \sim Hx) \supset \sim Lxc]$

3.6.13. If a pig lives in Cleveland, Ohio, it's happy.
$(\forall x)[(Px \;\&\; Lxc) \supset Hx]$

3.6.14. If some pigs live in Cleveland, Ohio, Sally is happy.
$(\exists x)(Px \;\&\; Lxc) \supset Hs$

3.6.15. Arnold doesn't live anywhere.
~(∃x)Lax or (∀x)~Lax

3.6.16. Pigs are happy.
(∀x)(Px ⊃ Hx).
This interprets the English statement as saying that *all* pigs are happy. But that statement is ambiguous. It might just mean that some pigs are happy, in which case it would be translated (∃x)(Px & Hx)

EXERCISE 3.7

3.7.1. (∀x)(Px ⊃ Ixc)
False. It says that all pigs are in Canada. Clearly there are some pigs somewhere else.

3.7.2. (∀x)[Px ⊃ (Ixc v ~Ixc)]
True. This says that each pig is either in Canada or not. (It's even logically true.)

3.7.3. (∀x)[Ixc ⊃ (Mx v ~Mx)]
True. This says that everything in Canada is either a mammal or not a mammal.

3.7.4. (∃x)[Px & (Ixc & ~Ixc)]
False. This says that at least one pig is both in and not in Canada. (It's even logically false.)

3.7.5. (∃x)(Px ⊃ ~Mx)
True. This says that there's something such that if it's a pig, then it's not a mammal. This is true of lots of things: everything that's not a mammal, for example. Consider the substitution instance Pd ⊃ ~Md, where d stands for Denmark. The antecedent is false, so this conditional statement is true.

3.7.6. (∀x)[Px ⊃ (Mx ≡ Ixc)]
False. This says, each pig is a mammal if and only if it's in Canada. All that's needed is one false substitution instance to make it false. Consider the individual p, namely Porcino the Italian pig. Porcino is a mammal, but not in Canada. So Pp ⊃ (Mp ≡ Ipc) is false. (Make sure you see why.)

EXERCISE 3.8.

As you've noticed, several equivalent translations are possible for each English sentence. I can't give all of them here; I'll just give one correct one for each. Check with your instructor if you want to know if your different translation is correct.

Translate the following:

3.8.1. Every cat likes some mouse or other.
   $(\forall x)[Cx \supset (\exists y)(My \ \& \ Lxy)]$

3.8.2. There's a mouse that's liked by all cats.
   $(\exists x)[Mx \ \& \ (\forall y)(Cy \supset Lyx)]$

3.8.3. No mouse likes any cat.
   $\sim(\exists x)[Mx \ \& \ (\exists y)(Cy \ \& \ Lxy)]$

3.8.4. No mouse likes every cat.
   $\sim(\exists x)[Mx \ \& \ (\forall y)(Cy \supset Lxy)]$

3.8.5. Some cats like some mice.
   $(\exists x)[Cx \ \& \ (\exists y)(My \ \& \ Lxy)]$

3.8.6. Each cat doesn't like some mice.
   $(\forall x)[Cx \supset (\exists y)(My \ \& \sim Lxy)]$

3.8.7. Mice don't like cats.
   $(\forall x)(Mx \supset (\forall y)(Cy \supset \sim Lxy))$

3.8.8. Some cats don't like any mice.
   $(\exists x)(Cx \ \& \sim(\exists y)(My \ \& \ Lxy))$

EXERCISE 3.9

3.9.1. Arthur likes cats and dogs.
   $(\forall x)[(Cx \lor Dx) \supset Lax]$

3.9.2. Beth owns cats and dogs.
   $(\exists x)(Cx \ \& \ Obx) \ \& \ (\exists x)(Dx \ \& \ Obx)$
   Note that 1 is taken to mean that Arthur likes all cats and all dogs; but that 2 is taken to mean that Beth owns some cats and some dogs. This is probably what the English sentences mean, but the logic of English sentences is sometimes quite ambiguous. 3.9.1., for example, might be taken to mean that Arthur likes some cats and dogs. In several of the sentences considered below, I've given what I take to be the most plausible logical interpretation of the English sentence; but there are several somewhat ambiguous cases.

3.9.3. Cats and dogs like Beth
$(\forall x)[(Cx \lor Dx) \supset Lxb]$

3.9.4. Not all mammals are cats or dogs.
$\sim(\forall x)[Mx \supset (Cx \lor Dx)]$
Note that this English sentence doesn't mean that every mammal is neither a cat nor a dog. It means merely that not all of them are: at least some of them aren't.

3.9.5. Not all mammals owned by Beth are cats or dogs.
$\sim(\forall x)[(Mx \& Obx) \supset (Cx \lor Dx)]$

3.9.6. If it's a dog, then Beth likes it.
$(\forall x)(Dx \supset Lbx)$
I take this sentence to be a way of expressing the thought that Beth likes every dog. But it's possible that it mean something else. Imagine, for example, that Fred is looking at a very strange sort of dog-like animal, and says this to Arnold. Then the best way of translating this sentence would be to assign that odd animal an individual constant, say g, and to translate Arnold's sentence as
$Dg \supset Lbg$

3.9.7. If Arthur owns a dog, he doesn't own any cats.
$(\exists x)(Dx \& Oax) \supset \sim(\exists x)(Cx \& Oax)$
Again, there's a chance for ambiguity. Is the speaker referring to a particular dog—one, for example, who's so anti-cat that Arthur couldn't own any cats if he owns that dog? But it seems that a more ordinary use of that sentence would mean: *If Arthur owns any dogs, then he doesn't own any cats* That's the way it's translated here.

3.9.8. If Arthur owns a dog, he likes it.
$(\forall x)[(Dx \& Oax) \supset Lax]$
The best interpretation here is again to take this to mean *If Arthur owns any dogs....*

Notice in this case that you can't translate this sentence by beginning it in what might seem to be the obvious way, the way 3.9.7 began, with $(\exists x)(Dx \& Oax) \supset$ ...If you do, then the dog referred to in the consequent of this conditional won't necessarily be the same one as the one mentioned in the antecedent, because it's not in the scope of that initial existential quantifier.

3.9.9. No cats or dogs like Arthur.
$\sim(\exists x)[(Cx \lor Dx) \& Lxa]$

3.9.10. Arthur doesn't like anything he owns.
$(\forall x)(Oax \supset \sim Lax)$

3.9.11. Any cat owned by Beth doesn't like Arthur.
($\forall$x)[(Cx & Obx) $\supset$ ~Lxa]

3.9.12. Beth likes her sister.
($\exists$x)(Sxb & Lbx)

3.19.13. Beth and her sister like each other.
($\exists$x)[Sxb & (Lxb & Lbx)]

3.19.14. Beth likes her sister's dog.
($\exists$x)(Sxb & ($\exists$y)[(Dy & Oxy) & Lby])

3.19.15 Beth likes whatever Arthur owns.
($\forall$x)(Oax $\supset$ Lbx)

3.19.16. Beth and Arthur are co-owners of a dog.
($\exists$x)[Dx & (Oax & Obx)]

3.9.17. Arthur likes Beth sometimes.
($\exists$x)(Tx & Labx)

3.9.18. Nobody likes Arthur ever.
~($\exists$x)[Tx & ($\exists$y)(Py & Lyax)]

3.9.19. Beth never likes anyone.
~($\exists$x)[Tx & ($\exists$y)(Py & Lbyx)]

3.9.20. Everybody likes somebody sometime.
($\forall$x)(Px $\supset$ ($\exists$y)[Py & ($\exists$z)(Tz & Lxyz)])

EXERCISE 3.10

Hmm, well. I guess that points in space are existing things—individuals—so if the universe is infinite, then the answer is yes. If instants of time are individuals, and if time continues forever (even after everything in the physical universe is destroyed) then the answer is yes. If the positive integers 1, 2, 3, etc. are individuals, then the answer is yes. (But are they existing things? A deep question.)

EXERCISE 3.11

3.11.1. Logical truth/falsity/indeterminacy. You can prove indeterminacy by finding two interpretations: one on which the sentence is true, and one on which the sentence is false. A logically true sentence will have no interpretations on which the sentence is false; you can't prove that by this method. A logically false sentence will have no interpretations on which the sentence is true; you can't prove that by this method.

3.11.2. Consistency/inconsistency. You can prove consistency by finding an interpretation on which all the sentences in the set are true. An inconsistent set is one which has no such interpretation; you can't prove that by this method.

3.11.3. Equivalence/non-equivalence. You can prove non-equivalence of a pair of sentences by finding an interpretation on which one of them is true, and the other is false. Equivalency means there is no such interpretation, so you can't prove that by this method.

EXERCISE 3.12 (There are of course any number of different interpretations that will do, so yours might be right too. But here are some answers to look at if you're stumped.)

3.12.1. $(\forall x)(Ax \supset Bx)$
          $(\forall x)(\sim Ax)$
          ―――――――――
          $(\forall x)(\sim Bx)$

   Ax: x is a unicorn
   Bx: x is blue

3.12.2. $(\forall x)[Ax \supset (Bx \lor Cx)]$
          $Ag \& \sim Bg$
          ―――――――
          $\sim Cg$

   Ax: x is a dog
   Bx: x is blue
   Cx: x is a mammal
   g: Lassie

3.12.3. $(\forall x)[Ax \supset (Bx \lor Cx)]$
          $Ag \& Bg$
          ―――――――
          Cg

   Ax: x is a city
   Bx: x is smaller than Europe
   Cx: x is bigger than Brazil
   g: Cleveland, Ohio

3.12.4. $(\forall x)[(Ax \lor Bx) \supset Cx]$
$\dfrac{(\exists x)Ax}{(\exists x)Bx}$

  Ax: x is a city in Canada
  Bx: x is a unicorn
  Cx: x is north of Brazil

(Note that this makes the first premise true: if anything is a city in Canada or a unicorn, it's north of Brazil. Every city in Canada is north of Brazil; and so is every unicorn (vacuously)).

3.12.5. $\dfrac{(\exists x)(Ax \lor Bx)}{(\exists x)(Ax \,\&\, Bx)}$

  Ax: x is a dog
  Bx: x is a cat

3.12.6. $\dfrac{(\forall x)(Ax \supset Bgx)}{Ag \,\&\, \sim Bgg}$

  Ax: x is a city
  Bxy: x is bigger than y
  g: Brazil

Under this interpretation, the premise is true (Brazil is bigger than every city). And the conclusion is false: $\sim Bgg$ is true because Brazil is not bigger than itself; but Ag is false.

3.12.7.   Ag
$\dfrac{(\forall x)[Ax \supset (\exists y)(Ay \,\&\, Byx)]}{(\exists x)(Ax \,\&\, Bgx)}$

  Ax: x is a positive integer
  Bxy: x is a bigger number than y
  g: 1

The relevant fact of arithmetic here is that 1 is the smallest positive integer (0 is not a positive integer). If you're familiar with the elementary facts of arithmetic, you might find that interpretations involving numbers (including predicates such as x is a positive integer, x is an odd number, x is a prime, and so on) are handy for this method.

3.12.8. $\dfrac{(\forall x)(Ax \supset Bx)}{(\exists x)(Ax \,\&\, Bx)}$

  Ax: x is a unicorn
  Bx: x is blue

3.12.9. $(\forall x)(Ax \supset Bx)$
$(\forall x)(Cx \supset Bx)$
$\overline{(\exists x)(Ax \, \& \, Cx)}$

Ax: x is a pig
Bx: x is a mammal
Cx: x is a dog

3.12.10. $(\exists x)(Ax \, \& \, Bx)$
$(\exists x)(Ax \, \& \, Cx)$
$\overline{(\exists x)(Bx \, \& \, Cx)}$

Ax: x is an integer
Bx: x is bigger than 12
Cx: x is smaller than 12

3.12.11. $(\forall x)(Axa \supset Axb)$
$(\forall x)(Axc \supset Axb)$
$\overline{(\forall x)(Axa \supset Axc)}$

Axy: x is a number bigger than y
a: 2
b: 1
c: 3

3.12.12. $(\exists x)(Ax \, \& \, Bx)$
$(\forall x)(Ax \supset Cx)$
$\overline{\sim(\exists x)(Bx \, \& \, \sim Cx)}$

Ax: x is a university
Bx: x is located in Canada
Cx: x has students

EXERCISE 3.13

3.13.1. $\{ (\forall x)(Ax \supset Bx) , (\exists x)Ax , (\exists x)\sim Bx \}$
Ax: x is a pig
Bx: x is a mammal

3.13.2. $\{ (\exists x)(Ax \, \& \, Bxg) , \sim(\exists x)(Ax \, \& \, Bgx) \}$
Ax: x is a positive integer
Bxy: x is bigger than y
g: 0

3.13.3.   { (∀x)[Ax ⊃ (∃y)(Ay & Bxy)] , Ag & Bgg }
Ax: x is a number
Bxy: x is equal to y
g: 17

3.13.4.   { (∀x)(Ax ⊃ Bx) , (∀x)(Ax ⊃ ~Bx) }

Ax: x is a unicorn
Bx: x is blue

EXERCISE 3.14   NOTE: Did you remember that you have to find *two* interpretations to show a sentence logically indeterminate? (One on which it's true, another on which it's false.)

3.14.1. (∃x)(Ax & Bx)

TRUE:
Ax: x is a dog
Bx: x is brown
FALSE:
Ax: x is a dog
Bx: x can fly

3.14.2. (∀x)[Ax ⊃ (Bx v Cx)]

TRUE:
Ax: x is a positive integer
Bx: x is odd
Cx: x is even
FALSE:
Ax: x is a pig
Bx: x is a reptile
Cx: x is an insect

3.14.3. (∀x)[Ax ⊃ (∃y)(By & Cxy)]

TRUE:
Ax: x is an elephant
Bx: x is an earthworm
Cxy: x is bigger than y
FALSE:
Ax: x is a student
Bx: x is a dog
Cxy: x owns y

3.14.4. (∃x)[Ax & Bxg]

   TRUE:
      Ax: x is a politician
      Bxy: x is President of y
      g: United States
   FALSE:
      Ax: x is a politician
      Bxy: x is Prime Minister of y
      g: United States

EXERCISE 3.15

3.15.1. (∃x)Axb , (∃x)Abx

   Axy: x is a larger positive integer than y
   b: zero

3.15.2. ~(∃x)Ax , (∃x)~Ax

   Ax: x is a pig

3.15.3. (∃x)(∀y)Axy , (∀y)(∃x)Axy

   Axy: x resembles y

This one is very hard to understand. The first sentence says that there exists something that resembles everything. I take it that that's false: nothing resembles *everything*. The second says that for each thing, there is something that it resembles. I take it that this is true (if only because each thing resembles itself—note that the x and the y things don't have to be different things).

3.15.4. (∃x)(Ax ⊃ Bx) , (∃x)(Ax & Bx)

   Ax: x is a pig
   Bx: x can fly

CHAPTER FOUR

QUANTIFIER DERIVATIONS

About Quantifier Derivations

We have now added quantified sentences to our logical system, turning what we're calling *Sentence Logic* into *Quantifier Logic.*

As we saw in the last chapter, truth tables don't work to show quantifier logical properties, and the method of Finding an Interpretation can prove only some of the properties we're interested in. For example, it can prove quantifier invalidity, but it can't prove quantifier validity. Derivations are available for quantified sentences, and they're extra important here, because they can prove things exactly when Finding an Interpretation can't.

Derivations for our language expanded to include quantifiers have exactly the same sort of structure as the ones for Sentential Logic we've studied already, and include those eleven rules. (If you didn't master derivation technique then, it's time to do so now!) All we need to add to that system now, you'll be happy to hear, is four new rules: an introduction and an elimination rule for each of the two quantifiers.

But before we get to the rules, it's important that you understand three concepts.

Undischarged Assumptions

The first is the notion of a **discharged / undischarged assumption**. An assumption is undischarged in every step following the assumption within the same scope—that is, in every step to the right of the same scope line as the assumption. Here's a derivation left over from Sentential Logic, but it will do to illustrate discharged and undischarged assumptions:

```
1. | A ⊃ B              Ass
2. | ~A ⊃ ~B            Ass
3. |  | A               Ass
4. |  | B               3, 1, ⊃E
5. |  | B               Ass
6. |  |  | ~A           Ass
7. |  |  | ~B           6, 2, ⊃E
8. |  |  | B            5, R
9. |  | A               6-8, ~E
10.| A ≡ B              3-4, 5-9, ≡I
```

The assumption A, on line 3, is undischarged at line 4, but because that scope line ends after line 4, it's discharged at all the rest of the following steps. The assumption B, on line 5, is undischarged at lines 6 through 9, but is discharged at line 10. The assumption ~A, line 6, is undischarged at lines 7 and 8, and discharged at lines 9 and 10. The two primary assumptions for the derivation, on lines 1 and 2, are always undischarged, at every following line. (Primary assumptions are never discharged.)

Exercise 4.1.

Consider each assumption in this derivation; list the lines at which that assumption is undischarged.

```
1. | I v J              Ass
2. | I ≡ (~I v J)       Ass
3. |  | I               Ass
4. |  | ~I v J          3, 2, ≡E
5. |  | ~I              Ass
6. |  |  | ~J           Ass
7. |  |  | I            3, R
8. |  |  | ~I           5, R
9. |  | J               6-8, ~E
10.|  | J               Ass
11.|  | J               10, R
12.|  | J               4, 5-9, 10-11, vE
13.|  | J               Ass
14.|  | J               13, R
15.| J                  1, 3-12, 13-14, vE
```

Main Connective

The second concept extends the notion of the *main connective* to sentences with quantifiers in them.

You'll remember (I hope) that the introduction and elimination rules for each of the sentential connectives apply only to particular sentences: for example, the conjunction elimination rule can be used only on conjunctions—that is, on sentences whose main connective is &. Thus you can use &E on

A & B

or on

[(H v J) & (L v [G ⊃ K])]

But you can't use it on

~(A & B)

which is a negation, not a conjunction.

Nor can you use it on

(A & B) v C

which is a disjunction.

The situation is similar for the quantifier rules. The universal introduction and elimination rules can be used only on universal sentences. A universal sentence is a sentence whose main connective (so to speak) is the universal quantifier. In other words: if a sentence is composed by an initial universal quantifier (with nothing to its left), and the scope of that quantifier is the whole rest of the sentence, then it's a universal sentence. Otherwise it isn't. These are universal sentences:

(∀x)(Ax v Ba)

(∀y)[Ay ⊃ (∃z)(Az)]

Universal Introduction (∀I) can be used to get universal sentences, and Universal Elimination (∀E) can be used if you already have one. But these are not universal sentences:

~(∀x)(Ax v Ba) This is a negation.

(∀x)Ax v Ba This is a disjunction.

(∀y)Ay ⊃ (∃z)(Az) This is a conditional.

(∃y)(∀x)Axy This is an existential sentence.

You can't use Universal Elimination on any of the last four, and you can't use Universal Introduction to get any of them. You can, however, involve the negation in a Negation Elimination; or you can get it through negation introduction. The disjunction can be involved in the usual sorts of ways in vI or vE. You can get the conditional by ⊃I, and use it in ⊃E. Existential sentences can be derived by Existential Introduction (∃I), and can be used for Existential Elimination (∃E).

Exercise 4.2.

Circle the main connective in each sentence. Say what sort of sentence each is (Universal, Existential, Conjunction, Disjunction, Conditional, Biconditional, Negation.)

4.2.1. [Bab ⊃ (∃y)(Cy & Dya)]

4.2.2. (∃x)[Ax ⊃ (∃y)(Cy & Db)]

4.2.3. ~(∃x)[Ax ⊃ (∃y)(Cy & Db)]

4.2.4. (∃x)Ax ⊃ (∃y)(Cy & Db)

4.2.5. ~(∃x)Ax ⊃ (∃y)(Cy & Db)

4.2.6. (∀x)[(∀y)Bxy & C]

4.2.7. (∀x)(∀y)Bxy & C

4.2.8. (∀x)(∀y)[Bxy & C]

Substitution Instance

The third concept is that of a **substitution instance** of a quantified sentence. A substitution instance of a quantified sentence is a sentence in which the quantifier that is the main connective is removed, and in which each variable quantified by that quantifier is replaced by the same constant, called the **instantiating constant**. Consider the existential sentence

(∃z)[Azb & (∀y)(By ⊃ Czyza)]

When we remove the main-connective existential quantifier and replace each z by a, we get this substitution instance:

Aab & (∀y)(By ⊃ Cayaa)

a is the instantiating constant in this substitution instance. When b is the instantiating constant we get:

Abb & (∀y)(By ⊃ Cbyba)

When c is the instantiating constant we get:

Acb & (∀y)(By ⊃ Ccyca)

The following replaces one z by a, and the rest by b; so it is not a substitution instance of the original:

Aab & (∀y)(By ⊃ Cbyba)

The following replaces one z by a, but leaves the rest of the zs as they were, so it's not a substitution instance of the original.

Aab & (∀y)(By ⊃ Czyza)

It's not even a well-formed sentence: all those zs are unbound.

Note that a constant that's already in a quantified sentence may replace the quantified variable to produce a substitution instance. So, for example, we can take this sentence:

(∀z)[Aza ⊃ (∃y)(By & Czyb)]

And produce these correct substitution instances:

Aaa ⊃ (∃y)(By & Cayb)
Aba ⊃ (∃y)(By & Cbyb)

Note that you can't produce a substitution instance of this:

(∀x)Fx ⊃ (∃y)Gya

because it's not a universal (or an existential) sentence: neither quantifier is its main connective. Its main connective is the horseshoe.

Exercise 4.3.

Consider this universal sentence:

(∀x)[Bxab ⊃ (∃y)(Cyxa & Dxxyb)]

Which of the following are substitution instances of it? In each substitution instance, identify the instantiating constant.

4.3.1. [Bbab ⊃ (∃y)(Cyba & Dbbyb)]

4.3.2. [Bxab ⊃ (∃y)(Cyxa & Dxxyb)]

4.3.3. [Baaa ⊃ (Caaa & Daaaa)]

4.3.4. (∀x)[Bxab ⊃ (Ccxa & Dxxcb)]

Now consider the following sentence:

Caabc ⊃ (∃x)Bxabc

Of which of the following is this a substitution instance?
When it is, identify the instantiating constant.

4.3.5. (∀y)[Cxxbc ⊃ (∃x)Bxybc]

4.3.6. (∃w)[Caawc ⊃ (∃x)Bxxbc]

4.3.7. (∃w)[Cwwwc ⊃ (∃x)Bxwwc]

The general way we shall refer, in the derivation rules, to any universally quantified sentence is $(\forall \chi)\mathcal{P}\chi$, and to any existentially quantified sentence is $(\exists \chi)\mathcal{P}\chi$. The χ after the $\mathcal{P}$ in each refers to the quantified variable(s) in each. You should understand that this does not merely mean sentences which quantify over the variable x—any other variable will do; and that $\mathcal{P}$ can stand for any formula in the scope of that quantifier. So all the following are of the general form $(\forall \chi)\mathcal{P}\chi$:

(∀x)(Px)
(∀y)(Hy⊃Gba)
(∀z)[Mza ≡ (∃y)(Nyz ⊃ Ryya)]

but these aren't:

(∃x)(Px)
(∀y)Hy⊃Gba
(∀x)Mza ≡ (∃y)(Nyb ⊃ Ryya)

And the way we refer, in the derivation rules, to any substitution instance of a quantified sentence is $\mathcal{P}a$. What this means is that the quantifier is dropped off, and the quantified variable(s) inside the $\mathcal{P}$, referred to as χ in the general formula $\mathcal{P}\chi$, are replaced by a single constant—the instantiating constant—(referred to as a in the general formula $\mathcal{P}a$). The instantiating constant may be any constant, not just a.

Universal Elimination

Okay, now we're ready to look at a quantifier rule.

Universal Elimination (∀E)

$$(\forall x) Px$$
$$Pa$$

This one is simple. It represents the fact that if something is true of everything, then it's true for each individual. So for example, from the statement *Everything is a pig* you can derive *Arnold is a pig*. If the first is true, the second must be also. In more technical terms, this rule says that when you have any universal statement, you can get any substitution instance of that statement. So, for instance, when you have the statement

(∀x)(Gxxbc)

you can get any of these:

Gaabc
Gbbbc
Gccbc
Gddbc etc.

Here's a derivation using ∀E:

1.	(∀x)Axp	Ass
2.	Agp ⊃ M	Ass
3.	Agp	1, ∀E
4.	M	3, 2, ⊃E

You'll notice that the old rules (for example ⊃E in this derivation) are still in force.

Exercise 4.4 *Prove by derivation:*

4.4.1. { (∀y)(Agy ⊃ M) , Agg } ⊢ M

4.4.2. { (∀w)(Bw ≡ Gw) , (∀z)(Az ⊃ Bz) } ⊢ Ar ⊃ Gr

Existential Introduction

This one is also simple:

Existential Introduction (∃I)

$$\mathcal{P}a$$
$$(\exists x)\mathcal{P}x$$

This rule represents the fact that if something is true of a particular individual, then it's true of something—of at least one thing. So for example, from the statement *Arnold is a pig* you can derive *Something is a pig.* If the first is true, the second must be also. In more technical terms, this rule says that you can get an existential sentence from a substitution instance of it.

So for example if you have

Gaabc

you can get any of the following:

(∃w)Gwwbc
(∃x)Gaaxc
(∃y)Gaaby
(∃z)Gzabc etc.

But make sure you understand that (and why) you cannot get:

(∃x)Gxxc
(∃y)Gyaby
(∃z)Gzxbc

And from (∃y)Gaaby you can get

(∃z)(∃y)Gzzby

Note carefully the scopes of the quantifiers in that last sentence. Putting in (optional) parentheses may make them more obvious:

(∃z)[(∃y)(Gzzby)]

The scope of (∃z) is (∃y)(Gzzby). The scope of (∃y) is (Gzzby). (Do you remember what the scope of a quantifier is? If not review the material on that in Chapter Three.)

Here's a derivation incorporating both of these new rules:

1. $(\forall x)[Gabxx \supset (\exists y)(Haxy)]$ Ass
2. $Gabaa \supset (\exists y)(Haay)$ 1, $\forall$E
3. $(\exists z)[Gabzz \supset (\exists y)(Hzay)]$ 2, $\exists$I

The only tricky thing in this one is remembering what has to be a substitution instance of what. Note that *all* the xs in 1 must be replaced by the same instantiating constant in 2, when $\forall$E is used. But that only some of the **as** in 2 correspond to quantified zs in 3. Even though 2 precedes 3, you have to think of 2 as representing the replacement of variables in 3.

Here's another derivation using both of these rules, to prove $\{ (\forall x)Gx \} \vdash (\exists y)[Gy \& (Gb \lor Ry)]$

1. $(\forall x)Gx$ Ass
2. Ga 1, $\forall$E
3. Gb 1, $\forall$E
4. $Gb \lor Ra$ 3, $\lor$I
5. $Ga \& (Gb \lor Ra)$ 2, 4, &I
6. $(\exists y)[Gy \& (Gb \lor Ry)]$ 5, $\exists$I

Here's a fairly common mistake you should make sure to avoid:

1. $(\forall x)Gxs \supset Hs$ Ass
2. $Gbs \supset Hs$ 1, $\forall$E 👎👎👎

Step 2 has that thumbs-down symbol again, indicating a mistaken step. Note very carefully that the sentence in step 1 is not a universal sentence: the scope of the universal quantifier does not extend beyond Gxs. The main connective in the sentence in step 1 is the $\supset$. If we had the antecedent

$(\forall x)Gxs$

we could do a $\supset$E on it and get the consequent

Hs

If instead the sentence in line 1 were

$(\forall x)(Gxs \supset Hs)$

you could use $\forall$E (but not $\supset$E) on it.

Exercise 4.5 *Prove the following by doing derivations.*

4.5.1. { Dd & Bd } ⊢ (∃x)(Bx & Dx)

4.5.2. { (∀w)(∀x)(Cwx) } ⊢ (∃x)(∃w)(Cxw)

4.5.3. { (∀w)(∀x)(Cwx) } ⊢ (∃x)(Cxx)

4.5.4. { (∀x)(Gx ⊃ Hx) , Gg } ⊢ Hg

4.5.5. { (∀x)(Gx ⊃ Hx) , Gg } ⊢ B ⊃ (∃y)Hy

Universal Introduction

The remaining two derivation rules are more complicated, because they come with restrictions for use. Here's one:

Universal Introduction (∀I)

$$\mathcal{P}a$$
$$(\forall x)\mathcal{P}x$$

Provided:

(i): *a* does not occur in an undischarged assumption.

(ii): *a* does not occur in $(\forall x)\mathcal{P}x$

The restrictions for use are those two items listed under "Provided:" Universal Introduction can be used only if those two restrictions hold. They are both restrictions on the instantiating constant, referred to here as *a*, but which, as we've seen, need not actually be **a**—might be any constant—in your derivation. The first one, (i), tells you that the instantiating constant may not occur in an undischarged assumption—in an assumption, that is, which is undischarged as yet at the point you're using the ∀I step. Here's an example of a use of ∀I that violates this restriction:

1. | Gk   Ass
2. | (∀x)Gx   2, ∀I ❦❦❦—restriction (i)

And of course this should be a mistake. The argument

Kermit is green
Everything is green

is obviously invalid. This is a violation of Restriction (i) because the instantiating constant, in this case is k, *does* occur in an undischarged assumption: step 1.

Here's another mistake which is a violation of Restriction (i):

1. | ~(∀x)(Gx)   Ass
2. | | Gk   Ass
3. | | (∀x)Gx   2, ∀I   ☞☞☞—Restriction (i)
4. | | ~(∀x)(Gx)   1, R
5. | ~Gk   2-4, ~I

The ∀I in line 3 uses the instantiating constant k. At that point in the derivation, there are two undischarged assumptions, in lines 1 and 2. But the instantiating constant k occurs in line 2, so that use of ∀I violates Restriction (i). And that's a good thing, because the derivation attempts to prove something invalid:

> *Not everything is green (that is, at least some things aren't*
> ___*green)*___
> *Kermit isn't green.*

Restriction (ii) says that the instantiating constant is not allowed to occur in the universal sentence which is obtained by using ∀I. So, for example, if you already have a Gff, then (provided Restriction (i) is obeyed) it's okay to get

(∀y)Gyy

but it's not okay to get

(∀y)Gyf

In this case, the instantiating constant is f, and that occurs in the universal sentence obtained, so Restriction (ii) is violated. Were it not for Restriction (ii), this derivation would be allowed:

1. | (∀x)Sxx   Ass
2. | Skk   1, ∀E
3. | (∀x)(Sxk)   2, ∀I   ☞☞☞—Restriction (ii)

This argument is clearly invalid: from the fact that everything is the same size as itself it doesn't follow that everything is the same size as Kermit.

(How, you might be wondering, could it be that a universal statement ever follows from a substitution instance of it? It follows only when the individual named in the substitution instance is a *completely arbitrary* one. The two restrictions guarantee that the individual is completely arbitrary. You may see the logic behind this, or it may become clearer when we do exercises; but the more important thing here that you must know is how to apply this rule with its restrictions.)

Here's a correct use of ∀I, one which obeys the restrictions.

```
1. | (∀x)(Ax & Bx)      Ass
2. | Ag & Bg            1, ∀E
3. | Bg                 2, &E
4. | (∀y)By             3, ∀I
```

Let's check those restrictions on ∀I. The instantiating constant is g.

(i)   When ∀I is used in line 4, the only undischarged assumption is line 1, and there's no g in there.

(ii)   The universal sentence we get using ∀I in line 4 is (∀y)By; and there's no g in there.

The restrictions for ∀I are respected. The argument is valid, and that makes sense: from the premise that everything is both A and B, it does follow that everything is B.

Exercise 4.6 *Find the mistakes in these derivations:*

4.6.1.

```
1. | (∀x)Hx ⊃ ~(∃y)Ky      Ass
2. | Ha ⊃ Na               Ass
3. | Ha                    1, ∀E
4. | Na                    2, 3 ⊃E
```

4.6.2.

```
1. | Bk                    Ass
2. | (∀x)Mx                Ass
3. | Mk                    2, ∀E
4. | Bk & Mk               1, 3, &I
5. | (∀x)(Bx & Mx)         4, ∀I
```

4.6.3.

```
1. | (∀x)(∀y)(Jx & Gy)     Ass
2. | (∀x)(Jx & Gc)         1, ∀E
3. | (∀x)(Jx & Gc) v Lc    2, vI
```

4.6.4

1.	$(\forall x)Rxx$	Ass
2.	$(\forall x)(\forall y)Rxy \supset \sim Sg$	Ass
3.	Raa	1, $\forall$E
4.	$(\forall y)Ray$	3, $\forall$I
5.	$(\forall x)(\forall y)Rxy$	4, $(\forall$I
6.	$\sim Sg$	2, 5, $\supset$E

Exercise 4.7 *Prove by derivations:*

4.7.1. $\{ (\forall x)(Abx \supset Ba) \} \vdash (\forall y)(Aby \supset Ba)$

4.7.2. $\{ [G \& (\forall x)Dx] , Da \} \vdash [G \& (\forall x)(Dx \vee Cb)]$

Existential Elimination

The last rule is slightly more complicated.

Existential Elimination ($\exists$E)

$$\begin{array}{|l}
(\exists x)Px \\
\quad \begin{array}{|l} Pa \\ \hline Q \end{array} \\
Q
\end{array}$$

Provided:

(i) *a* does not occur in an undischarged assumption

(ii) *a* does not occur in $(\exists x)Px$

(iii) *a* does not occur in Q

This rule works something like vE: it "eliminates" a sentence by using a subderivation (two for vE, only one in this case) which comes to a different conclusion (the $\mathcal{R}$ sentence in vE; the Q sentence here) which is then repeated outside the subderivation.

The justification for the $\exists$E step, the last one in this routine, when the Q sentence is written outside the subderivation, must include the step where $(\exists x)Px$ (the existential sentence being used) is found, plus reference to the whole subderivation.

∀I has two restrictions, but ∃E has three.

(i)   prohibits the instantiating constant's appearing in an undischarged assumption.

(ii)   prohibits its appearing in $(\exists x)Px$ (the existential sentence being used in the ∃E).

(iii)   prohibits its appearing in the Q sentence (the sentence appearing as the last step of the subderivation, and again outside its scope as the conclusion of this whole routine).

As in the case of ∀I, then, you have to identify a, the instantiating constant, and check those places where it's prohibited from appearing. In the case of ∃E, however, you choose the instantiating constant: it's the one that appears in the assumption of the subderivation. When you choose what is to be that assumption, make sure at that point that the a you choose doesn't already appear in any undischarged assumptions, or in $(\exists x)Px$ (the existential sentence you plan on using for the ∃E), or in the Q sentence you're aiming at. All this is rather cumbersome, involving several things to look out for, but nothing is terribly difficult here.

Here's a very simple derivation using ∃E:

```
1. │ (∃x)Gx          Ass
2. │ │ Gk            Ass
3. │ │ (∃y)Gy        2, ∃I
4. │ (∃y)(Gy)        1, 2-3, ∃E
```

The instantiating constant, the one that replaces the existentially bound variable in 1 to make 2 (which is the assumption of the subderivation), is k. Checking all three restrictions:

(i)   At step 4, the one justified by ∃E, there's only one undischarged assumption, step 1, and there's no k in there. Note that the instantiating constant will *always* appear in the assumption of the subderivation used for ∃E (step 2 in here) but by the time you get to the ∃E step that assumption will *always* be discharged.

(ii) $(\exists x)Px$, the existential sentence used in this ∃E, is step 1, and there's no k in there. Yes, we've already checked this. In this case, but not always, $(\exists x)Px$ is also an undischarged assumption checked for restriction (i).

(iii) The Q sentence is in both steps 3 and 4, and there's no k in that sentence.

The restrictions have all been respected, and the derivation is correct. (You'll notice that it proves something obvious: that one sentence that says *Something is* G follows from another that says exactly the same thing.)

Here's a slightly more complicated derivation using ∃E:

```
1.│ (∃y)(Gy & Hyk)  Ass
2.│ (∀z)(Gz ⊃ Hzn)  Ass
  │
3.│  │ Gj & Hjk       Ass
  │  │
4.│  │ Gj             3, &E
5.│  │ Gj ⊃ Hjn       2, ∀E
6.│  │ Hjn            4, 5, ⊃E
7.│  │ (∃x)(Hxn)      6, ∃I
8.│ (∃x)Hxn          1, 3-7, ∃E
```

It was necessary to be careful in the choice of the instantiating constant to go in the assumption in step 3. Steps 1 and 2 would be undischarged when the ∃E step occurred, and constants k and n occur in those steps; so we couldn't use k or n. The existential sentence we're using is step 1; this tells us again that we can't use k for the constant. The Q sentence we're aiming at as conclusion to the derivation is (∃x)Hxn, and this tells us again that we can't use n for the constant. So we have to pick some constant other than k or n. The arbitrary choice made here is j, but any other one—other than k or n—would do.

Exercise 4.8 *Find the mistakes in each of the following derivations:*

4.8.1.

```
1.│ (∃x)Qx            Ass
2.│ (∀x)(Zx ≡ Qx)    Ass
  │
3.│ │ Zd ≡ Qd        2, ∀E
4.│ │ Qd             1, ∃E
5.│ │ Zd             3, 4, ≡E
6.│ │ (∃x)Zx         5, ∃I
```

4.8.2.

1.	(∀x)(Fx ⊃ Gx)	Ass
2.	~(∃x)Fx	Ass
3.	Fi	Ass
4.	Fi ⊃ Gi	1, ∀E
5.	Gi	3, 4, ⊃E
6.	(∃x)Gx	5, ∃I
7.	(∃x)(Gx)	2, 3-6, ∃E

4.8.3.

1.	(∀x)(∃y)(Dx & Sy)	Ass
2.	(∃y)(Da & Sy)	1, ∀E
3.	Da & Sz	Ass
4.	Sz	3, &E
5.	(∃y)Sy	4, ∃I
6.	(∃y)Sy	2, 3-5, ∃E

4.8.4.

1.	(∃w)(∃y)Awy	Ass
2.	(∃y)Aky	Ass
3.	Akj	Ass
4.	(∃z)Azj	3, ∃I
5.	(∃z)Azj	2, 3-4, ∃E
6.	(∃x)(∃z)Azx	5, ∃I
7.	(∃x)(∃z)Azx	1, 2-6, ∃E

Exercise 4.9

Given the following start of a derivation

1.	(∀x)Saaxx	Ass
. 2.	Saabb	1 ∀E

Which of the following sentences could be derived on line 3 by one of the quantifier introduction or elimination rules? For each that can be derived, give justification.

4.9.1.   Saacc

4.9.2.   Saaaa

4.9.3.   Saaab

4.9.4.   (∃x)Saxbb

4.9.5.   (∃x)Sxabb

4.9.6.   (∃y)Saayb

4.9.7.   (∃w)Swwbb

4.9.8.   (∃x)Sxaxb

4.9.9.   (∀x)Sxxbb

4.9.10. (∀x)Saaxx

4.9.11. (∀x)Saxxb

4.9.12. (∀z)Saabz

List of All the Additional Quantifier Rules

Universal Introduction (∀I)

$$\mathcal{P}a$$
$$(\forall x)\mathcal{P}x$$

Provided:

(i): *a* does not occur in an undischarged assumption.

(ii): *a* does not occur in $(\forall x)\mathcal{P}x$

Universal Elimination (∀E)

$$(\forall x)\mathcal{P}x$$
$$\mathcal{P}a$$

Existential Introduction (∃I)

$$\mathcal{P}a$$
$$(\exists x)\mathcal{P}x$$

Existential Elimination (∃E)

$$
\begin{array}{|l}
(\exists x)\mathcal{P}x \\
\quad\begin{array}{|l} \mathcal{P}a \\ \hline \\ Q \end{array} \\
Q
\end{array}
$$

Provided:

(i) *a* does not occur in an undischarged assumption

(ii) *a* does not occur in $(\exists x)\mathcal{P}x$

(iii) *a* does not occur in Q

Using Derivations (Again)

A large number of derivation exercises follow in a moment, but before we get to them, remind yourself how to prove logical properties using derivations.

- <u>Validity</u> { $\mathcal{P}$, Q } ⊢ $\mathcal{R}$ Derive the conclusion $\mathcal{R}$ using premises $\mathcal{P}$, Q as primary assumptions.

- <u>Logical truth</u> ⊢ $\mathcal{P}$ Derive sentence $\mathcal{P}$ without any primary assumptions.

- <u>Logical falsity</u> of a sentence $\mathcal{P}$. With the sentence $\mathcal{P}$ as a primary assumption, derive a contradiction in the main scope: some sentence Q on one step, its negation ~Q on another.

- <u>Inconsistency</u> of a set of sentences { $\mathcal{P}$, Q ... } Assume those sentences $\mathcal{P}$, Q , ... as primary assumptions, and derive a contradiction in the main scope: some sentence $\mathcal{R}$ on one step, its negation ~$\mathcal{R}$ on another.

- <u>Equivalence</u> of a pair of sentences $\mathcal{P}$, Q : do two derivations: { $\mathcal{P}$} ⊢ Q and { Q } ⊢ $\mathcal{P}$

Okay, now for lots of derivation exercises. As in Chapter 2, these are are sorted into categories of increasing difficulty; of course, you should try the easy ones first. If you can't do any in the VERY EASY category, read this chapter—and perhaps Chapter Two again, very carefully, doing all the exercises preliminary to this one. If you can do the VERY EASY derivations but run into a lot of trouble in the next category, you might pass the test on derivations, but you won't do well. In the last category, the derivations are VERY DIFFICULT indeed, and you might not be able to do at least some of these if time were limited. Ask your instructor how important ability to do the most difficult derivations is for getting a good grade.

Exercise 4.10. *Prove the following by doing derivations.*

GROUP 1: VERY EASY

4.10.1.　{ (∃x)Ax ⊃ Aa , (∃x)Ax } ⊦ Aa

4.10.2.　{ (∀x)(Bx & Cx) } ⊦ Ca

4.10.3.　{ (∀x)[Dx & (Ex ≡ Fx)] } ⊦ (∀x)(Ex ≡ Fx)

4.10.4.　{ Ga & Ha } ⊦ (∃z)(Hz & Gz)

4.10.5.　{ (Ia ⊃ Ja) & Ia } ⊦ (∃x)(∃y)(Ix & Jy)

4.10.6.　{ (∀x)[Kx & (Kx ⊃ Lx)] } ⊦ (∃y)[Ly & (∃x)Kx]

4.10.7.　{ (∃y)My , (∀x)(Nx ≡ Mx) } ⊦ (∃z)Nz

4.10.8.　⊦ (∃x)(Ox ≡ Oa)

4.10.9.　{ (∀x)(∀y)Pxy } ⊦ (∀y)(∀x)Pxy

4.10.10.　{ (∀x)[Qx ⊃ (∃y)Rxy] , Qa } ⊦ (∃z)Raz

GROUP II: EASY

4.10.11. { (∀x)(Sx ⊃ Tx) , (∀x)(Tx ⊃ Ux) } ⊦ (∀x)(Sx ⊃ Ux)

4.10.12. { (∀x)(Ax & Bx) } ⊦ (Ab & Bh) & Ad

4.10.13. { (∀z)(Cz ⊃ Dz) , (∀w)(~Ew ≡ Dw) } ⊦ ~(Cb & Eb)

4.10.14. { (∀x)(Fx ⊃ Gx) , Fa } ⊦ Ha ⊃ Ga

4.10.15. { (∀x)(Ix ⊃ ~Jx) , (∀x)(Ix & Kx) } ⊦ (∃x)~Jx

4.10.16. { La ⊃ (∀x)Mx , (∃x)Mx ⊃ La } ⊦ (∀x)(La ≡ Mx)

4.10.17. { (∀x)(Nx ≡ Ox) } ⊦ (∀x)Nx ≡ (∀x)Ox

4.10.18. { (∀x)(Px ≡ Qx) } ⊦ (∃x)Px ≡ (∃x)Qx

4.10.19. { (∃x)(Rx ⊃ Sx) } ⊦ (∀x)Rx ⊃ (∃x)Sx

4.10.20. ⊦ (∀x)Tx ≡ (∀x)(Tx & Tx)

4.10.21. ⊢ $(\forall x)(Ax \supset \sim \sim Ax)$

4.10.22. ⊢ $(\forall x)(Bx \supset Cx) \supset [(\forall x)Bx \supset (\forall x)Cx]$

4.10.23. ⊢ $(\exists x)(Dx \& Ex) \supset ((\exists x)Dx \& (\exists x)Ex)$

4.10.24. ⊢ $(\forall x)(Fa \supset Gx) \equiv (Fa \supset (\forall x)Gx)$

4.10.25. Prove equivalent: $(\forall x)(\forall y)(Hx \& Iy)$, $(\forall x)Hx \& (\forall y)Iy$

4.10.26. Prove inconsistent: $\{ (\forall x)Jx , (\forall y)\sim(Jy \vee Kyy) \}$

4.10.27. Prove logically false: $(\forall x)(Lx \equiv \sim Lx)$

4.10.28. Prove logically false: $(\forall w)(\forall z)(Mwz \equiv \sim Mwz)$

GROUP III: MEDIUM DIFFICULTY

4.10.29. $\{ (\forall z)(\forall y)Nzy , (\forall x)(\forall y)(Nxy \supset \sim Ox) \}$ ⊢ $(\forall w)\sim Ow$

4.10.30. $\{ (\exists x)Px \}$ ⊢ $(\exists y)(Py \vee Qy)$

4.10.31. $\{ (\forall x)(Rx \supset Sx) , (\exists x)Rx \}$ ⊢ $(\exists x)Sx$

4.10.32. $\{ (\exists y)(\forall x)Txy \}$ ⊢ $(\forall x)(\exists y)Txy$

4.10.33. $\{ (\exists x)(\exists y)Uxy \}$ ⊢ $(\exists y)(\exists x)Uxy$

4.10.34. $\{ (\forall x)[(\exists y)Axy \supset Bbx] , (\forall x)(\forall y)Ayx \}$ ⊢ $(\exists x)Bxx$

4.10.35. $\{ (\exists x)Cx \supset (\forall x)Dx \}$ ⊢ $(\forall x)(\sim Dx \supset \sim Cx)$

4.10.36. $\{ (\exists x)Exb \supset (\forall x)Fx , (\forall x)Eax \}$ ⊢ $(\forall x)(Gxc \supset Fx)$

4.10.37. $\{ Hmm \& \sim Imr , (\exists y)\sim(Hmy \supset Iyr) \supset (\forall x)Jxx \}$ ⊢ Jaa

4.10.38. $\{ (\forall z)[(Kz \vee (\forall x)Lxz) \equiv Mzzz] , Mggg \}$
$\qquad$ ⊢ $((\forall x)Lxg \vee Kg) \vee Ng$

4.10.39. $\{ (\exists x)Ox \supset (\exists x)Px \}$ ⊢ $(\forall x)[Ox \supset (\exists y)Py]$

4.10.40. $\{ (\exists x)Qx \& (\forall x)Rx \}$ ⊢ $(\exists x)(Qx \& Rx)$

4.10.41. $\{ (\exists x)Sx , (\exists x)Tx \}$ ⊢ $(\exists x)[(\exists y)Sy \& Tx]$

4.10.42. $\{ (\exists x)[Ax \supset (\exists y)By] \}$ ⊢ $(\forall x)Ax \supset (\exists x)Bx$

4.10.43. $\{ (\forall x)(Cx \supset Dx), (\forall x)[(\exists y)(Dy \& Exy) \supset Fx]$,
$\qquad (\exists x)[Gx \& (\exists y)(Cy \& Exy)] \}$ ⊢ $(\exists x)(Gx \& Fx)$

4.10.44. $\{ (\forall x)(Hxa \supset Hxb) \}$
$\qquad$ ⊢ $(\forall x)[(\exists y)(Ixy \& Hya) \supset (\exists y)(Ixy \& Hyb)]$

4.10.45. { (∀x)[Jx ⊃ (∀y)(Ky ⊃ Lxy)] ,
(∀x)[Mx ⊃ (∀y)(Lxy ⊃ Ny)] }
⊢ (∃x)(Jx & Mx) ⊃ (∀y)(Ky ⊃ Ny)

4.10.46. { (∃x)[Ox & (∀y)(Py ⊃ Rxy)] } ⊢ (∃x)[Ox & (Pa ⊃ Rxa)]

4.10.47. { (∀x)(∀y)(Sxy ≡ (Ty ⊃ Ux)) , (∀z)Saz }
⊢ (∃x)Tx ⊃ (∃x)Ux

4.10.48. { (∀x)[(∃y)Axy ⊃ (∃y)~By] , (∃x)(∃y)Axy ,
(∀x)(Bx ≡ ~Cx) } ⊢ (∃x)Cx

4.10.49. ⊢ (∀x)(∃y)(Dy ⊃ Dx)

4.10.50. ⊢ (∀x)(Ex ⊃ Fa) ≡ ((∃x)Ex ⊃ Fa)

4.10.51. Prove equivalent: (∃x)(Gx v Hx) , (∃x)Gx v (∃x)Hx

4.10.52. Prove equivalent: (∀x)~Ix , ~(∃x)Ix

4.10.53. Prove inconsistent: { (∀x)Jx , (∃x)~Jx }

4.10.54. Prove inconsistent: { (∀y)(∃z)Kyz , (∀w)~Kaw }

4.10.55. Prove inconsistent: { (∀x)(∃y)(Lx ⊃ My) ,
~(∃y)(∀x)(Lx ⊃ My) }

4.10.56. Prove logically false: (∃x)(Nx & ~Nx)

GROUP IV: DIFFICULT

4.10.57. { ~(∀x) ~Ox } ⊢ (∃x)Ox

4.10.58. { Pnn v (Qn & Rj) , ~(∀z)Ssz ⊃ ~Qn }
⊢ (∃x)(~Pxx ⊃ (∀z)Ssz)

4.10.59. { (∃x)(∃y)Txy v (∀x)(∀y)Uyx }
⊢ (∃x)(∃y)(Txy v Uxy)

4.10.60. { (∀x)(~Ax ⊃ Bx) , (∀x)[(~Bx v Ax) ≡ ~Bx] ,
(∃x)(Cx ≡ Ax) } ⊢ ~(∀x)(Cx ≡ Bx)

4.10.61. { (∀x)(∀y)[(Dx & Ey) ⊃ Fxy] ,
(∃x)(∃y)[(Dx & ~Dy) & ~Fxy] }
⊢ (∃x)(~Dx & ~Ex)

4.10.62. Prove equivalent: ~(∀x)Gx , (∃x)~Gx

4.10.63. Prove equivalent: (∀x)(∀y)[(Hxy & Hyx) ⊃ Hxx] ,
(∀x)[(∃y)(Hxy & Hyx) ⊃ Hxx]

4.10.64. Prove equivalent: (∃x)Ix ⊃ ((∃y)Jy ⊃ (∀z)Kz) ,
         (∀x)(∀y)(∀z)[(Ix & Jy) ⊃ Kz]

4.10.65. Prove inconsistent: { (∃x)(∀y)Lxy ,
         ~(∀y)(∃x)Lxy }

Answers to Exercises in Chapter Four

EXERCISE 4.1

Ass on line 1: undischarged at all lines.
Ass on line 2: undischarged at all lines
Ass on line 3: undischarged at lines 3 – 12.
Ass on line 5: undischarged at lines 5 – 9.
Ass on line 6: undischarged at lines 6 – 8.
Ass on line 10: undischarged at lines 10-11.
Ass on line 13: undischarged at lines 13-14.

EXERCISE 4.2.

4.2.1. [Bab ⊃ (∃y)(Cy & Dya)]   Conditional

4.2.2. (∃x)[Ax ⊃ (∃y)(Cy & Db)]   Existential

4.2.3. ~(∃x)[Ax ⊃ (∃y)(Cy & Db)]   Negation

4.2.4. (∃x)Ax ⊃ (∃y)(Cy & Db)   Conditional

4.2.5. ~(∃x)Ax ⊃ (∃y)(Cy & Db)   Conditional

4.2.6. (∀x)[(∀y)Bxy & C]   Universal

4.2.7. (∀x)(∀y)Bxy & C   Conjunction

4.2.8. (∀x)(∀y)[Bxy & C]   Universal

EXERCISE 4.3

4.3.1.. [Bbab ⊃ (∃y)(Cyba & Dbbyb)]
Yes. The instantiating constant is b, and it replaces every x.

4.3.2.. [Bxab ⊃ (∃y)(Cyxa & Dxxyb)]
No—this leaves all those xs unbound.

4.3.3. [Baaa ⊃ (Caaa & Daaaa)]
No—this substitutes as for the bs—a substitution instance replaces only variables. This one also improperly removes the existential quantifier and instantiates the variables it binds (the ys).

4.3.4. (∀x)[Bxab ⊃ (Ccxa & Dxxcb)]
No—a substitution instance can only be done on a quantifier which is the
main connective of the sentence.

4.3.5. (∀y)[Cxxbc ⊃ (∃x)Bxybc]
Yes. It substitutes the instantiating constant a for each x.

4.3.6. (∃w)[Caawc ⊃ (∃x)Bxxbc]
Yes. b is the instantiating constant; it replaces each w.

4.3.7. (∃w)[Cwwwc ⊃ (∃x)Bxwwc]
No. The sentence substitutes a for some ws, b for others.

EXERCISE 4.4

4.4.3. { (∀y)(Agy ⊃ M) , Agg } ⊢ M

1.	(∀y)(Agy ⊃ M)	Ass
2.	Agg	Ass
3.	Agg ⊃ M	1, ∀E
4.	M	2, 3, ⊃E

4.4.2. { (∀w)(Bw ≡ Gw) , (∀z)(Az ⊃ Bz) } ⊢   Ar ⊃ Gr

1.	(∀w)(Bw ≡ Gw)	Ass
2.	(∀z)(Az ⊃ Bz)	Ass
3.	Ar	Ass
4.	Ar ⊃ Br	2, ∀E
5.	Br	3, 4, ⊃E
6.	Br ≡ Gr	2, ∀E
7.	Gr	5, 6, ≡E
8.	Ar ⊃ Gr	3-7, ⊃I

EXERCISE 4.5

4.5.1. { Dd & Bd } ⊢   (∃x)(Bx & Dx)

1.	Dd & Bd	Ass
2.	Dd	1, &E
3.	Bd	1, &E
4.	Bd & Dd	2, 3, &I
5.	(∃x)(Bx & Dx)	4, ∃I

4.5.2. { (∀w)(∀x)(Cwx) } ⊢ (∃x)(∃w)(Cxw)

1.| (∀w)(∀x)(Cwx)   Ass
2.| (∀x)Cax   1, ∀E
3.| Cab   2, ∀E
4.| (∃w)Caw   3, ∃I
5.| (∃x)(∃w)(Cxw)   4, ∃I

In this derivation, you should pay careful attention to the order of the two
∀E steps and the order of the two ∃I steps. ∀E has to remove the initial
quantifier first. Because this results in another universal sentence, the result
can in turn be used in ∀E. Step 4 starts putting on the *inside* quantifier first,
because step 5 can only add an existential quantifier to the left of that one.
Pay attention to which constant you're replacing with which variable, in
order to get the desired result in 5.

4.5.3 { (∀w)(∀x)(Cwx) } ⊢ (∃x)(Cxx)

1.| (∀w)(∀x)(Cwx)   Ass
2.| (∀x)Cax   1, ∀E
3.| Caa   2, ∀E
4.| (∃x)(Cxx)   3, ∃I

Note that in moving from step 2 to step 3 using ∀E, you need to use the
same instantiating constant that you used in moving from step 1 to step 2. If
you got Cab in step 3, by ∀E from step 2, that would be correct, but then
the difference in the two constants wouldn't allow you to get step 4.

4.5.4. { (∀x)(Gx ⊃ Hx) , Gg } ⊢ Hg

1.| (∀x)(Gx ⊃ Hx)   Ass
2.| Gg   Ass

3.| Gg ⊃ Hg   1, ∀E
4.| Hg   2, 3, ⊃E

4.5.5 { (∀x)(Gx ⊃ Hx) , Gg } ⊢ B ⊃ (∃y)Hy

1.| (∀x)(Gx ⊃ Hx)   Ass
2.| Gg   Ass

3.| Gg ⊃ Hg   1, ∀E
4.| Hg   2, 3, ⊃E
5.| B   Ass
6.| (∃y)Hy   4, ∃I
7.| B ⊃ (∃y)Hy   5-6, ⊃I

EXERCISE 4.6

4.6.1.

```
1.| (∀x)Hx ⊃ ~(∃y)Ky      Ass
2.| Ha ⊃ Na               Ass

3.| Ha                    1 ∀E ☞☞☞
4.| Na                    2, 3 ⊃E ☞☞☞
```

∀E can be used only on universal sentences. The scope of the quantifier in 1 extends only over the Hx; its main connective is the ⊃, and it's a conditional sentence, not a universal sentence.

Do you see the problem with line 4? No?? The problem here is that it's missing a comma, after the 3 in the justification.

What? You must be kidding. How can you be so picky? What difference does the comma make?

The idea throughout what we've been doing is to produce a system that sets the exact form that everything has to take, with a complete set of rigorous rules that need to be followed exactly. That's what's involved in a formal system like this. So you can't just bend things a little. Those of you who have worked a bit with computers know how this works: small errors that humans would generously ignore, understanding what you meant, make computers fall into disarray. Think of what we're doing as computer input.

4.6.2.

```
1.| Bk                    Ass
2.| (∀x)Mx                Ass

3.| Mk                    2, ∀E
4.| Bk & Mk               1, 3 &I
5.| (∀x)(Bx & Mx)         4, ∀I ☞☞☞
```

Line 5 violates **restriction** (i) of ∀I. The instantiating constant, k, appears in an undischarged assumption: line 1.

4.6.3.

1. | (∀x)(∀y)(Jx & Gy)   Ass
2. | (∀x)(Jx & Gc)   1, ∀E ☞☞☞
3. | (∀x)(Jx & Gc) v Lc   2, vI

Line 2 is not a substitution instance of line 1. To make a substitution instance of line 1, you have to remove the first quantifier. The conclusion on line 3 can, however, be correctly derived. Try doing it before you look at the correct version, just below.

CORRECTED

1. | (∀x)(∀y)(Jx & Gy)   Ass
2. | (∀y)(Jn & Gy)   1, ∀E
3. | Jn & Gc   2, ∀E
4. | (∀x)(Jx & Gc)   3, ∀I
5. | (∀x)(Jx & Gc) v Lc   4, vI

4.6.4.

1. (∀x)Rxx   Ass
2. (∀x)(∀y)Rxy ⊃ ~Sg   Ass
3. Rdd   1, ∀E
4. (∀y)Rdy   3, ∀I ☞☞☞
5. (∀x)(∀y)Rxy   4, ∀I
6. ~Sg   2, 5, ⊃E

The ∀I step here violates restriction (ii): the instantiating constant is d, and it occurs in the universal sentence introduced in step 4. This derivation attempts to prove an invalid argument, so there's no way this can be done correctly.

EXERCISE 4.7

4.7.1. { (∀x)(Abx ⊃ Ba) } ⊢ (∀y)(Aby ⊃ Ba)

1. | (∀x)(Abx ⊃ Ba)   Ass
2. | Abc ⊃ Ba   1, ∀E
3. | (∀y)(Aby ⊃ Ba)   2, ∀I

The only trick here is to choose an instantiating constant in step 2 that will not get you into trouble when you do ∀I in step 3: it has to be a constant that does not occur either in 1 or 3. So it can't be either b or a.

4.7.2. { [G & (∀x)Dx] , Da } ⊢ [G & (∀x)(Dx v Cb)]

1.	G & (∀x)Dx	Ass
2.	Da	Ass
3.	(∀x)Dx	1, &E
4.	Dn	3, ∀E
5.	Dn v Cb	4, vI
6.	(∀x)(Dx v Cb)	5, ∀I
7.	G	1, &E
8.	G & (∀x)(Dx v Cb)	6, 7, &I

Again, care is necessary to choose an instantiating constant in step 4: you must avoid a (in undischarged assumption 2) and b (in the sentence resulting from ∀I later on, step 6). Also, note that ∀E can't be done on step 1 which is a conjunction; and ∀I can't get you step 8, another conjunction.

EXERCISE 4.8

4.8.1.

1.	(∃x)Qx	Ass
2.	(∀x)(Zx ≡ Qx)	Ass
3.	Zd ≡ Qd	2, ∀E
4.	Qd	1, ∃E ❧❧❧
5.	Zd	3, 4, ≡E
6.	(∃x)Zx	5, ∃I

Line 4 misuses ∃E, which requires a subderivation. This derivation can be done correctly; maybe you should try to do it before looking at the correct version, just below.

CORRECTED:

1.	(∃x)Qx	Ass
2.	(∀x)(Zx ≡ Qx)	Ass
3.	Zd ≡ Qd	2, ∀E
4.	Qd	Ass
5.	Zd	3, 4, ≡E
6.	(∃x)Zx	5, ∃I
7.	(∃x)Zx	1, 4-6, ∃E

4.8.2.

1.	(∀x)(Fx ⊃ Gx)	Ass
2.	~(∃x)Fx	Ass
3.	Fi	Ass (ok, but won't allow ∃E)
4.	Fi ⊃ Gi	1, ∀E
5.	Gi	3, 4, ⊃E
6.	(∃x)Gx	5, ∃I
7.	(∃x)(Gx)	2, 3-6, ∃E 👣👣👣

This one would be fine if there weren't that pesky tilde in line 2. As it is, the tilde is the main connective of line 2, so it's a negation, not an existential statement, and you can't do ∃E using it. All the steps are correct as far as the rules go (though useless) through line 6, however.

4.8.3.

1.	(∀x)(∃y)(Dx & Sy)	Ass
2.	(∃y)(Da & Sy)	1, ∀E
3.	Da & Sz	Ass 👣👣👣
4.	Sz	3, &E 👣👣👣
5.	(∃y)Sy	4, ∃I
6.	(∃y)Sy	2, 3-5, ∃E

This one would be fine if the instantiating constant introduced in the assumption, line 3, were really a constant: z is a variable. This makes lines 3 and 4 not-well-formed, because of unbound variables. Replace z in this derivation with a real constant, say g, and everything is correct.

4.8.4.

1.	(∃w)(∃y)Awy	Ass
2.	(∃y)Aky	Ass
3.	Akj	Ass
4.	(∃z)Azj	3, ∃I
5.	(∃x)Azj	2, 3-4, ∃E 👣👣👣
6.	(∃x)(∃z)Azx	5, ∃I
7.	(∃x)(∃z)Azx	1, 2-6, ∃E

The ∃E attempted in line 5 violates restriction (iii). The instantiating constant j, replacing the existentially bound variable y, occurs in the Q sentence, found in lines 4 and 5. This derivation can be done correctly; try to do so before you look at the corrected version on the next page.

CORRECTED

```
1. │ (∃w)(∃y)Awy              Ass
2. │ │ │ (∃y)Aky              Ass
3. │ │ └ Akj                  Ass
4. │ │ │ ┌ (∃z)Azj            3, ∃I
5. │ │ │ │ (∃x)(∃z)Azx        4, ∃I
6. │ │ │ (∃x)(∃z)Azx          2, 3-5, ∃E
7. │ (∃x)(∃z)Azx              1, 2-6, ∃E
```

The idea here, applicable elsewhere to prevent this sort of restriction violation, is to get rid of the instantiating constant before you end the subderivation for ∃E.

EXERCISE 4.9

```
4.9.1. Saacc          1, ∀E
4.9.2. Saaaa          1, ∀E
4.9.3. Saaab          ♥♥♥  Not a substitution instance of 1
4.9.4. (∃x)Saxbb      2, ∃I
4.9.5. (∃x)Sxabb      2, ∃I
4.9.6. (∃y)Saayb      2, ∃I
4.9.7. (∃w)Swwbb      2, ∃I
4.9.8. (∃x)Sxaxb      ♥♥♥  Step 2 is not a substitution instance of this.
4.9.9. (∀x)Sxxbb      ♥♥♥  ∀I can't be used to derive this from step 2
       because a occurs as an undischarged assumption in step 1.
4.9.10. (∀x)Saaxx     2, ∀I  (or 1, R)
4.9.11. (∀x)Saxxb     ♥♥♥  Step 2 is not a substitution instance of this.
4.9.12. (∀z)Saabz     ♥♥♥  Attempting to derive this from step 2 by ∀I
       would violate restriction (ii).
```

EXERCISE 4.10.

4.10.1 { (∃x)Ax ⊃ Aa , (∃x)Ax } ⊢ Aa

```
1. │ (∃x)Ax ⊃ Aa    Ass
2. │ (∃x)Ax         Ass
3. │ Aa             1, 2, ⊃E
```

4.10.2 { (∀x)(Bx & Cx) } ⊢ Ca

```
1. │ (∀x)(Bx & Cx)  Ass
2. │ Ba & Ca        1, ∀E
3. │ Ca             2, &E
```

4.10.3. { (∀x)[Dx & (Ex ≡ Fx)] } ⊢ (∀x)(Ex ≡ Fx)

1. | (∀x)[Dx & (Ex ≡ Fx)] Ass

2. | Da & (Ea ≡ Fa)   1, ∀E
3. | Ea ≡ Fa   2, &E
4. | (∀x)(Ex ≡ Fx)   3, ∀I

4.10.4. { Ga & Ha } ⊢ (∃z)(Hz & Gz)

1. | Ga & Ha   Ass

2. | Ga   1, &E
3. | Ha   1, &E
4. | Ha & Ga   2, 3, &I
5. | (∃z)(Hz & Gz)   4, ∃I

4.10.5. { (Ia ⊃ Ja) & Ia } ⊢ (∃x)(∃y)(Ix & Jy)

1. | (Ia ⊃ Ja) & Ia   Ass

2. | Ia ⊃ Ja   1, &E
3. | Ia   1, &E
4. | Ja   2, 3, ⊃E
5. | Ia & Ja   3, 4, &I
6. | (∃y)(Ia & Jy)   5, ∃I
7. | (∃x)(∃y)(Ix & Jy) 6, ∃I

4.10.6. { (∀x)[Kx & (Kx ⊃ Lx)] } ⊢ (∃y)[Ly & (∃x)Kx]

1. | (∀x)[Kx & (Kx ⊃ Lx)]   Ass

2. | Ka & (Ka ⊃ La)   1, ∀E
3. | Ka   2, &E
4. | (∃x)Kx   3, ∃I
5. | Ka ⊃ La   2, &E
6. | La   3, 5, ⊃E
7. | La & (∃x)Kx   4, 6, &I
8. | (∃y)[Ly & (∃x)Kx]   7, ∃I

4.10.7. { (∃y)My , (∀x)(Nx ≡ Mx) } ⊢ (∃z)Nz

1. | (∃y)My   Ass
2. | (∀x)(Nx ≡ Mx)   Ass

3. | | Ma   Ass

4. | | Na ≡ Ma   2, ∀E
5. | | Na   3, 5, ≡E
6. | | (∃z)Nz   5, ∃I
7. | (∃z)Nz   1, 3-6, ∃E

4.10.8. ⊢ $(\exists x)(Ox \equiv Oa)$

1.		Oa	Ass
2.		Oa	1, R
3.		Oa	Ass
4.		Oa	3, R
5.	Oa ≡ Oa		1-2, 3-4, ≡I
6.	$(\exists x)(Ox \equiv Oa)$		5, ∃I

4.10.9. $\{ (\forall x)(\forall y)Pxy \}$ ⊢ $(\forall y)(\forall x)Pxy$

1.	$(\forall x)(\forall y)Pxy$	Ass
2.	$(\forall y)Pay$	1, ∀E
3.	Pab	2, ∀E
4.	$(\forall x)Pxb$	3, ∀I
5.	$(\forall y)(\forall x)Pxy$	4, ∀I

4.10.10. $\{ (\forall x)[Qx \supset (\exists y)Rxy] , Qa \}$ ⊢ $(\exists z)Raz$

1	$(\forall x)[Qx \supset (\exists y)Rxy]$	Ass
2	Qa	Ass
3	$Qa \supset (\exists y)Ray$	1, ∀E
4	$(\exists y)(Ray)$	2, 3, ⊃E
5	Rab	Ass
6	$(\exists z)Raz$	5, ∃I
7	$(\exists z)Raz$	4, 5-6, ∃E

4.10.11. $\{ (\forall x)(Sx \supset Tx) , (\forall x)(Tx \supset Ux) \}$ ⊢ $(\forall x)(Sx \supset Ux)$

1.	$(\forall x)(Sx \supset Tx)$	Ass
2.	$(\forall x)(Tx \supset Ux)$	Ass
3.	Sb	Ass
4.	$Sb \supset Tb$	1, ∀E
5.	Tb	3, 4, ⊃E
6.	$Tb \supset Ub$	2, ∀E
7.	Ub	5, 6, ⊃E
8.	$Sb \supset Ub$	3-7, ⊃I
9.	$(\forall x)(Sx \supset Ux)$	8, ∀I

4.10.12. { (∀x)(Ax & Bx) } ⊢ (Ab & Bh) & Ad

1.	(∀x)(Ax & Bx)	Ass
2.	Ab & Bb	1, ∀E
3.	Ab	2, &E
4.	Ah & Bh	1, ∀E
5.	Bh	4, &E
6.	Ab & Bh	3, 5, &I
7.	Ad & Bd	1, ∀E
8.	Ad	7, &E
9.	(Ab & Bh) & Ad	6, 8, &I

4.10.13. { (∀z)(Cz ⊃ Dz) , (∀w)(~Ew ≡ Dw) } ⊢ ~(Cb & Eb)

1.	(∀z)(Cz ⊃ Dz)	Ass
2.	(∀w)(~Ew ≡ Dw)	Ass
3.	Cb & Eb	Ass
4.	Cb ⊃ Db	1, ∀E
5.	Cb	3, &E
6.	Db	5, 4, ⊃E
7.	~Eb ≡ Db	2, ∀E
8.	~Eb	6, 7, ≡E
9.	Eb	3, &E
10.	~(Cb & Eb)	3-9, ~I

4.10.14. { (∀x)(Fx ⊃ Gx) , Fa } ⊢ Ha ⊃ Ga

1.	(∀x)(Fx ⊃ Gx)	Ass
2.	Fa	Ass
3.	Ha	Ass
4.	Fa ⊃ Ga	1, ∀E
5.	Ga	2, 4, ⊃E
6.	Ha ⊃ Ga	3-5, ⊃I

4.10.15. { (∀x)(Ix ⊃ ~Jx) , (∀x)(Ix & Kx) } ⊢ (∃x)~Jx

1.	(∀x)(Ix ⊃ ~Jx)	Ass
2.	(∀x)(Ix & Kx)	Ass
3.	In & Kn	2, ∀E
4.	In	3, &E
5.	In ⊃ ~Jn	1, ∀E
6.	~Jn	4, 5, ⊃E
7.	(∃x)~Jx	6, ∃I

4.10.16. { La ⊃ (∀x)Mx , (∃x)Mx ⊃ La } ⊢ (∀x)(La ≡ Mx)

1.	La ⊃ (∀x)Mx	Ass
2.	(∃x)Mx ⊃ La	Ass
3.	La	Ass
4.	(∀x)Mx	3, 1 ⊃E
5.	Mb	4, ∀E
6.	Mb	Ass
7.	(∃x)Mx	6, ∃I
8.	La	7, 2, ⊃E
9.	La ≡ Mb	3-5, 6-8, ≡I
10.	(∀x)(La ≡ Mx)	9, ∀I

4.10.17. { (∀x)(Nx ≡ Ox) } ⊢ (∀x)Nx ≡ (∀x)Ox

1.	(∀x)(Nx ≡ Ox)	Ass
2.	Na ≡ Oa	1, ∀E
3.	(∀x)Nx	Ass
4.	Na	3, ∀E
5.	Oa	4, 2, ≡ E
6.	(∀x)Ox	5, ∀I
7.	(∀x)Ox	Ass
8.	Oa	7, ∀E
9.	Na	8, 2, ≡E
10.	(∀x)Nx	9, ∀I
11.	(∀x)Nx ≡ (∀x)Ox	3-6, 7-10, ≡I

4.10.18. { (∀x)(Px ≡ Qx) } ⊢ (∃x)Px ≡ (∃x)Qx

1.	(∀x)(Px ≡ Qx)	Ass
2.	Pa ≡ Qa	1, ∀E
3.	(∃x)Px	Ass
4.	Pa	Ass
5.	Qa	4, 2, ≡E
6.	(∃x)Qx	5, ∃I
7.	(∃x)Qx	3, 4-6, ∃E
8.	(∃x)Qx	Ass
9.	Qa	Ass
10.	Pa	9, 2, ≡E
11.	(∃x)Px	10, ∃I
12.	(∃x)Px	8, 9-11, ∃E
13.	(∃x)Px ≡ (∃x)Qx	3-7, 8-12, ≡I

4.10.19.{ (∃x)(Rx ⊃ Sx) } ⊢ (∀x)Rx ⊃ (∃x)Sx

1.	(∀x)(Rx ≡ Sx)	Ass
2.	Rn ≡ Sn	1, ∀E
3.	(∀x)Rx	Ass
4.	Rn	3, ∀E
5.	Sn	4, 2, ≡E
6.	(∃x)Sx	5, ∃I
7.	(∀x)Rx ⊃ (∃x)Sx	3-6, ⊃I

4.10.20. ⊢ (∀x)Tx ≡ (∀x)(Tx & Tx)

1.	(∀x)Tx	Ass
2.	Ta	1, ∀E
3.	Ta	2, R
4.	Ta & Ta	2, 3, &I
5.	(∀x)(Tx & Tx)	4, ∀I
6.	(∀x)(Tx & Tx)	Ass
7.	Ta & Ta	6, ∀E
8.	Ta	7, &E
9.	(∀x)Tx	8, ∀I
10.	(∀x)Tx ≡ (∀x)(Tx & Tx)	1-5, 6-9, ≡I

4.10.21. ⊢ (∀x)(Ax ⊃ ~ ~Ax)

1.	Aa	Ass
2.	~Aa	Ass
3.	Aa	1, R
4.	~Aa	2, R
5.	~ ~Aa	2-4, ~I
6.	Aa ⊃ ~ ~Aa	1-5, ⊃I
7.	(∀x)(Ax ⊃ ~ ~Ax)	6, ∀I

4.10.22. ⊢ (∀x)(Bx ⊃ Cx) ⊃ [(∀x)Bx ⊃ (∀x)Cx]

1.	(∀x)(Bx ⊃ Cx)	Ass
2.	(∀x)Bx	Ass
3.	Ba	2, ∀E
4.	Ba ⊃ Ca	1, ∀E
5.	Ca	3, 4, ⊃E
6.	(∀x)Cx	5, ∀I
7.	(∀x)Bx ⊃ (∀x)Cx	2-6, ⊃I
8.	(∀x)(Bx ⊃ Cx) ⊃ [(∀x)Bx ⊃ (∀x)Cx]	1-7, ⊃I

4.10.23. ⊢ (∃x)(Dx & Ex) ⊃ ((∃x)Dx & (∃x)Ex)

1.	(∃x)(Dx & Ex)	Ass
2.	Dk & Ek	Ass
3.	Dk	2, &E
4.	(∃x)Dx	3, ∃I
5.	Ek	2, &E
6.	(∃x)Ex	5, ∃I
7.	(∃x)Dx & (∃x)Ex	4, 6, &I
8.	(∃x)Dx & (∃x)Ex	1, 2-7, ∃E
9.	(∃x)(Dx & Ex) ⊃ [(∃x)Dx & (∃x)Ex]	1-8, ⊃I

4.10.24. ⊢ (∀x)(Fa ⊃ Gx) ≡ (Fa ⊃ (∀x)Gx)

1.	(∀x)(Fa ⊃ Gx)	Ass
2.	Fa	Ass
3.	Fa ⊃ Gg	1, ∀E
4.	Gg	2, 3, ⊃E
5.	(∀x)Gx	4, ∀I
6.	Fa ⊃ (∀x)Gx	2-5, ⊃I
7.	Fa ⊃ (∀x)Gx	Ass
8.	Fa	Ass
9.	(∀x)Gx	7, 8, ⊃E
10.	Gg	9, ∀E
11.	Fa ⊃ Gg	8-10, ⊃I
12.	(∀x)(Fa ⊃ Gx)	11, ∀I
13.	∀x)(Fa ⊃ Gx) ≡ (Fa ⊃ (∀x)Gx)	1-6, 7-12, ≡I

4.10.25. Prove equivalent: (∀x)(∀y)(Hx & Iy) , (∀x)Hx & (∀y)Iy

1.	(∀x)(∀y)(Hx & Iy)	Ass
2.	(∀y)(Ha & Iy)	1, ∀E
3.	Ha & Ib	2, ∀E
4.	Ha	3, &E
5.	(∀x)Hx	4, ∀I
6.	Ib	3, &E
7.	(∀y)Iy	6, ∀I
8.	(∀x)Hx & (∀y)Iy	5, 7, &I

1.	(∀x)Hx & (∀y)Iy	Ass
2.	(∀x)Hx	1, &E
3.	Ha	2, ∀E
4.	(∀y)Iy	1, &E
5.	Ib	4, ∀E
6.	Ha & Ib	3, 5, &I
7.	(∀y)(Ha & Iy)	6, ∀I
8.	(∀x)(∀y)(Hx & Iy)	7, ∀I

4.10.26. Prove inconsistent: { (∀x)Jx , (∀y)~(Jy v Kyy) }

1.	(∀x)Jx	Ass
2.	(∀y)~(Jy v Kyy)	Ass
3.	Ja	1, ∀E
4.	Ja v Kaa	2, vI
5.	~(Ja v Kaa)	2, ∀E

4.10.27. Prove logically false: (∀x)(Lx ≡ ~Lx)

1.	(∀x)(Lx ≡ ~Lx)	Ass
2.	La ≡ ~La	1, ∀E
3.	La	Ass
4.	La	3, R
5.	~La	4, 2, ≡E
6.	~La	3-5, ~I
7.	La	6, 2, ≡E

4.10.28. Prove logically false: (∀w)(∀z)(Mwz ≡ ~Mwz)

1.	(∀w)(∀z)(Mwz ≡ ~Mwz)	Ass
2.	(∀z)(Maz ≡ ~Maz)	1, ∀E
3.	Mab ≡ ~Mab	2, ∀E
4.	Mab	Ass
5.	~Mab	4, 3, ≡E
6.	Mab	4, R
7.	~Mab	4-6, ~I
8.	Mab	7, 3, ≡E

4.10.29. { (∀z)(∀y)Nzy , (∀x)(∀y)(Nxy ⊃ ~Ox) } ⊢ (∀w)~Ow

1.	(∀z)(∀y)Nzy	Ass
2.	(∀x)(∀y)(Nxy ⊃ ~Ox)	Ass
3.	(∀y)(Ngy)	1, ∀E
4.	Ngh	3, ∀E
5.	(∀y)(Ngy ⊃ ~Og)	2, ∀E
6.	Ngh ⊃ ~Og	5, ∀E
7.	~Og	4, 6, ⊃E
8.	(∀w)~Ow	7, ∀I

4.10.30. { (∃x)Px } ⊢ (∃y)(Py v Qy)

1.	(∃x)Px	Ass
2.	Pk	Ass
3.	Pk v Qk	2, vI
4	(∃y)(Py v Qy)	3, ∃I
5.	(∃y)(Py v Qy)	1, 2-4, ∃E

4.10.31. { (∀x)(Rx ⊃ Sx) , (∃x)Rx } ⊢ (∃x)Sx

1.	(∀x)(Rx ⊃ Sx)	Ass
2.	(∃x)Rx	Ass
3.	Rn	Ass
4.	Rn ⊃ Sn	1, ∀E
5.	Sn	3, 4, ⊃E
6.	(∃x)Sx	5, ∃I
7.	(∃x)Sx	2, 3-6, ∃E

4.10.32. { (∃y)(∀x)Txy } ⊢ (∀x)(∃y)Txy

1.	(∃y)(∀x)Txy	Ass
2.	(∀x)Txr	Ass
3.	Tqr	2, ∀E
4.	(∃y)Tqy	3, ∃I
5.	(∃y)Tqy	1, 2-4, ∃E
6.	(∀x)(∃y)Txy	5, ∀I

4.10.33. { (∃x)(∃y)Uxy } ⊢ (∃y)(∃x)Uxy

1.	(∃x)(∃y)Uxy	Ass
2.	(∃y)Uny	Ass
3.	Uno	Ass
4.	(∃x)Uxo	3, ∃I
5.	(∃y)(∃x)Uxy	4, ∃I
6.	(∃y)(∃x)Uxy	2, 3-5, ∃E
7.	(∃y)(∃x)Uxy	1, 2-6, ∃E

4.10.34. { (∀x)[(∃y)Axy ⊃ Bbx] , (∀x)(∀y)Ayx } ⊢ (∃x)Bxx

1.	(∀x)[(∃y)Axy ⊃ Bbx]	Ass
2.	(∀x)(∀y)Ayx	Ass
3.	(∃y)Aby ⊃ Bbb	1, ∀E
4.	(∀y)Ayn	2, ∀E
5.	Abn	4, ∀E
6.	(∃y)Aby	5, ∃I
7.	Bbb	6, 3, ⊃E
8.	(∃x)Bxx	7, ∃I

4.10.35. { (∃x)Cx ⊃ (∀x)Dx } ⊢ (∀x)(~Dx ⊃ ~Cx)

1.	(∃x)Cx ⊃(∀x)Dx	Ass
2.	~Da	Ass
3.	Ca	Ass
4.	(∃x)Cx	3, ∃I
5.	(∀x)Dx	4, 1, ⊃E
7.	Da	5, ∀E
8.	~Da	2, R
9.	~Ca	3-8, ~I
10	~Da ⊃ ~Ca	2-9, ⊃I
11	(∀x)(~Dx ⊃ ~Cx)	10, ∀I

4.10.36. { (∃x)Exb ⊃ (∀x)Fx , (∀x)Eax } ⊢ (∀x)(Gxc ⊃ Fx)

1.	(∃x)Exb ⊃ (∀x)Fx	Ass
2.	(∀x)Eax	Ass
3.	Eab	2, ∀E
4.	(∃x)Exb	3, ∃I
5.	(∀x)Fx	4, 1, ⊃E
6.	Gjc	Ass
7.	Fj	5, ∀E
8.	Gjc ⊃ Fj	6-7, ⊃I
9.	(∀x)(Gxc ⊃ Fx)	8, ∀I

4.10.37. { Hmm & ~Imr , (∃y)~(Hmy ⊃ Iyr) ⊃ (∀x)Jxx } ⊢ Jaa

1.	Hmm & ~Imr	Ass
2.	(∃y)~(Hmy ⊃ Iyr) ⊃ (∀x)Jxx	Ass
3.	Hmm ⊃ Imr	Ass
4.	Hmm	1, &E
5.	Imr	3, 4, ⊃E
6.	~Imr	1, &E
7.	~(Hmm ⊃ Imr)	3-6, ~I
8.	(∃y)~(Hmy ⊃ Iyr)	7, ∃I
9.	(∀x)Jxx	8, 2, ⊃E
10.	Jaa	9, ∀E

4.10.38. { (∀z)[(Kz v (∀x)Lxz) ≡ Mzzz] , Mggg }
⊢ ((∀x)Lxg v Kg) v Ng

1.	(∀z)[(Kz v (∀x)Lxz) ≡ Mzzz]	Ass
2.	Mggg	Ass
3.	(Kg v (∀x)Lxg) ≡ Mggg	1, ∀E
4.	Kg v (∀x)Lxg	2, 3, ≡E
5.	Kg	Ass
6.	(∀x)Lxg v Kg	5, vI
7.	(∀x)Lxg	Ass
8.	(∀x)Lxg v Kg	7, vI
9.	(∀x)Lxg v Kg	4, 5-6, 7-8, vE
10.	((∀x)Lxg v Kg) v Ng	9, vI

4.10.39. { (∃x)Ox ⊃ (∃x)Px } ⊢ (∀x)[Ox ⊃ (∃y)Py]

1.	(∃x)Ox ⊃ (∃x)Px	Ass
2.	Oa	Ass
3.	(∃x)Ox	2, ∃I
4.	(∃x)Px	3, 1, ⊃E
5.	Pb	Ass
6.	(∃y)Py	5, ∃I
7.	(∃y)Py	4, 5-6, ∃E
8.	Oa ⊃ (∃y)Py	2-7, ⊃I
9.	(∀x)[Ox ⊃ (∃y)Py]	9, ∀I

4.10.40. { (∃x)Qx & (∀x)Rx } ⊢ (∃x)(Qx & Rx)

1.	(∃x)Qx & (∀x)Rx	Ass
2.	(∃x)Qx	1, &E
3.	Qk	Ass
4.	(∀x)Rx	1, &E
5.	Rk	4, ∀E
6.	Qk & Rk	3, 5, &I
7.	(∃x)(Qx & Rx)	6, ∃I
8.	(∃x)(Qx & Rx)	2, 3-7, ∃E

4.10.41. { (∃x)Sx , (∃x)Tx } ⊢ (∃x)[(∃y)Sy & Tx]

1.	(∃x)Sx	Ass
2.	(∃x)Tx	Ass
3.	⎜ Sa	Ass
4.	⎜ (∃y)Sy	3, ∃I
5.	⎜ ⎜ Tb	Ass
6.	⎜ ⎜ (∃y)Sy & Tb	4, 5, &I
7.	⎜ ⎜ (∃x)[(∃y)Sy & Tx]	6, ∃I
8.	⎜ (∃x)[(∃y)Sy & Tx]	2, 5-7, ∃E
9.	(∃x)[(∃y)Sy & Tx]	1, 3-8, ∃E

4.10.42. { (∃x)[Ax ⊃ (∃y)By] } ⊢ (∀x)Ax ⊃ (∃x)Bx

1.	(∃x)[Ax ⊃ (∃y)By]	Ass
2.	Aa ⊃ (∃y)By	Ass
3.	(∀x)Ax	Ass
4.	Aa	3, ∀E
5.	(∃y)By	4, 2, ⊃E
6.	Bb	Ass
7.	(∃x)Bx	6, ∃I
8.	(∃x)Bx	5, 6-7, ∃E
9.	(∀x)Ax ⊃ (∃x)Bx	3-8, ⊃I
10.	(∀x)Ax ⊃ (∃x)Bx	1, 2-9, ∃E

4.10.43. { (∀x)(Cx ⊃ Dx), (∀x)[(∃y)(Dy & Exy) ⊃ Fx],
　　　(∃x)[Gx & (∃y)(Cy &.Exy)] } ⊢ (∃x)(Gx & Fx)

1.	(∀x)(Cx ⊃ Dx)	Ass
2.	(∀x)[(∃y)(Dy & Exy) ⊃ Fx]	Ass
3.	(∃x)[Gx & (∃y)(Cy & Exy)]	Ass
4.	Ga & (∃y)(Cy & Eay)	Ass
5.	Ga	4, &E
6.	(∃y)(Cy & Eay)	4, &E
7.	Cb & Eab	Ass
8.	Cb	7, &E
9.	Cb ⊃ Db	1, ∀E
10.	Db	8, 9, ⊃E
11.	Eab	7, &E
12.	Db & Eab	10, 11, &I
13.	(∃y)(Dy & Eay)	12, ∃I
14.	(∃y)(Dy & Eay) ⊃ Fa	2, ∀E
15.	Fa	13, 14, ⊃E
16.	Ga & Fa	15, 5, &I
17.	(∃x)(Gx & Fx)	16, ∃I
18.	(∃x)(Gx & Fx)	6, 7-17, ∃E
19.	(∃x)(Gx & Fx)	3, 4-18, ∃E

4.10.44. { (∀x)(Hxa ⊃ Hxb) }
　　　⊢ (∀x)[(∃y)(Ixy & Hya) ⊃ (∃y)(Ixy & Hyb)]

1.	(∀x)(Hxa ⊃ Hxb)	Ass
2.	(∃y)(Idy & Hya)	Ass
3.	Idm & Hma	Ass
4.	Idm	3, &E
5.	Hma	3, &E
6.	Hma ⊃ Hmb	1, ∀E
7.	Hmb	5, 6, ⊃E
8.	Idm & Hmb	4, 7, &I
9.	(∃y)(Idy & Hyb)	8, ∃I
10.	(∃y)(Idy & Hyb)	2, 3-9, ∃E
11.	(∃y)(Idy & Hya) ⊃ (∃y)(Idy & Hyb)	2-10, ⊃I
12.	(∀x)[(∃y)(Ixy & Hya) ⊃ (∃y)(Ixy & Hyb)]	11, ∀I

4.10.45. { (∀x)[Jx ⊃ (∀y)(Ky ⊃ Lxy)] , (∀x)[Mx ⊃ (∀y)(Lxy ⊃ Ny)] }
        ⊢ (∃x)(Jx & Mx) ⊃ (∀y)(Ky ⊃ Ny)

1.	(∀x)[Jx ⊃ (∀y)(Ky ⊃ Lxy)]	Ass
2.	(∀x)[Mx ⊃ (∀y)(Lxy ⊃ Ny)]	Ass
3.	(∃x)(Jx & Mx)	Ass
4.	Ja & Ma	Ass
5.	Ja	4, &E
6.	Ja ⊃ (∀y)(Ky ⊃ Lay)	1, ∀E
7.	(∀y)(Ky ⊃ Lay)	5, 6, ⊃E
8.	Kb ⊃ Lab	7, ∀E
9.	Ma	4, &E
10.	Ma ⊃ (∀y)(Lay ⊃ Ny)	2, ∀E
11.	(∀y)(Lay ⊃ Ny)	9, 10, ⊃E
12.	Lab ⊃ Nb	11, ∀E
13.	Kb	Ass
14.	Lab	13, 8, ⊃E
15.	Nb	14, 12, ⊃E
16.	Kb ⊃ Nb	13-15, ⊃I
17.	(∀y)(Ky ⊃ Ny)	16, ∀I
18.	(∀y)(Ky ⊃ Ny)	3, 4-17, ∃E
19.	(∃x)(Jx & Mx) ⊃ (∀y)(Ky ⊃ Ny)	3-18, ⊃I

4.10.46. { (∃x)[Ox & (∀y)(Py ⊃ Rxy)] } ⊢ (∃x)[Ox & (Pa ⊃ Rxa)]

1.	(∃x)[Ox & (∀y)(Py ⊃ Rxy)]	Ass
2.	Ob & (∀y)(Py ⊃ Rby)	Ass
3.	Ob	2, &E
4.	(∀y)(Py ⊃ Rby)	2, &E
5.	Pa ⊃ Rba	4, ∀E
6.	Ob & (Pa ⊃ Rba)	3, 5, &I
7.	(∃x)[Ox & (Pa ⊃ Rxa)]	6, ∃I
8.	(∃x)[Ox & (Pa ⊃ Rxa)]	1, 2-7, ∃E

NOTE: In this one, because you need a in the conclusion which will be gotten by ∃E, it's important not to use a as the instantiating constant in step 2.

4.10.47. $\{ (\forall x)(\forall y)(Sxy \equiv (Ty \supset Ux)) , (\forall z)Saz \} \vdash (\exists x)Tx \supset (\exists x)Ux$

1.	$(\forall x)(\forall y)[Sxy \equiv (Ty \supset Ux)]$	Ass
2.	$(\forall z)Saz$	Ass
3.	$(\exists x)Tx$	Ass
4.	Tb	Ass
5.	$(\forall y)[Say \equiv (Ty \supset Ua)]$	1, $\forall$E
6.	$Sab \equiv (Tb \supset Ua)$	5, $\forall$E
7.	Sab	2, $\forall$E
8.	$Tb \supset Ua$	6, 7, $\equiv$E
9.	Ua	4, 8, $\supset$E
10.	$(\exists x)Ux$	9, $\exists$I
11.	$(\exists x)Ux$	3, 4-10, $\exists$E
12.	$(\exists x)Tx \supset (\exists x)Ux$	3-11, $\supset$I

4.10.48. $\{ (\forall x)[(\exists y)Axy \supset (\exists y)\sim By] , (\exists x)(\exists y)Axy , (\forall x)(Bx \equiv \sim Cx) \}$
$\vdash (\exists x)Cx$

1.	$(\forall x)[(\exists y)Axy \supset (\exists y)\sim By]$	Ass
2.	$(\exists x)(\exists y)Axy$	Ass
3.	$(\forall x)(Bx \equiv \sim Cx)$	Ass
4.	$(\exists y)Aay$	Ass
5.	$(\exists y)Aay \supset (\exists y)\sim By$	1, $\forall$E
6.	$(\exists y)\sim By$	4, 5, $\supset$E
7.	$\sim Bb$	Ass
8.	$Bb \equiv \sim Cb$	3, $\forall$E
9.	$\sim Cb$	Ass
10.	Bb	8, 9, $\equiv$E
11.	$\sim Bb$	7, R
12.	Cb	9-11, $\sim$E
13.	$(\exists x)Cx$	12, $\exists$I
14.	$(\exists x)Cx$	6, 7-13, $\exists$E
15.	$(\exists x)Cx$	2, 4-14, $\exists$E

4.10.49. $\vdash (\forall x)(\exists y)(Dy \supset Dx)$

1.	Da	Ass
2.	Da	1, R
3.	$Da \supset Da$	1-2, $\supset$I
4.	$(\exists y)(Dy \supset Da)$	3, $\exists$I
5.	$(\forall x)(\exists y)(Dy \supset Dx)$	4, $\forall$I

4.10.50. ⊢ (∀x)(Ex ⊃ Fa) ≡ ((∃x)Ex ⊃ Fa)

1.	(∀x)(Ex ⊃ Fa)	Ass
2.	(∃x)Ex	Ass
3.	Eb	Ass
4.	Eb ⊃ Fa	1, ∀E
5.	Fa	3, 4, ⊃E
6.	Fa	2, 3-5, ∃E
7.	(∃x)Ex ⊃ Fa	2-6, ⊃I
8.	(∃x)Ex ⊃ Fa	Ass
9.	Eb	Ass
10.	(∃x)Ex	9, ∃I
11.	Fa	10, 8, ⊃E
12.	Eb ⊃ Fa	9-11, ⊃I
13.	(∀x)(Ex ⊃ Fa)	12, ∀I
14.	(∀x)(Ex ⊃ Fa) ≡ ((∃x)Ex ⊃ Fa)	1-7, 8-14, ≡I

4.10.51. Prove equivalent: (∃x)(Gx v Hx) , (∃x)Gx v (∃x)Hx

1.	(∃x)(Gx v Hx)	Ass
2.	Ga v Ha	Ass
3.	Ga	Ass
4.	(∃x)Gx	3, ∃I
5.	(∃x)Gx v (∃x)Hx	4, vI
6.	Ha	Ass
7.	(∃x)Hx	6, ∃I
8.	(∃x)Gx v (∃x)Hx	7, vI
9.	(∃x)Gx v (∃x)Hx	2, 3-5, 6-8, vE
10.	(∃x)Gx v (∃x)Hx	1, 2-9, ∃E

1.	(∃x)Gx v (∃x)Hx	Ass
2.	(∃x)Gx	Ass
3.	Ga	Ass
4.	Ga v Ha	3, vI
5.	(∃x)(Gx v Hx)	4, ∃I
6.	(∃x)(Gx v Hx)	2, 3-5, ∃E
7.	(∃x)Hx	Ass
8.	Ha	Ass
9.	Ga v Ha	8, vI
10.	(∃x)(Gx v Hx)	9, ∃I
11.	(∃x)(Gx v Hx)	7, 8-10, ∃E
12.	(∃x)(Gx v Hx)	1, 2-6, 7-11, vE

4.10.52. Prove equivalent: (∀x)~Ix , ~(∃x)Ix

1.	(∀x)~Ix		Ass
2.		(∃x)Ix	Ass
3.		Ia	Ass
4.		~(M & ~M)	Ass
5.		Ia	3, R
6.		~Ia	1, ∀E
7.		M & ~M	4-6, ~E
8.		M & ~M	2, 3-7, ∃E
9.		M	8, &E
10.		~M	8, &E
11.	~(∃x)Ix		2-10, ~I

This last derivation contains a special and not obvious technique you should take note of. We're looking for a contradiction in that subderivation starting on step 2. We assume Ia on step 3, to do a ∃E on step 2, and we can get ~Ia from step 1; and of course these can be joined to get (Ia & ~Ia); but this will not work as the *R*-sentence for that ∃E, because the instantiating constant **a** is in it. But this contradiction, Ia and ~Ia, can be used inside the subderivation for ∃E to get a different arbitrary contradiction, M & ~M, using ~E, and this one doesn't have that instantiating constant in it, so it can be used as the *R*-sentence. Examine this derivation carefully to see how this works. This routine will be used in several other derivations so it's a good idea to bear it in mind. When it's used in the rest of these exercises, the arbitrary contradiction is always (M & ~M), so that you'll recognize this technique; though, of course, any contradiction without the instantiating constant in it would do. Other exercises in here that need this technique are 4.10.53, 4.10.54, 4.10.56, 4.10.60, and 4.10.62.

Well, at last, here's the second derivation needed to prove equivalence in 4.10.52.

1.	~(∃x)Ix		Ass
2.		Ia	Ass
3.		(∃x)Ix	2, ∃I
4.		~(∃x)Ix	1, R
5.	~Ia		2-4, ~I
6.	(∀x)~Ix		5, ∀I

4.10.53. Prove inconsistent: { (∀x)Jx , (∃x)~Jx }

1.	(∀x)Jx	Ass
2.	(∃x)~Jx	Ass
3.	~Ja	Ass
4.	~(M & ~M)	Ass
5.	~Ja	3, R
6.	Ja	1, ∀E
7.	M & ~M	4-6, ~E
8.	M & ~M	2, 3-7, ∃E
9.	M	8, &E
10.	~M	8, &E

4.10.54. Prove inconsistent: { (∀y)(∃z)Kyz, (∀w)~Kaw }

1.	(∀y)(∃z)Kyz	Ass
2.	(∀w)~Kaw	Ass
3.	(∃z)Kaz	1, ∀E
4.	Kab	Ass
5.	~(M & ~M)	Ass
6.	Kab	4, R
7.	~Kab	2, ∀E
8.	M & ~M	5-7, ~E
9.	M & ~M	3, 4-8, ∃E
10.	M	9, &E
11.	~M	9, &E

4.10.55. Prove inconsistent: { (∀x)(∃y)(Lx ⊃ My) , ~(∃y)(∀x)(Lx ⊃ My) }

1.	(∀x)(∃y)(Lx ⊃ My)	Ass
2.	~(∃y)(∀x)(Lx ⊃ My)	Ass
3.	(∃y)(La ⊃ My)	1, ∀E
4.	La ⊃ Mb	Ass
5.	(∀x)(Lx ⊃ Mb)	4, ∀I
6.	(∃y)(∀x)(Lx ⊃ My)	5, ∃I
7.	(∃y)(∀x)(Lx ⊃ My)	3, 4-6, ∃E
8.	~(∃y)(∀x)(Lx ⊃ My)	2, R

4.10.56. Prove logically false: (∃x)(Nx & ~Nx)

1.	(∃x)(Nx & ~Nx)		Ass
2.		Na & ~Na	Ass
3.			~(M & ~M)	Ass
4.			Na	2, &E
5.			~Na	2, &E
6.		M & ~M	3-5, ~E
7.	M & ~M		1, 2-6, ∃E
8.	M		7, &E
9.	~M		7, &E

4.10.57. { ~(∀x) ~Ox } ⊢ (∃x)Ox

1.	~(∀x)~Ox		Ass
2.		~(∃x)Ox	Ass
3.			On	Ass
4.			(∃x)Ox	3, ∃I
5.			~(∃x)Ox	2, R
6.		~On	3-5, ~I
7.		(∀x)~Ox	6, ∀I
8.		~(∀x)~Ox	1, R
9.	(∃x)Ox		2-8, ~E

4.10.58. { Pnn v (Qn & Rj) , ~(∀z)Ssz ⊃ ~Qn }
    ⊢ (∃x)(~Pxx ⊃ (∀z)Ssz)

1.	Pnn v (Qn & Rj)	Ass
2.	~(∀z)Ssz ⊃ ~Qn	Ass
3.	Pnn	Ass
4.	~Pnn	Ass
5.	~(∀z)Sxz	Ass
6.	Pnn	3, R
7.	~Pnn	4, R
8.	(∀z)Ssz	5-7, ~E
9.	~Pnn ⊃ (∀z)Ssz	4-8, ⊃I
10.	(∃x)[~Pxx ⊃ (∀z)Ssz]	9, ∃I
11.	Qn & Rj	Ass
12.	~(∀z)Ssz	Ass
13.	~Qn	12, 2, ⊃E
14.	Qn	11, &E
15.	(∀z)Ssz	12-14, ~E
16	~Pgg	Ass
17.	(∀z)Ssz	15, R
18.	~Pgg ⊃ (∀z)Ssz	16-17, ⊃I
19.	(∃x)[~Pxx ⊃ (∀z)Ssz]	18, ∃I
20.	(∃x)(~Pxx ⊃ (∀z)Ssz)	1, 2-10, 11-19, vE

4.10.59. { (∃x)(∃y)Txy v (∀x)(∀y)Uyx } ⊢ (∃x)(∃y)(Txy v Uxy)

1.	(∃x)(∃y)Txy v (∀x)(∀y)Uyx	Ass
2.	(∃x)(∃y)Txy	Ass
3.	(∃y)Tay	Ass
4.	Tab	Ass
5.	Tab v Uab	4, vI
6.	(∃y)(Tay v Uay)	5, ∃I
7.	(∃x)(∃y)(Txy v Uxy)	6, ∃I
8.	(∃x)(∃y)(Txy v Uxy)	3, 4-7, ∃E
9.	(∃x)(∃y)(Txy v Uxy)	2, 3-8, ∃E
10.	(∀x)(∀y)Uyx	Ass
11.	(∀y)Uya	10, ∀E
12.	Uba	11, ∀E
13.	Tba v Uba	12, vI
14.	(∃y)(Tby v Uby)	13, ∃I
15.	(∃x)(∃y)(Txy v Uxy)	14, ∃I
16.	(∃x)(∃y)(Txy v Uxy)	1, 2-9, 10-15, vE

4.10.60. { $(\forall x)(\ \sim Ax \supset Bx)$, $(\forall x)[(\ \sim Bx \lor Ax) \equiv \sim Bx)]$, $(\exists x)(Cx \equiv Ax)$ }
⊢ $\sim (\forall x)(Cx \equiv Bx)$

1.	$(\forall x)(\ \sim Ax \supset Bx)$	Ass
2.	$(\forall x)[(\ \sim Bx \lor Ax) \equiv \sim Bx)]$	Ass
3.	$(\exists x)(Cx \equiv Ax)$	Ass
4.	$\sim Aa \supset Ba$	1, $\forall$E
5.	$(\sim Ba \lor Aa) \equiv \sim Ba$	2, $\forall$E
6.	$(\forall x)(Cx \equiv Bx)$	Ass
7.	$Ca \equiv Ba$	6, $\forall$E
8.	$Ca \equiv Aa$	Ass
9.	Ba	Ass
10.	Ca	9, 7, $\equiv$E
11.	Aa	10, 8, $\equiv$ E
12.	$\sim Ba \lor Aa$	11, $\lor$I
13.	$\sim Ba$	5, 12, $\supset$E
14.	$\sim Ba$	9-13, $\sim$I
15.	$\sim Aa$	Ass
16.	Ba	15, 4, $\supset$E
17.	$\sim Ba$	14, R
18.	Aa	15-17, $\sim$E
19.	Ca	18, 8, $\equiv$E
20.	Ba	19, 7, $\equiv$E
21.	$\sim(M \ \& \sim M)$	Ass
22.	Ba	20, R
23.	$\sim Ba$	14, R
24.	$M \ \& \sim M$	21-23, $\sim$E
25.	$M \ \& \sim M$	3, 8-24, $\exists$E
26.	M	25, &E
27.	$\sim M$	25, &E
28.	$\sim(\forall x)(Cx \equiv Bx)$	6-27, $\sim$I

4.10.61. { (∀x)(∀y)[(Dx & Ey) ⊃ Fxy] , (∃x)(∃y)[(Dx & ~Dy) & ~Fxy] }
⊢ (∃x)(~Dx & ~Ex)

1.	(∀x)(∀y)[(Dx & Ey) ⊃ Fxy]	Ass
2.	(∃x)(∃y)[(Dx & ~Dy) & ~Fxy]	Ass
3.	(∃y)[(Da & ~Dy) & ~Fay]	Ass
4.	(Da & ~Db) & ~Fab	Ass
5.	Da & ~Db	4, &E
6.	(∀y)[(Da & Ey) ⊃ Fay]	1, ∀E
7.	(Da & Eb) ⊃ Fab	6, ∀E
8.	Da & Eb	Ass
9.	Fab	8, 7, ⊃E
10.	~Fab	4, &E
11.	~(Da & Eb)	8-10, ~I
12.	Eb	Ass
13.	Da	5, &E
14.	Da & Eb	12, 13, &I
15.	~(Da & Eb)	11, R
16.	~Eb	12-15, ~I
17.	~Db	5, &E
18.	~Db & ~Eb	16, 17, &I
19.	(∃x)(~Dx & ~Ex)	18, ∃I
20.	(∃x)(~Dx & ~Ex)	3, 4-19, ∃E
21.	(∃x)(~Dx & ~Ex)	2, 3-20, ∃E

4.10.62. Prove equivalent: ~(∀x)Gx , (∃x)~Gx

1.	~(∀x)Gx	Ass
2.	~(∃x)~Gx	Ass
3.	~Ga	Ass
4.	(∃x)~Gx	3, ∃I
5.	~(∃x)~Gx	2, R
6.	Ga	3-5, ~E
7.	(∀x)Gx	6, ∀I
8.	~(∀x)Gx	1, R
9.	(∃x)~Gx	1-8, ~E

Second derivation for equivalence on next page.

1.	(∃x)~Gx	Ass
2.	(∀x)Gx	Ass
3.	~Ga	Ass
4.	~(M & ~M)	Ass
5.	Ga	2, ∀E
6.	~Ga	3, R
7.	M & ~M	4-6, ~E
8.	M & ~M	1, 3-7, ∃E
9.	M	8, &E
10.	~M	8, &E
11.	~(∀x)Gx	2-10, ~I

4.10.63. Prove equivalent: (∀x)(∀y)[(Hxy & Hyx) ⊃ Hxx] ,
       (∀x)[(∃y)(Hxy & Hyx) ⊃ Hxx]

1.	(∀x)(∀y)[(Hxy & Hyx) ⊃ Hxx]	Ass
2.	(∀y)[(Hay & Hya) ⊃ Haa]	1, ∀E
3.	(Hab & Hba) ⊃ Haa	2, ∀E
4.	(∃y)(Hay & Hya)	Ass
5.	Hab & Hba	Ass
6.	Haa	5, 3, ⊃E
7.	Haa	4, 5-6, ∃E
8.	(∃y)(Hay & Hya) ⊃ Haa	4-7, ⊃I
9.	(∀x)[(∃y)(Hxy & Hyx) ⊃ Hxx]	8, ∀I

1.	(∀x)[(∃y)(Hxy & Hyx) ⊃ Hxx]	Ass
2.	(∃y)(Hay & Hya) ⊃ Haa	1, ∀E
3.	Hab & Hba	Ass
4.	(∃y)(Hay & Hya)	3, ∃I
5.	Haa	4, 2, ⊃E
6.	(Hab & Hba) ⊃ Haa	3-5, ⊃I
7.	(∀y)[(Hay & Hya) ⊃ Hxx]	6, ∀I
8.	(∀x)(∀y)[(Hxy & Hyx) ⊃ Hxx]	7, ∀I

4.10.64. Prove equivalent: $(\exists x)Ix \supset ((\exists y)Jy \supset (\forall z)Kz)$,
$(\forall x)(\forall y)(\forall z)[(Ix \; \& \; Jy) \supset Kz]$

1.	$(\exists x)Ix \supset ((\exists y)Jy \supset (\forall z)Kz)$	Ass
2.	$Ia \; \& \; Jb$	Ass
3.	Ia	2, &E
4.	$(\exists x)Ix$	3, $\exists$I
5.	$(\exists y)Jy \supset (\forall z)Kz$	4, 1, $\supset$E
6.	Jb	2, &E
7.	$(\exists y)Jy$	6, $\exists$I
8.	$(\forall z)Kz$	7, 5, $\supset$E
9.	Kc	8, $\forall$E
10.	$(Ia \; \& \; Jb) \supset Kc$	2-9, $\supset$I
11.	$(\forall z)[(Ia \; \& \; Jb) \supset Kz]$	10, $\forall$I
12.	$(\forall y)(\forall z)[(Ia \; \& \; Jy) \supset Kz]$	11, $\forall$I
13.	$(\forall x)(\forall y)(\forall z)[(Ix \; \& \; Jy) \supset Kz]$	12, $\forall$I

1.	$(\forall x)(\forall y)(\forall z)[(Ix \; \& \; Jy) \supset Kz]$	Ass
2.	$(\exists x)Ix$	Ass
3.	Ia	Ass
4.	$(\exists y)Jy$	Ass
5.	Jb	Ass
6.	$(\forall y)(\forall z)[(Ia \; \& \; Jy) \supset Kz]$	1, $\forall$E
7.	$(\forall z)[(Ia \; \& \; Jb) \supset Kz]$	6, $\forall$E
8.	$(Ia \; \& \; Jb) \supset Kc$	7, $\forall$E
9.	$Ia \; \& \; Jb$	3, 5, &I
10	Kc	8, 9, $\supset$E
11	$(\forall z)Kz$	10, $\forall$I
12	$(\forall z)Kz$	4, 5-11, $\exists$E
13	$(\exists y)Jy \supset (\forall z)Kz$	4-12, $\supset$I
14	$(\exists y)Jy \supset (\forall z)Kz$	2, 3-13, $\exists$E
15	$(\exists x)Ix \supset ((\exists y)Jy \supset (\forall z)Kz)$	2-14, $\supset$I

4.10.65. Prove inconsistent: $\{ (\exists x)(Ay)Lxy , \sim(\forall y)(\exists x)Lxy \}$

1.	$(\exists x)(\forall y)Lxy$	Ass
2.	$\sim(\forall y)(\exists x)Lxy$	Ass
3.	$(\forall y)Ldy$	Ass
4.	Lde	3, $\forall$E
5.	$(\exists x)Lxe$	4, $\exists$I
6.	$(\forall y)(\exists x)Lxy$	5, $\forall$I
7.	$(\forall y)(\exists x)Lxy$	1, 3-6, $\exists$E
8.	$\sim(\forall y)(\exists x)Lxy$	2, R